Sanford M. (Sanford Moon) Green

**Crime: its nature, causes, treatment, and prevention**

Sanford M. (Sanford Moon) Green

**Crime: Its nature, causes, treatment, and prevention**

ISBN/EAN: 9783743417373

Manufactured in Europe, USA, Canada, Australia, Japa

Cover: Foto ©Suzi / pixelio.de

Manufactured and distributed by brebook publishing software (www.brebook.com)

Sanford M. (Sanford Moon) Green

**Crime: its nature, causes, treatment, and prevention**

# CRIME:

ITS

# NATURE, CAUSES, TREATMENT, AND PREVENTION.

BY

SANFORD M. GREEN,

LATE JUDGE OF THE SUPREME AND CIRCUIT COURTS OF MICHIGAN;
AUTHOR OF "GREEN'S PRACTICE," ETC, ETC.

PHILADELPHIA:
J B. LIPPINCOTT COMPANY.
1889.

# PREFATORY.

THE leading ideas expressed in the following pages, in regard to the nature and appropriate treatment of crime, were enunciated by the writer more than forty years ago in giving instructions to juries in the trial of criminal cases, and in the sentencing of persons convicted of crime, and have been publicly expressed by me hundreds of times in the presence of thousands of people during the long period of my service as a judge, without eliciting, so far as I have ever heard, any serious dissent or adverse criticism. Jurors were advised that their duties required no violation of the golden rule; that the prisoner was alleged to be morally diseased, and that they were summoned as a council of physicians to diagnose his case, and determine whether or not he was really diseased as supposed; and that if such was proven to be his condition, the proper treatment ought to be administered for his cure and the protection of the community upon the same principle in all respects as in the case of an insane person. Juries were further instructed that if in fact the prisoner was found to be thus diseased, it was most merciful as well as just to the prisoner himself that they should so declare by their verdict, in order that he should receive the treatment his condition required; and that though it were better that ninety and nine guilty persons should escape than that one innocent person should suffer, yet it were still better that no guilty person should be allowed to escape the just consequences of his evil conduct.

Deeply impressed with the truth of these propositions, I had for several years contemplated preparing an essay for the purpose of illustrating and enforcing them, when I should be able to find the necessary time and opportunity to do so. While engaged in the attempt to prepare such an essay, the idea of a more comprehensive work on the subject of crime occurred to me, and the following treatise on the nature, causes, treatment, and prevention of crime has been the result.  It was commenced without any definite idea of its publication.  I was then seventy-eight, and might not be able to complete it.  But favorable conditions have enabled me to present it to the public.  It was, as I believed, the last work I should attempt to write, and as it progressed I became intensely interested in the subjects treated of, and inspired with the hope that it might be of some value in aiding to solve some of the great social problems that are now agitating the civilized world.

The treatment and cure of those moral diseases from which all sin and crime proceed are subjects of more interest and importance to mankind than all others.  Sin may never be entirely eliminated from this world, but I believe that, by means which have been proven to be practicable, it may be reduced to a small fraction of its present magnitude; and if this book shall be a means of contributing in some small degree to that end, I shall be more than satisfied with the result of my labor.

Some apparent anachronisms will be found in references made to recent or transpiring events.  These are explained by the fact that the preparation of the work has extended over some four years, and the events thus referred to were recent or passing at the time of the allusions made to them.

I avail myself of this occasion to express my most sincere thanks to those friends who have aided me in this work by candid criticisms and suggestions, and by assisting me in my researches after historical and scientific facts.

THE AUTHOR.

BAY CITY, October, 1889.

# CONTENTS.

## ARTICLE I.

### OF THE NATURE OF CRIME.

#### CHAPTER I.

## ARTICLE II.

### CAUSES OF CRIME.

#### CHAPTER I.

#### CHAPTER II.

#### CHAPTER III.

#### CHAPTER IV.

#### CHAPTER V.

#### CHAPTER VI.

#### CHAPTER VII.

# A TREATISE

## ON THE

## NATURE, CAUSES, TREATMENT, AND PREVENTION

### OF

# CRIME.

## ARTICLE I.

### OF THE NATURE OF CRIME.

" This grim topic still claims precedence over all others, whether personal or general. It is at once the most catholic and the most individual of human attributes. It confronts us alike in crowded cities and on lonely prairies, in peaceful villages and on stormy oceans; and when we seek the privacy of our chamber it passes with us across the threshold. Its beginning was in the earliest dawn of history, and he were a bold optimist who should foretell the day of its departure. It was a mystery at the first, and, after so many thousand years of experience and analysis, we still ask ourselves what it is, and why? It is the darkest and the hardiest growth that has ever sprouted from the human heart. All the nostrums of the usual pharmacopœia have been tried upon it, with scarce an abatement of its sinister luxuriance. No other phenomenon is so bewildering in its manifestations. Civilizations have been based upon it, and it has destroyed civilizations. We call it the child of ignorance, but many of the most highly trained and gifted minds have been steeped in this sable vat of crime. . . . Paganism suckled it, but Christianity has slain for it the fatted calf."—JULIAN HAWTHORNE, " Address on Crime before the National Conference of Charities and Correction," at Washington, 1885.

## CHAPTER I.

### NATURE OF CRIME.

CRIME is said to consist of those wrongs which the government notices as injurious to the public, and punishes in what is called a criminal proceeding in its own name. A crime or misdemeanor has also been defined to be, " An act committed or omitted in violation of a public law forbidding or commanding it." In considering the nature of crime, we shall not be limited to what the laws treat as such, but shall include as within the meaning of that term all wrongs committed against persons and property, public health, justice, decency, and morality, whether forbidden by a public law or not. In the course of our discussion of the nature and causes of crime, we think it will appear manifest that some great wrongs are tolerated and upheld by the laws of States and nations, while many smaller ones are made punishable as public offences. The main reason why governments do not treat all great wrongs as criminal, and subject the offenders to punishment, is the difficulty of defining them in such a way as to distinguish them from those acts which may be beneficial or injurious, according to surrounding circumstances, and their ultimate results. Such are those wrongs which constantly occur in trade and commerce and business transactions, in which the strong take advantage of the weak and the shrewd of the simple and credulous, and by which the former wrests from the latter the proceeds of his honest industry and labor, giving no adequate return therefor, the law in many cases applying the rule of *caveat emptor*, and affording no redress, even by a civil suit for damages.

Under our institutions of republican government, all are theoretically equal, and possess an inalienable right to life, liberty, and the pursuit of happiness ; and it is the duty of the whole collectively, as represented by the government, to protect every individual in the enjoyment of this right. In the political compact constituting the government, which is supposed to be based upon the consent of the governed, the common right and common interest of all to be secure in their persons and property is fully recognized, and it is the principal object of civil government to guard and protect

this right. It is for this purpose that laws are enacted forbidding those acts which are subversive of these recognized
rights, or which endanger the welfare of the community,
and provide redress according to the nature of the wrong
committed. If such wrong is of a private nature, affecting
the rights of an individual or individuals only, it may, in
general, be redressed by a civil action in favor of the party
wronged; but if it be one affecting the public in general and
tending to disturb the peace and good order of society, it
is denominated a crime or misdemeanor, and is redressed by
means of a prosecution in the name and behalf of the people
of the State.

We can best comprehend the nature of crime by contrasting its consequences with those of well-doing. Being a wrong
done to the injury of others, its fruits are evil, resulting in
pain and suffering; whereas the fruits of well-doing are
good, tending to promote happiness and relieve or prevent
suffering. Thus crime is evil because it is hurtful, and well-
doing good because it is beneficial. By contrasting these
results we arrive at a knowledge of what is good and what
is evil, and this knowledge can be gained in no other way.
If, therefore, there ever was a time in the history of our race
when man knew not evil, it is certain that he did not know
good. The author of the book of Genesis illustrates this
great truth in his account of Adam and Eve in the garden
of Eden. The tree which was planted in the midst of the
garden, and the fruit of which they were forbidden to partake, was the tree of knowledge of *good* and *evil*, and by
partaking of that fruit they are assumed to have become as
gods, knowing good and evil.

So if "the fruit of that forbidden tree brought death into
the world and all our woe," as the poet assumes, it also
brought a knowledge of all the good that man can ever
know. This law of contrast, or comparison, runs through
all the daily experiences of our lives. By lawless violence

and disorder in the community we learn the value of peace
and security; by sickness, the value of health; by hunger,
the enjoyment of food; by weariness, of rest; by poverty
and destitution, the value of a competence; by darkness,
that of light; by ugliness, the charm of beauty.   And so
of every conceivable thing that can subserve the good of
man and promote his enjoyment,—he can only appreciate
it as good by comparing it with that which is evil.   It is
by this law that intellect itself has its development.   Herbert
Spencer, Bain, and other eminent writers on biology and
physiology, who have analyzed the modes of intellect and
the conditions of its development, have shown that all intellectual processes, from the highest and most complex to
the most elementary and simple, consist in apprehending
resemblances and differences.   To assimilate and dissimilate,
to integrate and disintegrate, is its fundamental process,
which is exemplified in all its operations.

The serpent, which is represented as tempting the woman
to eat of the fruit of the tree of knowledge, was to the He-
brews the emblem of wisdom.   It was a brazen serpent that
Moses lifted up in the wilderness for the healing of those
who had been bitten by the flying reptiles that afflicted
them.   The disciples of Jesus were admonished to be wise
as serpents and harmless as doves.   The wisdom attributed
to the serpent was therefore something to be desired, and
was a necessary qualification for the successful preaching of
the gospel of righteousness.   If, then, good could only be
known by a knowledge of evil, are we to conclude that evil
should be accounted as good? or shall we then do evil that
good may come?   The voice of wisdom answers, Nay.
The tree is known by its fruit; a good tree cannot bring
forth evil fruit, neither do men gather grapes from thorns
or figs of thistles.   It is said that "In this world offences
must needs come; but woe unto him by whom the offence
cometh."   We know by our daily experiences and observa-

tion that good and evil are opposites in their nature and effects. Whatever incidental good may, in some way not foreseen or designed, grow out of the commission of a wrong, the character of the act remains the same. It is still a wrong, and the perpetrator is equally guilty, even if good should result from it. An act proceeding from pure motives, and which is beneficial in its results to individuals or the public in general, we denominate good, and an act proceeding from an evil purpose, and injurious to individuals or the public, we denominate an evil or criminal act, and all enlightened peoples recognize these opposite qualities as characterizing human actions and conduct.

In order to fully comprehend the nature and effects of crime, it is necessary that we consider the duty of all to each and each to all. The obligation of the government to protect every citizen in the enjoyment of his recognized rights, whatever his character or condition may be, arises from the very nature of organized society, and presupposes the power as existing in the body politic to adopt all such measures as are requisite for the attainment of this object. This obligation and duty on the part of the aggregated body of the citizens of a State implies a correlative duty on the part of each of its members not only to refrain from all acts which tend to interfere with or obstruct it in the performance of its duties, but to aid the whole body in the attainment of its objects. Upon the faithful and intelligent performance of those reciprocal obligations and duties depends the happiness and prosperity of the people of a State.

In our complex state of society a condition of independence is impossible, and no individual can, if he would, escape the duties which he owes to it with impunity; nor can there be any adequate motive for his desiring to do so if it were possible. Without the active support of the citizens of a republic the government cannot perform its appropriate functions. Those who are elected or appointed to make or administer the laws must perform the duties assigned them, or the constitution of government must cease to exist. The duty of every one not only to contribute his fair proportion of the expenses of administering the government, if he has property upon which it can be apportioned or assessed, but, if he have no property to be assessed, and be capable of doing so, to labor for his own support, is fully recognized as the just equivalent of the protection which the government is intended to afford to the person and property of each individual,—a protection, the right to which, as we have above indicated, cannot be alienated or forfeited, even by the commission of crime however flagrant.

The mutual relations of all to each and each to all establish a common interest and tend to inspire a feeling of common brotherhood among men. No public wrong can be committed without an injury to every member of the community, and no wrong can be done to one without an injury to all.

As society progresses in knowledge, science, and useful arts and inventions, it becomes more and more complex, and new wants and new sources of enjoyment are developed, and each individual becomes more and more dependent upon others for essential requisites of his support and comfort. When the primitive man clothed himself with fig-leaves, or the skins of wild beasts, and fed upon the spontaneous productions of the earth, his condition was that of comparative independence during the period of his manhood and strength; yet in his infancy and childhood he was as dependent for the preservation of his life and the supply of his physical needs as the infant of the present period. But the arts and inventions, and improved social conditions of an advanced civilization, and the multiplication of the race, have destroyed the independence which the savage man possessed and bound the interests of all together in one common weal, and thus made each dependent upon all and

all upon each, while they have increased the means of happiness according to the ratio of such advancement. Thus
there exists both a necessity and a motive for recognizing
the common brotherhood of the social body. In our habits
and modes of thought none are independent. A man may
be, and certainly ought to be, honest in the expression of
his convictions of truth and right, but how far his opinions
have been the result of independent ratiocination, or how
they may have been formed or influenced by the thoughts
and opinions of others, none can determine. He is indebted
to the intellectual and moral culture of the ages for all the
intellectual and moral power he possesses above those of
the savage or primitive man. Knowledge and wisdom are
of slow growth, and their development in man has occupied
all the vast period of time since man's advent upon the
earth; and yet his greatest wisdom and highest degree of
knowledge only serves to reveal to him the fact that he is
still groping in darkness and ignorance. When, therefore,
we speak of independence of thought and opinion, we clearly
can do so only in a very limited and qualified sense. An
original thought, says Emerson, is the rarest thing in the
world. In supplying our physical wants and necessities we
find ourselves absolutely dependent upon others. Not one
of all the vast multitude of civilized men can furnish himself with the food he consumes, or a single article of the
clothing he wears, or the house he dwells in, without the
aid of others; and when we consider what a multitude of
people have contributed their labor and skill in the production of every garment we wear, the number appears amazing.
From the acquisition of the land, its clearing and cultivation,
the sowing of the seed, and the care of the plants that yield
the fibre, or food, for the fleecy tribes that furnish the raw
material; the preparation of the material and the manufacture
of it into cloth, including the invention, manufacture, and
operation of the machinery by which it is manufactured;

the preparation of the cloth for its destined uses; its sale, transportation, and distribution to the points where it is needed; the cutting, fitting, and making up into the garments with which we are clothed, the number of those who have thus labored for our benefit appears almost beyond our power to compute. Each one of this immense number has done a part, however small; but it required them all to accomplish the completed work. We thus see and ought to be profoundly impressed with the truth of the proposition, that it is the interest as well as the duty of each to seek his own happiness in promoting the welfare of all. In a community where all should act intelligently for the accomplishment of this purpose, the highest attainable degree of human happiness would be reached. The person, property, and individual rights would be held sacred, and would be safe, and none would be permitted to suffer where suffering could be averted. As, however, we do not expect to find absolute perfection in any individual, neither do we expect to see a perfect nation or community of people. Individuals and communities will always be subject to defects and imperfections, and the effort to overcome the evils men see in themselves, or the body politic of which they are a part, will ever be, to those who make it, an inspiring source of gratification. As humanity ascends from one moral elevation to another, the view broadens, and while the lower conditions from which man has arisen are more clearly seen, a view is gained of more elevated positions still to be attained, and the motive for higher effort is seen in the " coming events" which " cast their shadows before."

In all ages of the world, since the dawn of civilization, there has existed in the minds of the wisest and best an ideal of a social state wherein righteousness, peace, harmony, and good-will should prevail, and an abiding faith that such a state would eventually be realized by mankind. The " Republic" of Plato, the " Cyropædia" of Xenophon, the "Republic" of Cicero in imitation of that of Plato, Dante's "De Monarchia," Sir Thomas More's "Utopia," Bacon's "New Atlantis," the "Argenis" of Barclay, Saint-Pierre's "Arcadia," and the schemes of Fourier, Proudhon, Robert Owen, Saint-Simon, Ruskin, and others, represent the ideas of their several authors and promoters in regard to a social state or condition which would be promotive of the highest degree of human happiness. The early Christians believed that a great change was soon to take place over the whole earth, and that in the new state about to be inaugurated righteousness and peace should everywhere prevail, and universal love and good-will should fill all hearts and govern all actions. This was to be the millennial state, and there are many who still look forward with faith and hope that such a condition will some time be realized upon the earth. While the Utopias, Arcadias, and ideal commonwealths of former ages appear extravagant and absurd in many of their characteristics, some of them contain suggestions of needed reforms which have been practically adopted in later times for the amelioration and improvement of the condition of men.

When we come face to face with society as it now is, and consider the vast amount of ignorance, folly, and iniquity everywhere manifest, even among those who are deemed the most enlightened, it is apparent that we may not hope for an immediate realization of that exalted condition which we believe the race is capable of reaching. But when we also contemplate the progress it has made within the historic period, from a condition of savage and barbaric brutality to civilization and enlightenment, as exhibited in the character of the English, French, German, and American peoples, and especially since the beginning of the present century, we are justified in predicting a continuance of progression until our highest ideal shall be realized. As the means of knowledge have increased, man's progress has

been accelerated in a constantly increasing ratio; and although his practical standard of morals has not kept pace
with his progress in science and arts, discoveries and inventions, and needs to be greatly elevated, yet, taking the world
at large, it was perhaps never so high as now, and should
and must continue to rise as intelligence is increased.

Man's physical needs were the first to be felt and provided
for, and the effort to provide for these developed his intellectual faculties.   When these became sufficiently unfolded
he began to acquire ideas of moral obligation and duty,
and to advance from the sensual and purely selfish plane of
animal life towards that condition which constitutes the
ideal of a perfect social state.

The experiences of one condition of the race have prepared it for a higher one.   The light and knowledge of one
age could not be comprehended by a preceding age, and
wherever a people have advanced so far as to be capable of
receiving more knowledge of truth, a teacher has never
failed to appear to dispense it to the world.   Confucius,
Zoroaster, Socrates, Plato, and Jesus were far in advance of
the ages in which they lived, and the great principles of
right and justice which they taught were received by a
few only, and were but imperfectly understood by those
who became their disciples.   Their light shone upon darkness, and the darkness comprehended it not.   Although
the light was perfect, the perception of it in the minds of
men has been so feeble, or distorted, that it has led them
into the greatest errors, superstitions, and perversions of
the truth.   The Prophet of Nazareth taught that men should
love not only their friends, but their enemies also, and seek
to do good to them; that each should do to others as he
would that others should do to him; that wars should cease,
and that peace and good-will should prevail upon the earth.
A religion professedly based upon the teachings of Jesus
has for centuries been the prevailing religion in the most

powerful and enlightened nations of the world.  But of all
the sects and denominations which have assumed the name
of Christianity, and each one claiming to have the true
light, which one has ever understood the teachings of the
Master?  Instead of organizing churches upon the principle
that love is the fulfilling of the law, and the qualification
for membership a pure and holy life devoted to the welfare
of all,—a principle so in accord with human reason and
experience that the wayfaring man, though a fool, need not
err therein,—creeds, dogmas, and articles of faith the most
abhorrent to human reason and repulsive to every kindly
impulse of the heart of man have been adopted, taught,
and their acceptance insisted upon as the only means of
escape from the vengeful anger of an offended Deity and of
salvation from endless woe.  To one who looks at the history of Christendom from the stand-point of a moral phi-
losopher and historian merely, it scarcely seems wonderful
that for more than a decade of centuries, under ecclesiastical
rule,—when to reason was a crime worthy of death, and
hundreds of thousands were put to death with excruciating
tortures for the supposed glory of God, as heretics, because they had outgrown the ignorance, bigotry, and superstitions of their age, and become wiser than their generation,
—a pall of thick moral and intellectual darkness covered
the earth during that long and terrible period justly denominated "the dark ages."  But the light continued to shine
and the minds of men have gradually been opened to receive it, so that during the eighteenth and nineteenth centuries, and more especially during the last half-century,
thought has asserted its supremacy and exulted in a freedom never accorded to it before, and the progress of the
race in material wealth and comfort as well as intellectual
and moral improvement has been unprecedented.

Thus we see that ignorance has been the mother of crime,
and that crime has perpetuated and rendered the moral

darkness and depravity more dense and horrible.  It matters
not that men were burned at the stake, or crucified, or otherwise slain as heretics or non-conformists, because of their
opinions in matters of religious belief, under the authority
or protection of the power constituting the goverment, or
according to the forms of law, nor how sincere were the
convictions of those who perpetrated or sanctioned the deeds
of blood, that the God they professed to worship required
such sacrifice of human life, their acts stand out in all their
hideous and ghastly deformity as crimes against humanity.

It is the nature and necessary effect of crime to obstruct
and oppose progress in knowledge and virtue; and hence,
by contrasting his present state or any former condition
with that ideal state in which peace, order, and universal
love shall prevail, and to which we believe man will eventually attain, see that the only practical means of his advancement must be to overcome evil with good.  Had that vast
number of men who suffered martyrdom because of their
indomitable integrity and courage been allowed the exercise
of freedom in the expression of their thoughts, and to continue their example before the world, we cannot doubt but
what it would have been centuries in advance of its present
state in intelligence, morals, religion, and everything that
tends to promote human welfare.  " Who can pretend," says
Darwin, "to say why the Spanish nation, so dominant at
one time, has been distanced in the race?  The awakening
of the nations of Europe from the dark ages is a still more
perplexing problem.  At this early period, as Mr. Galton
has remarked, almost all the men of gentle nature, those
given to meditation or culture of the mind, had no refuge
except in the bosom of the church, which demanded celibacy,
and this could hardly fail to have a deteriorating influence
upon each successive generation.  During this same period
the Holy Inquisition selected with extreme care the finest
and boldest men in order to burn and imprison them.  In

Spain alone some of the best men—those who doubted and questioned (and without doubt and questioning there can be no progress)—were eliminated during three centuries at the rate of a thousand a year."

The way of progression is to oppose and endeavor to eradicate all wrong, oppression, injustice, and crime, wherever or in whatever form it may exist. When we come to consider the causes of crime which constitute the root of all these evils, it will be apparent that strong convictions and clear perceptions of right and justice, with courage, energy, charity, and patience, and that enthusiasm which is inspired by the consciousness of being engaged in a great and good work, will all be demanded as qualifications for effective service. There are evil habits and customs so deeply embedded in the constitution of society as it now exists, and which have been cherished for ages, to be corrected and removed, and great wrongs to be exposed and righted, against the assumed rights and interests of great masses of our people who will wish to be let alone, that the philanthropist or reformer who undertakes to go to the bottom of things and set them right may expect to encounter most strenuous resistance and rancorous and determined opposition.

Crime works injury to the perpetrator. When it affects others in their persons, property, or social rights, its tendency is to excite indignation and induce retaliation. It not infrequently sets in operation a train of events resulting in the greatest calamities. A great wrong done, or believed to have been done, not infrequently awakens a feeling of vindictiveness in the minds of masses of people, who, moved by a common impulse, become a maddened, lawless mob, who with reckless violence cause the destruction of lives and property and inspire universal terror throughout a municipality. A murder or other atrocious crime, committed or attempted, often inspires a multitude of men, who have never before been thought capable of committing crime or thought themselves to be so, with the determination to murder the supposed perpetrator, and vengeance is thus often blindly executed upon an innocent victim, who is given no opportunity to make his innocence appear.

We most firmly believe also that no man ever did, or can, derive any substantial benefit from the commission of wrong, whether done consciously or otherwise, and we sincerely believe that whoever commits a wrong to the injury of another will in his own person suffer for the wrong he has committed, and that no atonement will or can be made for it by another. If his conscience is so clouded that he does not at the time realize the moral guiltiness of his acts, we believe that the time will come when his moral conscious-ness will be awakened, and that he will then suffer the just penalty of his evil doing. And moreover, to our apprehen-sion, this immutable law which declares that " though hand join in hand, the wicked shall not be unpunished," and that " the soul that sinneth it shall die," is not only according to perfect justice, but according to the highest and most per-fect mercy and most supreme wisdom. These consequences of our actions are, to each individual, the discipline he needs, and which is indispensable in order to bring him into harmony with the laws of the universe, without which he cannot know happiness. A life of evil-doing is one of moral death. It may afford gratification to the sensual appetites and passions which man possesses in common with the brutes that are without moral sense; but when we consider that it is through man's moral consciousness that he is capable of rising from a low to a higher plane of existence, and that his happiness is increased in proportion to his moral elevation, and his knowledge of good as contrasted with evil, we perceive the supreme wisdom and mercy of the law by which just moral retribution is made a certain consequence of wrong or disregard of moral obligation.

# ARTICLE II.

## CAUSES OF CRIME.

---

## CHAPTER I.

### INTRODUCTION.

In the preceding article we have briefly considered the nature of crime with reference to its consequences to society and to its members individually, and the basis of man's individual obligation and duty in his relations to others in a social or civilized state. We have also adverted to the grounds upon which we may predicate the hope of his continued progression towards that ideal state which constitutes our conception of the highest and most perfect condition to which man is capable of attaining, and we have seen that in order to form a rational idea of his capacity for advancement, we must look back through the entire period of his history, and observe the progress he has made during the centuries through which we can trace his existence upon the earth. In this progress we have found the prophecy of that exalted state which seers and sages have predicted for the human race, and upon it we feel assured we may rest our faith in the ultimate emancipation of humanity from the thraldom of sin. We are now to treat of the causes which produce crime, and to consider the sources, so far as we are able to trace them, of the wrong and injustice, the tyranny, oppression, and cruelty men practise towards their fellow-men, and from which proceed most of the suffering which exists in the world.

In our endeavor to discover the causes of crime we shall

23

not undertake to solve the mystery of life, nor to search out the primal cause of sin. If an all-wise and all-powerful Creator permitted evil to enter into the constitution of man, and still permits it to exist in his nature and yield its fruitage of misery, our reason can guide us to no other conclusion than that infinite wisdom and goodness could devise no other means of securing for man that elevation in the scale of being to which he is destined. Or, if we assume that nature without a supreme guiding intelligence (as the materialists believe) has developed man from the elements of the material universe by infinite processes of evolution, we may conclude that she has done the best she could in making man what he has been, and what he is, but the origin of evil on this theory is none the less a mystery.

We are now mainly interested in inquiring into the nature and causes of crime, with reference to its prevention and treatment, and for this purpose we can only consider those proximate and secondary causes to which we can trace the commission of criminal actions; for until we shall have arrived at a true conception of the nature, and searched out the causes, of crime, we shall not understand what is necessary to its prevention or cure.

## CHAPTER II.

### HEREDITY AS A CAUSE OF CRIME.

In our researches after the causes of crime, the first, if not one of the principal, that attracts our attention is *heredity;* or the bodily, mental, and moral characteristics which proceed from ancestral antecedents, and which are planted as germs in the system of the child by his progenitors as a part of his nature, to grow with his growth and strengthen with his strength, unless overcome or counteracted by some more potent influence. An able writer and thinker has defined heredity as a law of biology, by which organisms tend to repeat themselves in their descendants. Every animal inherits the characteristics of the species to which it belongs; and mental heredity is just as much a fact of science as physical heredity. Animals inherit the physical as well as the psychological characteristics of the genus, species, and variety to which they belong.

Even atavism, resembling somewhat alternate generation in the lower forms, seems to show the tenacity with which heredity preserves and transmits what has been acquired, even when it has been repressed for generations.

Men and nations are generally subject to the law of heredity. An individual exhibits the traits of his race, his people, and his family. A State exhibits its national character. Historians have not failed to notice the essential identity of the character of a nation through all periods of its history. Ribot says that " In the absence of scientific researches, historians have long been accustomed to express decided judgments upon the national character, and the impossibility of altering it. Thus the French of the nineteenth century are in fact the Gauls described by Cæsar. In the commentaries by Strabo, and in Diodorous Siculus, we find all the essential traits of our national character: love of arms, taste for anything that glitters, extreme levity of mind, incurable vanity, address, great readiness of speech, and disposition to be carried away by phrases. There are in Cæsar some observations which might have been written yesterday. " The Gauls," says he, " have a love of revolution; they allow themselves to be led by false reports into acts they afterwards regret and into decisions on the most important events; they are depressed by reverses; they are as ready to go to war without a cause as they are weak and powerless in the hour of defeat."

History also shows that the other nations and peoples of the earth have perpetuated their peculiar characteristics, most of them, however, in a modified form, owing to the admixture of the blood of different nationalities, and other causes. Thus heredity is seen to be a law of conservation. Changes in environment, climate, soil, food, etc., produce changes, however slight, in the organism. Offspring cannot be wholly like both parents. The law by which paternal and maternal characteristics are transmitted necessitates variations from both the father and mother. Variations occur which, because we cannot discover their antecedents, are called spontaneous. These variations indicate the necessity of heredity to preserve and perpetuate beneficial changes, and to promote that progress which heredity would otherwise seem to render impossible. The newer modifications must necessarily be fluctuating until they become fully correlated with the reproductive system, and can only acquire stability and take their place as conservative inheritances, when sustained from without as well as from within. The same writer above referred to justly remarks, that " The knowledge now possessed in regard to the laws of heredity, were it diffused, would probably contribute something to prevent the transmission of physical, mental, and moral deformities and weaknesses ; but deep-rooted prejudices, time-honored customs, and hoary superstitions are obstacles to the practical application as well as the diffusion of this knowledge, not to be overcome easily, nor in a short time." But whatever obstacles may exist to retard the diffusion and appreciation of a knowledge of the laws of heredity, it is a subject of so great importance to the welfare of humanity, and so essential to human progress, that they cannot be overlooked, nor their investigation omitted. The prejudices, customs, and superstitions which have always stood opposed to the investigation of new truths in science, ethics, or philosophy, which are not in accord with preconceived opinions, are constantly being overcome or modified by deeper thought and the force of reason; and in this age of general freedom of opinion and speech they constitute no ground for discouragement to those who seek after knowledge for the purpose of applying it to the use and benefit of their fellowmen. The characteristics which distinguish nations, and which are called national characteristics, are formed by, and represent, the general character of the individuals constituting the nationality, and their perpetuation by the law of heredity indicates that by the same law individual and family traits of character are transmitted by parents to their descendants; and while each individual inherits the general character of his race or people, he also inherits, in a more marked degree, the physical and mental constitution of his parents or other ancestors." Mr. Ribot has shown that the sensorial qualities of touch, of sight, of hearing, smell and taste, as well as the faculties of memory, imagination, and intellect, are transmissible by heredity.

In treating of heredity as among the causes of crime, it will be sufficient for our purpose to consider the forms of transmission of those sentiments, appetites, and passions which tend to the commission of crime, either directly or indirectly. Ribot remarks that " the passion known as dipsomania, or alcoholism, is so frequently transmitted that all are agreed in considering its heredity as a rule. Not, however, that the passion for drink is always transmitted in that identical form, for it often degenerates into mania, idiocy, and hallucination. Conversely, insanity in parents may become alcoholism in the descendants. This continual metamorphosis shows how near passion comes to insanity, how closely the successive generations are connected, and, consequently, what a weight of responsibility rests on each individual."

Gall speaks of a Russian family in which the father and grandfather had died prematurely, the victims of this taste for strong drink. The grandson at the age of five manifested the same liking in the highest degree. In our own times Magnus Huss and Dr. Morel have collected many facts bearing on the heredity of alcoholism, a few instances only of which need to be cited.

A man belonging to the educated class, and charged with important functions, succeeded for a long time in concealing his alcoholic habits from the eyes of the public; his family being the only sufferers from it. He had five children, only one of whom lived to maturity. Instincts of cruelty were manifested in this child, and from an early age its sole delight was to torture animals in every conceivable way. He was sent to school, but could not learn. At the age of nineteen he had to be sent to an asylum for the insane.

Charles X——, son of an eccentric and intemperate father, manifested instincts of great cruelty from infancy. He was sent at an early age to various schools, but was expelled from all. Being forced to enlist in the army, he sold his uniform for drink, and only escaped a sentence of death on the testimony of physicians, who declared he was the victim of an irresistible appetite.

A man of an excellent family of laboring people was early addicted to drink, and died of chronic alcoholism, leaving seven children. The first two of these died at an early age of convulsions. The third became insane at twenty-two, and died an idiot. The fourth, after various attempts at suicide, fell into the lowest grade of idiocy. The fifth, of passionate and misanthropic temper, broke off all relations with his family. His sister suffered from various disorders which chiefly took the form of hysteria, with intermittent attacks of insanity. The seventh, a very intelligent workman, but of morose temperament, freely gives expression to the gloomiest foreboding as to his intellectual future.

Dr. Morel gives the history of another family, in which

the great-grandfather was a drunkard and died from the effects of intoxication, and the grandfather, subject to the same passion, died a maniac. He had a son far more sober than himself, but subject to hypochondria and homicidal tendencies, and the son of the latter was a stupid idiot. Here we see in the first generation alcoholic excess; in the second, hereditary dipsomania; in the third, hypochondria; in the fourth, idiocy and probable extinction of the race.

Ribot states the sad case of a lady of regular life and economical habits, who was subject to fits of uncontrollable dipsomania. Loathing her state, she called herself a miserable drunkard, and mixed the most disgusting substances with her wine, but all in vain; the passion was stronger than her will. Quite recently, says Ribot, Dr. Morel had again an opportunity of proving the hereditary effects of alcoholism in the children of the commune. He inquired into the mental state of one hundred and fifty children, ranging from ten to seventeen years of age, most of whom had been taken with arms in their hands behind the barricades. "This examination," he says, "has confirmed me in my previous convictions as to the baneful effects produced by alcohol, not only in the individuals who use this detestable drink to excess, but also in their descendants. On their depraved physiognomy is impressed the threefold stamp of physical, intellectual, and moral degeneracy."

Other propensities which, in their origin at least, are purely physical,—as gluttony, and even cannibalism,—as attested by Gall, Lordat, and Prosper Lucas, are transmissible to descendants. When we consider the more complex passions of avarice, theft, and murder, we find them also subject to the law of heredity. "The passion for play," says Ribot, "often attains such a pitch of madness as to be a form of insanity, and, like it, transmissible," and he cites from "Da Gama Machado" the case of a lady of large fortune who had a passion for gambling and spent whole nights at play, and who died young, of pulmonary disease. Her eldest son, who was very like his mother, had the same passion for play. He too, like his mother, died of consumption, and at about the same age. His daughter, who resembled him, inherited the same taste, and also died young.

Avarice produces similar consequences. " In several instances," says Dr. Maudsley, in his " Physiology and Pathology of the Mind," " in which the father has toiled upward from poverty to vast wealth, with the aim and hope of founding a family, I have witnessed the results in a physical and mental degeneracy, which has sometimes gone as far as the extinction of the family in the third or fourth generation. When the evil is not so extreme as madness or ruinous vice, the savor of a mother's influence having been present, it may still be manifest in an instinctive cunning and duplicity, and an extreme selfishness of nature,—a nature not having the capacity of a true moral perception or altruistic feeling." This distinguished author expresses the opinion that the extreme passion for getting rich, absorbing the whole energies of a life, predisposes to mental degeneration in the offspring, either to moral defect, or to intellectual or moral deficiency, or to outbreaks of positive insanity under the conditions of life. Ribot remarks that " the heredity of the tendency to thieving is so generally admitted that it would be superfluous to bring together facts which abound in every record of judicial proceedings." As an instance, the genealogy of the Christian family from Dr. Despine's " Psychologie Naturelle," is given as follows : " Jean Christian, the common ancestor, had three sons,—Pierre, Thomas, and Jean Baptiste. 1. Pierre had a son, Jean François, who was condemned for life to hard labor for robbery and murder. 2. Thomas had two sons, François, condemned to hard labor for murder, and Martin, condemned to death for murder. Martin's son died in Cayenne, whither he had been transported for robbery. 3. Jean Baptiste had a son, Jean François, whose wife was Marie Taure (belonging to a family of incendiaries). This Jean François had seven children: (1) Jean François, found guilty of several robberies, died in prison; (2) Benoit fell off a roof which he had scaled and was killed; (3) X——, nicknamed 'Clain,' found guilty of several robberies, died at the age of twenty-five; (4) Marie Reine, died in prison, whither she had been sent for theft; (5) Marie Rose, same deed, same fate; (6) Victor, in jail for theft; (7) Victorine, married one Lamaire; their son was condemned to death for murder and robbery." Many other facts of a like kind are related in this work, and which show a tendency in such families to unite, thus conferring hereditary transmission. Conflicting heredities may exist in families, as in the case referred to by Gall, where the one from the mother was good, the one from the father was bad, and where three out of the five children were condemned to severe and degrading penalties for thieving, and the other two possessed the good qualities of the mother and lived correct lives.

Kleptomania, which is defined to be "a supposed species of moral insanity, exhibiting itself in an irresistible desire to pilfer," is an infirmity with which our merchants and tradesmen generally are acquainted; and that it is subject to the laws of heredity there can be no more doubt than in the case of dipsomania. It may be, and probably in many cases is, the inheritance of avarice in one or both of the parents, and females as often as males are the subjects of this insane desire. Most unfortunately, too, many of the subjects of this mania are persons of education and intelligence, and otherwise of good character, and belonging to families of influence and respectability in the community.

What has been said above of the instinct of thieving may be applied to that for robbery or murder. Instances of hereditary transmission are generally conclusive, and equally

numerous.   We have already seen the heredity of homicide
added, in a portion of a family, to the heredity of theft.
Indeed, all great crimes, proceeding as they do from a depraved mind and an obscured moral sense, are more or less
correlated to each other.   The man who, armed with a re-
volver, breaks and enters a dwelling or shop in the night-time
with the intent to commit larceny of goods or money, may
not hesitate to murder any one who would be likely to prevent
the execution of his purpose ; and several notable cases have
occurred in this State recently in which members of a family
have been murdered by persons in pursuit of plunder.

Mr. Dugdale, in his examinations of prisons in New York,
traced back the genealogies of five hundred and forty persons
who had descended in seven generations from a woman who
is called " Margaret, Mother of Criminals," and one hundred
and sixty-nine who were related by marriage or cohabitation.
Of these seven hundred and nine persons, two hundred and
eighty were adult paupers and one hundred and forty were
criminals and offenders, guilty of murders, thefts, highway
robberies, and nearly every kind of offence known in the
calendar of crime.   Mr. Dugdale has estimated the cost of
supporting this vast family of paupers and criminals at one
million three hundred and eight thousand dollars, without
reckoning the cash paid for whiskey, or the entailment of
these evils upon posterity, or the incurable diseases, idiocy
and insanity, growing out of their debaucheries, and reaching further than we can calculate.   Commenting upon the
operations of the law of heredity, Papillon says, " The evo-
lutions of these hereditary maladies are exceedingly interesting and dramatic.   Planted in the children's systems as
germs, or as mere predispositions, they are sometimes destroyed beyond a possibility of returning by a multitude of
favorable conditions and precautions.   In other instances
they begin at once their fatal work of destruction.   Or,
again, they may be hidden for years, reappearing at length,

remorseless and terrible, under the influence of sundry exciting causes. Thus age, sex, temperament, practices, hygiene, surrounding conditions act a part in the development of hereditary morbid activities."

---

# CHAPTER III.

### ACCIDENTAL PRENATAL INFLUENCES.

ASIDE from these fixed habits and characteristics of the ancestors which are surely transmitted by heredity to descendants, there are often more transient causes which make an indelible impression upon the physical and mental constitutions of the child. The physical and mental conditions of the parents at the time of conception as surely affect the progeny for good or ill as the condition and character of the soil in which the seed is sown affect the plant which it causes to germinate. In the appendix to Combe, on the "Constitution of Man," a case is recited from the *Phrenological Journal* of intelligent parents who, on the evening of cohabitation, attended a social party, drank toddy, and danced and sang together during the evening until both became intoxicated, and when heated with the dance, and their nervous systems inflamed by the toddy, they left the cottage, and after the lapse of an hour they were found together in a state of insensibility, and the result of this interview was the birth of a low-grade idiot. Thousands of blighted lives may be traced to similar causes. Out of twenty-five epileptics, Voison found twelve to have had parents drunk on their honeymoon. This principle of transmission was understood by the people of ancient Carthage, who had a law forbidding the use of all beverages, except water, on the day of marital cohabitation.

c

Plutarch, in his work on morals, says, "The advice I am now about to give is indeed no other than what has been given by those who have undertaken this argument before me. You will ask me what is that? 'Tis this, that no man keep company with his wife, for issue sake, but when he is sober, or not having before drunk any wine, or at least, not to such a quantity as to distemper him, for they usually prove wine-bibbers, and drunkards, where parents beget them when they are drunk; whereupon Diogenes said to a stripling, somewhat crack-brained and half-witted, 'Surely, young man, thy father begot thee when he was drunk.'" Other prenatal causes influence or determine the character of the offspring. The environments of the mother, and her physical and mental condition during pregnancy, impress themselves upon the germ of manhood or womanhood in its embryonic or fœtal state. If the child is not wanted, and especially if, as occurs with fearful frequency among educated and fashionable married women (a fact which many of our experienced medical practitioners can attest), the mother persistently seeks its destruction, but the unconscious object of the parent's hate fights its way through to birth and recognized existence, the character of the man or woman coming into life under such adverse circumstances, unwelcome and unloved, cannot be expected to escape the baleful effects of the parent's malice.

Mr. Combe, in the appendix to the "Constitution of Man," relates the case of a shoemaker, who called and showed him his son, aged eighteen, who was in a state of idiocy. The father stated that the mother was sound in mind, as were also his three other children, and that the only account he could ever give of the condition of this son was, that while he was keeping a public house, and some months before the birth of this boy, an idiot had come around with a brewer's drayman, and helped him lift the casks off the cart; that that idiot made a strong impression on his wife, that she complained that she could not get his impression removed from her mind, and that she kept out of the way when he came to the house afterwards; that his son was weak in body from his birth, and silly in mind, and had the slouched and slovenly appearance of the idiot. Several cases are cited from the *Phrenological Journal* illustrative of the doctrine, that the faculties which predominate in power and activity in the parents when the organic existence of the child commences determine its future mental disposition,—a doctrine certainly of very great importance. It was remarked by the celebrated Esquirol that the children whose existence dated from the first French revolution turned out to be weak, nervous, irritable in mind, extremely susceptible of impressions, and liable to be thrown by the least extraordinary excitement into absolute insanity. Sometimes, too, family calamities produce serious effects upon the offspring. A very intelligent and reputable mother, during pregnancy, received information that the crew of the ship on board of which was her son had mutinied; that when the ship arrived in the West Indies, some of the mutineers, and also her son, had been put in irons, and that they were all to be sent home for trial. This intelligence acted so strongly upon her that she suffered a temporary alienation of judgment, and though the report turned out to be erroneous, this did not avert the consequences of the agitated state of the mother's feelings upon the daughter she afterwards gave birth to. When the daughter became a woman she was, and continued to be, a being of impulse, incapable of reflection, and in other respects greatly inferior to her sisters.

We could cite a number of well-authenticated cases which have come under our own observation, to show that circumstances strongly affecting the mother's feelings during pregnancy act upon, and frequently determine, the mental and physical constitution of the child. One is that of a young man of pleasing address, affectionate and obliging in disposition, who was sent to the reform school for theft at an early age. Shortly after he was discharged he repeated the offence, and finally committed a burglary, for which he was sentenced to the State House of Correction and Reformatory for a term of years. Before he was sentenced for the last offence, the mother, who was a very honest and respectable woman, and the mother of several other children of irreproachable moral character, related to us the following facts: Her husband was addicted to habits of intemperance, and though he was a good mechanic and earned large wages, he often spent so much for liquor as to leave the family in need, and during her pregnancy, and before the birth of this son, in order to supply her own pressing wants and those of her children, she several times took money clandestinely from her husband's pockets; and although in her own judgment she thought she was justified in doing so, yet she was greatly troubled in her conscience and felt that she was guilty of stealing, and it was to this condition of her feelings that she attributed the unfortunate propensity of her son, for whom she entertained the strongest affection.

# CHAPTER IV.

### INTEMPERANCE AS A CAUSE OF CRIME.

THAT the intemperate use of intoxicating liquors is an evil of immense and incalculable magnitude at the present day there are very few who will deny; nor will it be questioned by any who have had any participation in criminal proceedings, that it is one of the most fruitful sources of crime. It was said by a leading abolitionist a few years ago, that the institution of human slavery, as it then existed in some of our sister States, was "the sum of all villanies."

That institution, by means not then appearing probable, and perhaps entirely unthought of by any, has been abolished, and six millions of human beings, who were then regarded as mere chattels in the hands of their owners, have been made free American citizens, with all the rights and privileges, as such, which their former owners possess. In view of the enormous amount of poverty, crime, and consequent suffering growing out of the manufacture, sale, and intemperate use of intoxicating liquors, may it not with equal truth be said that they now constitute the most villanous system that the worst enemy of man could devise for the degradation and ruin of the human race?

It may be said that the evil arises from the consumption, and not from the manufacture and sale of intoxicants, and that if people did not use them there would of course be no manufacture of or traffic in them. But this does not lessen or at all mitigate the evil; nor is the manufacturer or dealer exempt from responsibility for the consequences of their use. By furnishing the means through which the end is accomplished, and foreseeing the inevitable consequences to the consumer and those who are affected by his acts resulting from such use, do they not make themselves accessories before the fact to the crime which he commits under their influence? If it be true—as physicians and physiologists of the highest authority, who have had the best means of observation, and have made the effects of alcohol upon the human system a subject of special study and investigation, declare—that its use as a beverage is not only injurious to the physical health of the body, but disastrous to the moral and intellectual faculties of those who use it, and that even as a medicine it is doubtful whether it is in any case beneficial, it may well be asked whether the manufacturer and the seller are not equally responsible with the man who commits a wrong in consequence of its use. The fact that alcohol, whether in the form of beer, wine, or spirits, has no

4

food value whatever has long been established by the most careful scientific tests. Every kind of substance employed by man as food, says Dr. Henry Monroe, consists of sugar, starch, oil, and glutinous matter, mingled together in various proportions. These are designed for the support of the animal frame. That alcohol contains none of these substances the most recent and carefully-conducted experiments of English, French, German, and American chemists and physiologists clearly attest. In answer to a memorial presented by the National Temperance Society to the International Medical Congress which convened at Philadelphia in 1886, and was composed of delegates from Europe and America, the section of that body on medicine returned the following:

1. "Alcohol is not shown to have a definite food value by any of the usual methods of chemical analysis or physiological investigation.

2. "Its use as a medicine is chiefly that of a cardiac stimulant, and often admits of substitution.

3. "As a medicine it is not well fitted for self-prescription by the laity, and the medical profession is not accountable for such administration or the enormous evils arising therefrom.

4. "The purity of alcoholic liquors is, in general, not as well assured as that of articles used for medicine should be. The various mixtures, when used as medicines, should have a definite and known composition, and should not be interchanged promiscuously."

Contrary to the commonly accepted opinion of the ignorant, alcohol is not a producer of heat. Dr. Hunt says that "The usual test for a force-producing food, and that to which other foods of that class respond, is the production of heat in the combination of oxygen therewith. This heat means vital force. Experiments have been conducted through long periods, and with the greatest care, and no

one has been able to discover that alcohol has ever under-
gone combustion, like food substances, and so given heat to
the body. On the contrary, it is now well known and admitted by the medical profession, that alcohol reduces the
temperature of the body instead of increasing it. This had
become well known to Arctic voyagers before physiologists
had demonstrated the fact by experiment."

Dr. Edward Smith says that "In the northern regions it
was proved that the entire exclusion of spirits was necessary
in order to retain heat under these unfavorable conditions."
It is safe to assume, in the light of what science has unfolded, and what it has failed to unfold upon the application
of the most careful analysis and experiment, that alcohol is
not in any sense an originator of vital force when taken into
the human system. On the contrary, "there can be no
doubt," says Dr. Hunt, "that alcohol does cause *defects* in
the processes of elimination which are natural to the healthy
body, and which in disease are often conservative of health.
In the pent-in evils which pathology so often shows concur-
rent in the case of spirit drinkers, in the vascular, fatty, and
fibroid degenerations which take place, in the accumulation
of rheumatic and scrofulous tendencies, there is the strongest
evidence that *alcohol acts as a disturbing element*, and is very
prone to initiate serious disturbances amid the normal conduct, both of organ and function." He also refers to Dick-
inson's able *exposé* of the effects of alcohol, in which, after
recounting with accuracy the structural changes which it
initiates, and the consequent derangement and suspension
of vital functions which it involves, he aptly terms it the
"genius of degeneration."

It is one of the most fundamental and universally recognized laws of organic life, that all vital phenomena are accompanied by, and depend on, molecular and atomic
changes, and whatever retards these retards the phenomena
of life, and whatever suspends these suspends life. That the

use of alcohol tends to these disastrous results, and that its use as a beverage can under no ordinary circumstances be beneficial or promotive of physical health, are propositions so well established upon incontrovertible medical testimony that it would be rashness and folly for any one in this age of advanced scientific knowledge and discovery to undertake to controvert them.

If, then, alcohol has no value as food, and is positively detrimental to physical health when taken into the system, and possesses no quality which can render it beneficial, these considerations alone, in view of the enormous tax it imposes upon the victims of a debasing appetite for intoxicants, would affix the stamp of crime upon the manufacturer and the seller of this "genius of degeneration," with the design that it shall be used as a beverage and with full knowledge of the evils which will surely follow such use. The man who discharges a loaded rifle among a crowd of people, though they may be all strangers to him, and he have no malice against any one in particular, and does not intend to destroy the life of any particular individual, is justly held guilty of murder if he thus inflict a mortal wound upon any ; and is it not fully as certain that the manufacture and sale of alcohol to be used as a beverage will cause crime and premature death as that death would ensue from the discharge of a loaded gun among a crowd of people ?

The cost to the consumer of the liquors manufactured in this country, as well as of those which are imported and used as a beverage by our people, cannot be accurately ascertained, but from the records of the Internal Revenue Department and records of the commerce and navigation of the country the quantity of spirits and beer upon which a government tax is collected is accurately known. From those records Dr. Wm. Hargreaves has compiled statements which may be taken as reliable, and from which the cost to consumers is computed. These show that the nation's drink bill in 1883 was $944,629,581, and that from 1880 to 1883, inclusive, it amounted to the enormous sum of $3,354,224,000, with a steady increase from year to year, as shown in the following tables:

| Year. | Dozens of bottles. | Gallons. | Estimated cost. |
|---|---|---|---|
| 1880 | 427,005 | 462,564,447 | $733,816,495 |
| 1881 | 487,815 | 498,038,084 | 800,112,580 |
| 1882 | 608,080 | 578,346,335 | 875,665,344 |
| 1883 | 890,591 | 610,195,505 | 944,629,581 |

The quantity and cost of liquors above given are based upon the supposition that such liquors are sold to the consumers as when taken from the bonded warehouses, except a deduction of twenty per cent. of alcohol by rectifiers and wholesale or retail dealers, and that no other reductions and no adulterations are made; and also upon the supposition that there are no illicit manufactories of liquors. But it is a well-established fact that vast quantities of liquor have been annually sold upon which no tax was paid. By the International Revenue Report of 1881, it appears that in the five years from 1887 to 1881, inclusive, there were 4769 illicit distilleries seized by the government, and that 8615 persons were arrested for operating them. It also appears that in making these seizures and arrests, twenty-eight officers and employés of the government were killed and sixty-four wounded. In the year 1882, 509 stills were seized and 1471 persons arrested for operating them; and four officers and other men killed in that year, in their endeavor to suppress illicit distilling. The product of these illicit stills, amounting to a very large sum, must be added to the cost of liquors on which the taxes were paid in order to form a true estimate of the entire expense to the consumer of the liquors used.

It is hardly possible for persons generally to comprehend the value of a million dollars. How, then, can we comprehend the value of the vast sum of three thousand three hun-

dred and fifty-four millions and upward ($3,354,224,000) ✗
which has been expended for drink by the people of this
country in four years, from 1880 to 1883, much less the
$21,286,525,458 expended for the same purpose in eighty-
four years, from 1800 to 1883 inclusive?  Probably the best
conception we can form of it is by comparing it with the
values of other products of human labor and enterprise.
During the eighty-four years specified, as shown from official sources, the value of our entire imports was $18,205,-
704,517, and that of our entire exports was $16,322,147,652.
Dr. Hargreaves, in his supplement to "Our Wasted Resources," by the same author, after giving tabulated statements to which he refers, makes the following comparisons
and statements :

" During the first quarter of this century there was spent
for intoxicating drinks nearly $2,000,000,000 ($1,948,205,487),
or $195,000,000 more than the value of all imports, including
coin and bullion, and $858,000,000 more than the value of
the merchandise, coin, and bullion exported ; and during the
next fifteen years, from 1825 to 1840, the value of the imports was over $1,547,000,000, and $375,000,000 more than
the cost of liquors ($1,172,609,790), and liquors cost $62,-
000,000 more than the value of all the domestic exports.

" During the next ten years over $1,130,000,000 were spent
for liquors, which was $30,000,000 more than the value of
all imports, and $34,000,000 more than the value of all
exports.   From 1850 to 1859 there were spent for liquors
$2,275,000,000, or $135,000,000 more than the value of all
domestic exports.   During the ten years from 1870 to 1879
the nation's drink bill was $6,717,000,000, or $1,497,000,000
more than all the domestic exports.   During eighty years
our nation's drink bills were nearly $18,000,000,000, which
was $2,485,000,000 more than all our domestic exports.   And
during the present century (eighty-four years) we have spent
for liquors $21,286,000,000, or $3,081,000,000 more than all

foreign imports, and $4,964,000,000 more than all domestic exports. By the tenth Census Report (1880) the assessed value of real and personal property was $16,902,993,543, or $4,384,000,000, less than the nation's drink bills for the century (eighty-four years). Thus more than $21,286,000,-000 of the hard-earned wages of our toiling millions, that should have been spent by our laboring classes for food and clothing for themselves and their families and to promote the prosperity of the country and the happiness of our people, were expended for strong drinks, from which have flowed poverty, misery, crime, disease, and death, and which have burdened our industrious and sober citizens with taxes which would not have been needed had not these thousands of millions been expended for drink.

"Then, again, by the Census Report (1880) the value of farm products sold, consumed, or on hand, was $2,212,540,-927, which was $197,000,000 less than the cost of drink for the three years, 1880, 1881, and 1882. The value of the products of our mechanical and manufacturing industries for the same period was $5,369,579,191, which was $198,-000,000 less than the nation's drink bill ($5,567,759,276) for eight years, from 1875 to 1882 inclusive. Then, again, the cost of liquors during the seventy-nine years from 1800 to 1879, inclusive, was $17,932,301,458, or over $1,000,000,000, more than the assessed value of all real estate and personal property in 1880 within the United States. Our people, in three years, spend for drink more than the value of the natural products of all our farms, and in eight years more than the value of all our mechanical and manufacturing industries; or in less than eleven years our people spend for drink the value of our farms and of all our mechanical and manufacturing industries. Then if a fire were to be kindled on the 1st of January of every eleventh year, and if during the year every article, as fast as produced in our factories workshops, etc., and all farm products as fast as they were gathered, were thrown into this fire and burned until nothing but their ashes remained, this destruction of the products of labor and capital would not inflict as much pecuniary injury to our people and country as is produced every eleven years by the sale of intoxicating drinks. If the products of our farms, factories, and workshops, of the value of the money spent annually for drink, were destroyed by fire and flood (in addition to all destroyed by casualties and other unavoidable causes), it would be a terrible loss, and a cry of woe, sorrow, and horror would be raised all over our land and would arouse and excite every feeling heart. Yet this destruction would not deprive our working-classes of the physical and mental power to supply their loss with others. To spend money for intoxicating drinks is not only a waste of the money, but the users of the drinks are, while under their influence, incapacitated to perform their duties in a greater or less degree."

As said already, the assessed value of real estate and personal property in 1880 was $16,902,993,543. The true value by the Census Report was $43,642,000,000. " During the present century, or in eighty-four years (from 1800 to 1883 inclusive), there were spent for liquors $21,286,525,458, which is nearly one-half of the true value of all the property, real and personal, that has been accumulated since the landing of the Pilgrim Fathers from the ' Mayflower' on Plymouth Rock and the first settlers at Jamestown. It may be safely asserted that if the true cost of liquors could be ascertained, more money has been spent for alcoholic poisons and their indirect cost since the Declaration of Independence than would buy to-day all our farms, factories, and workshops, and their machinery and other contents; all our railroads and their equipments; all our houses, furniture, clothing, and other articles of value in the United States, with the breweries and distilleries, liquor shops and liquors thrown into the bargain."

" The permanent investments in the 87,891 miles of railroad in operation, and owned by the 1482 railway companies in the United States in 1880, was $5,182,445,807. The drink bill of the nation for ten years (1870 to 1879) was $6,617,502,405, which was $1,436,000,000 more than the permanent investments of all the railroads in the United States in 1880. Indeed, our nation's drink bill for the last seven years was only $6,000,000 less than the investment in railroads. Thus in seven years our people spend for drink nearly as much money as is now invested in the 87,891 miles of railroads operated in the United States in 1880."

" Then, again, the average annual cost of liquors for the three years from 1880 to 1882, inclusive, was $803,000,000; the average cost of liquors for each man, woman, and child was $16, and for each family $80.75.

" There were in 1880, 8,955,812 dwellings, of which 163,522 were taxed retail liquor places, and 11,610 taxed retail malt-liquor shops, or a total of 175,133 places where intoxicating drinks were sold at retail. If the liquor shops in 1880 were in one place they would form a city having more dwellings than there are in Philadelphia (146,412) and Pittsburg (24,080) combined, and as many dwellings remaining as would make another city as large as Sacramento, California, or would make four cities as large as St. Louis, Missouri, or two cities larger than New York. Indeed, these drink shops would form a city larger than New York, Brooklyn, Rochester, Albany, and Syracuse, with 1307 dwellings to spare. To arrange them side by side, allowing each a frontage of thirty-four feet, they would form a street, with drinking shops on each side 497 miles long, or nearly the distance from Philadelphia, Pennsylvania, to Cleveland, Ohio; in other words, if placed side by side, they would extend on each side of the railroad track from Philadelphia nearly to Cleveland."

Every one who reflects a moment on the subject must be

convinced that no people, however favored, can continue to prosper who waste so large a proportion of the value of labor for drink. Money panics, hard times, and stagnation of business must inevitably follow such extravagance and waste, and people who violate every law of political economy must sooner or later become ruined and bankrupt.

"Money spent for drink adds nothing to the consumer's possessions,—nothing that really benefits in the present nor in the future, as do food, clothing, furniture, and other property. There is not the least doubt, if the money spent for intoxicating drinks in this country since the Declaration of Independence had been devoted to the purchase of necessary and useful articles, the real and personal property would be nearly double the present value, our people more happy and prosperous, besides being more intelligent, moral, and religious, and the sober and industrious classes free from taxation now imposed upon them for public charities and correction."

To one who has never given special attention to an investigation of the subject these figures and statements appear startling and almost incredible, but unfortunately their truthfulness is too well established by irrefragable evidence to admit of any doubt as to their substantial correctness.

Dr. Hargreaves estimates the loss of labor of persons engaged in the liquor trades, and loss by drinking, as follows : Loss of time and industry of 586,472 persons engaged in making and selling liquors, $293,236,000 ; loss of time and industry of 700,000 drunkards, $175,000,000 ; loss of time and industry of 2,138,391 male tipplers, $222,392,664 ; aggregate loss of time and industry, $690,628,664. He further remarks that "Closer investigation would doubtless show that this large aggregate is far below the true loss. Fifty years ago a committee of the English Parliament found, after close investigation, that one-sixth of the wealth-producing power of England was lost annually by drinking." The loss by the destruction of grain in the breweries and distilleries, in 1882, was 66,660,792 bushels, which at fifty cents a bushel would be $33,330,396. This grain would make about fifteen four-pound loaves of bread per bushel, and a grand total of 990,000,000 four-pound loaves, or more than ninety-nine and one-half loaves for each family in the United States in 1880. This calculation does not include the destruction of grain, etc., used in the production of imported liquors, nor that used in the manufacture of domestic liquors that are not reported to the revenue officers, nor the 30,000,000 gallons of wine as reported in the Agricultural Report of 1880.

The loss by sickness, etc., by the use of alcoholic drinks, amounts to many millions of dollars annually. Dr. Hargreaves says, " There is ample evidence that alcoholic drinks produce sickness, and in proportion to the quantity of liquors consumed is the sickness and death-rate of a people. It has, by careful investigation, been estimated that from one-third to one-half of the sickness of civilized nations is directly or indirectly the result of the use of alcoholic beverages. Dr. B. W. Richardson, President of the Health Section of the Social Science Congress, Brighton, England, October, 1875, stated that the duration of life in England was diminished to the extent of one-third by the sale of intoxicating drinks." Allowing one case of sickness in three hundred and fifty of the population of the United States, according to estimates carefully prepared, and it shows the average number simultaneously sick from drink in the United States to be 143,302 persons. The cost of medical attendance and medicine is not less than one dollar a day for each person sick, which, added to the loss of time for each working-man at one dollar and fifty cents per day, will make an annual loss from sickness caused by drink of $119,368,576.

Dr. Hargreaves says, " Drink not only predisposes the users to disease, but prevents their cure when taken sick, and hastens death, consequently deprives the State of the labor of its citizens, causing sorrow and suffering to the victims and their families or friends, and a loss to the whole nation." In 1880, as shown by the Census Report, 478,072 died under five years of age and 278,821 over five years. In the absence of the exact number we will say one-third of the latter died under twenty-one years, leaving 185,880 who lived to adult age. Applying Dr. Richardson's proportion of deaths from alcohol to the deaths in this country, then 61,962 deaths in 1880 were directly or indirectly due to intoxicating drinks, which fully bears out the estimate that "60,000 die annually in the United States by drink." More than sixty years ago we read among "short sentences" in our school-book this brief epigram, which we have recalled to memory a thousand times, that "Intemperance destroys more lives than war, pestilence, and famine." Dr. Hargreaves estimates the loss to employers by drinking employés at $10,000,000 annually, and, including other indirect losses, makes a total sum of $891,213,640 as the indirect annual cost and loss by drink. This sum, added to the direct cost of drinks in 1883 ($944,629,581), shows the grand total of loss and cost by drink to have been not less than $1,835,843,221 in a single year, not including the value of the grain destroyed to make the drink.

The arguments of the brewers and distillers, and those who favor the liquor traffic, that they give employment to large numbers of persons, is so fully answered by Dr. Hargreaves in the essay referred to, by showing that all the labor employed and capital invested in the manufacture and sale of liquors might be employed in the production of the necessaries and comforts which go to support health and produce happiness and enlarge the means of enjoyment, that we do not deem it necessary to do more than refer the reader to this essay for the perfect refutation of such an argument.

The results, which the most obtuse can see, of devoting the immense amount annually lost by liquor drinking to the purchase of food, clothing, building of comfortable homes, or other permanent improvements, education, etc., contrasted with the consequences of using it in the purchase of liquor, show how preposterous is the idea of the utility of manufacturing and selling intoxicating liquors to be used as a beverage, and the criminality to which the government becomes a party by legalizing and protecting the liquor traffic. For the destruction of a single life, when not justifiable or excusable, a man may be hung or incarcerated for life; but the destruction of sixty thousand lives every year (or one every two minutes) in the United States by strong drink, in a population of fifty millions, subjects no one to punishment by the State, except the unhappy victims of an insatiable appetite and of the cupidity and selfishness of those who compass their ruin and that of their families for gain. Does not every brewer, distiller, rectifier, and retailer of strong drinks well know the direful consequences inevitably resulting from the business in which he is engaged? Certainly to doubt this would be an insult to his understanding. What justification, then, can there be for the individual who engages in it, knowing that no good but only evil can grow out of it? To say that it is a legal business, sustained and protected by the laws of the State, and that the government makes itself a party to the iniquity by exacting a portion of the profits which is paid into the national, State, and municipal treasuries as an equivalent for legal immunity and protection, is only to assert a legal justification which no one questions, but does not in any degree affect the great moral question of man's right to bring upon his fellow-man the misery, degradation, and premature death which are the sure results of the use of alcoholic liquors. To answer that there is a demand for strong drink, and that, the business of supplying it being open to all who pay for the privilege, that

demand will be supplied by others if not by themselves, and
that therefore they might as well have the profit of it as
others, is equally fallacious as an argument to justify the
traffic.   If such an argument were sound, many of the
crimes which the law punishes as such could be easily justified for the same reason.   It entirely ignores the obligation
which rests upon all not to injure any, but to so act as to
benefit all who are affected by our actions.   The recognition
of this obligation lies at the foundation of all sound ethics
and of all genuine religion.

But more deplorable than the loss of the cost to the consumer, and the physical diseases, poverty, and destitution
which it brings upon the drinker, is the moral degradation
and crime which are caused by its use, especially in our
large cities.

Chief-Justice Noah Davis, of the New York Supreme
Court, in a paper carefully prepared and read by him in
December, 1878, in the parlors of the President of the
National Temperance Society, before many distinguished
guests, after remarking that there are other causes of crime,
such as hate, avarice, jealousy, lust, and revenge, says that
"Among all causes of crime, intemperance stands out the
unapproachable chief."   The passions named would probably cause more or less crime without the stimulating effect
of strong drink, but these are intensified by intemperance.
Intoxicating drinks enable men to commit crime by firing
the passions and quenching the conscience.   " Burke, the
Irish murderer, whose horrible mode of committing crime
has taken his own name, in his confession states that only
once did he feel any restraint of conscience.   That was when
he was about to kill an infant child.   The babe looked up
and smiled in his face; 'but,' said he, 'I took a large glass
of brandy, and then I had no remorse.'   His case," says
Judge Davis, "is one of thousands.   Many times in my experience have young men looked up to me, when asked

what they had to say why the sentence of the law should not be pronounced, and falteringly said, 'I was drunk; I would not and could not have done it had I not been drunk.'" In our own experience of over thirty-five years as circuit judge, when any response has been made to the question if he had anything to say why the sentence of the law should not be pronounced against him, the convicted criminal has stated that he was intoxicated at the time the crime was committed, else he should not have done it; and in several cases of larceny recently tried, the prisoners have testified that they were so overcome by the effects of long-continued drinking that they were not conscious of having committed the crime charged against them. The proofs in all such cases, however, satisfied the jury and the court that they had a "drunken consciousness," although obscured by intoxication, of the commission of the acts which constituted their crimes, and that they required the discipline and restraint which the law imposes for their own good.

"That habits of intemperance," says Judge Davis, "are the chief causes of crime is the testimony of all judges of large experience."

In 1670, Sir Matthew Hale, then Chief-Justice of England, and who was the author of a treatise on crimes, said, "The places of judicature I have long held in this kingdom have given me an opportunity to observe the original cause of most of the enormities that have been committed for the space of nearly twenty years; and by due observation I have found that if the murders and manslaughters, the burglaries and robberies, the riots and tumults, fornications, rapes, and other enormities that have happened in that time were divided into five parts, four of them have been the issue and product of excessive drinking—of tavern and alehouse drinking." The same testimony has been borne by judges of the highest and lowest courts exercising criminal jurisdiction during the intervening century. In a letter from

Lord Chief Baron Kelley to the Archdeacon of Canterbury, of recent date, he says, "Two-thirds of the crimes which come before the courts of law of this country are occasioned by intemperance." Equally explicit is the testimony of those whose official duties have brought them in contact with convicted criminals. The chaplain of the Preston House of Correction said, "Nine-tenths of the English crime requiring to be dealt with by law arises from the English sin (intemperance), which the law scarcely discourages." And the late inspector of English prisons says, "I am within the truth when I state that in four cases out of five, when an offence has been committed, intoxicating drink has been one of the causes." A committee of the House of Commons of the Dominion of Canada, in 1875, reported that "Out of 28,289 commitments to the jails of the Provinces of Ontario and Quebec during the three previous years, 21,236 were committed either for drunkenness or for crimes perpetrated under the influence of drink."

The State Board of Charities in Massachusetts, in their report for 1869, said, "The proportion of crime traceable to this great vice must be set down, as heretofore, at not less than four-fifths," and in 1868 the inspector of State prisons gave the same proportion. Dr. Harris, of New York, corresponding secretary of the Prison Association, after an inspection of the prisons of that State, in a paper on "The Relations of Drunkenness to Crime," says, "As a physician, familiar with the morbid consequences of alcoholic indulgence in thousands of sufferers from it, it was easy for the writer to believe that not less than one-half of all crimes and pauperism in the State depends upon alcoholic inebriety. But after two years of careful inquiry into the condition of the criminal population of the State, I find that the conclusion is inevitable that, taken in all its relations, alcoholic drinks may justly be charged with far more than half the crimes that are brought to conviction in the State of New York, and that full *eighty-five per cent.* of all convicts give evidence of having in some larger degree been prepared or enticed to do criminal acts because of the physical and distracting effects produced upon the human organism by alcohol." Dr. Harris also states that of seventeen cases of murder examined by him separately, fourteen were instigated by intoxicating drinks.

The Board of Police Justices of the city of New York, whose testimony is especially valuable because of their daily observation of crime and criminals, say, in their annual report of 1874, "We are fully satisfied that it (intoxication) is the one great leading cause which renders the existence of our police courts necessary."

"Three district attorneys of the county of Suffolk, embracing the city of Boston," says Judge Pittman, "speak to us with equal emphasis." The first in order of time, Hon. John C. Park, says, "While district attorney I formed the opinion (and it is not a mere matter of opinion, but is confirmed by every hour of experience since) that ninety-nine-one-hundredths of the crime in the Commonwealth is produced by intoxicating liquors." Hon. George P. Sanger (ex-Judge of the Court of Common Pleas and United States Attorney for the District of Massachusetts), speaking from his experience as the prosecuting officer for the same district, says, "There are very few cases into which the use of intoxicating liquors does not enter." The last attorney referred to, for the same district, J. Wilson May, writes, "According to my official observation, drinking in some form is directly responsible for about three-fourths of the crime that is brought to the cognizance of the country, and indirectly for about three-quarters of the other crimes." Dr. Hargreaves, in treating of intoxicating drinks as a cause of crime, says, "In whatever direction we look, in every State and Territory of the United States, and in every portion of the civilized world, the terrible results of the use of, and traffic in, alco-

holic drinks have been felt, and to which may be traced
most of the crime, misery, and disturbance of the public
peace. This cause, more than all others, fills our jails, poor-
houses, penitentiaries, and lunatic asylums, and does more
to frustrate the efforts of Christians and philanthropists than
all else combined." He refers to a paper written by Mr.
Fiske, and published in the report of the United States
Commission of Education for 1871, in which it is stated
that "at the Deer Island House of Industry (Boston), of
3514 committals, 3097, or eighty-eight per cent., were for
drunkenness; fifty-four more as idle and disorderly, which
commonly means under the influence of drink ; seventy-seven
for assault and battery, which means the same thing; and
forty-eight as common night-walkers, every one of whom
was a common drunkard. We have therefore in this prison
a full ninety-three per cent. whose confinement is connected
with the use of drink, and this may be taken as a not exaggerated sample of many municipal prisons. In the New
Hampshire State Prison, sixty-five out of ninety-one admit
themselves to have been intemperate. Reports were asked
from every State, county, and municipal prison in Connecticut in the spring of 1871, in reference to the statistics of
drinking habits among the inmates, and it was found that
more than ninety per cent. had been in the habit of drinking
by their own admission." "The Warden of the Rhode
Island State prison, and county jailer, estimated ninety per
cent. of the residents of his cells as drinkers. More than
three-fourths of the inmates of prisons attribute their fall to
the use of intoxicating drinks. Of thirty-nine cases of
murder, and one hundred and twenty-one cases of assault
to murder, in the city of Philadelphia, in 1868, in almost
every case the murderer was intoxicated when the deed was
committed."

In 1867 there was paid for liquor licenses in Pennsylvania
the sum of $320,015, and during the same year that State

paid for criminal and pauper expenses, caused directly by
liquor drinking, $2,259,910, or an average of five dollars
and eighty cents for each voter within her borders. In the
same year Philadelphia paupers and criminals cost $1,500,000,
or eleven dollars for each voter. The report of the Board
of State Charities of Pennsylvania, in 1871, on page 89 says,
"The most prolific source of disease, poverty, and crime,
observing men will acknowledge, is intemperance." Referring to the moneys received for licenses, the board asks,
"Should these wages of iniquity be put into the treasury?"
and says, "They are the price of blood, and in their aggregate would be inadequate to buy fields enough to bury the
multitude who are the victims of the dreadful traffic for
whose profits they sell the people's sanction."

Numerous other facts, derived from authentic sources,
are given by Dr. Hargreaves, all tending to establish the
conclusion that from four-fifths to nine-tenths of all the
crimes committed in the United States and other civilized
nations are the result, either directly or indirectly, of the
use of intoxicating liquors, and that probably an equal proportion of the pauperism proceeds from the same cause.
Our own observation, during an experience of more than
half a century as a practising lawyer, a prosecuting attorney,
and a circuit judge, leads us to the conclusion that this estimate is not exaggerated, and that fully nine-tenths of the
crime committed in this State is caused, directly or indirectly,
by the use of intoxicating liquors. As Judge Davis says,
"The line of witnesses might stretch out to the crack of
doom. The case would only be a little stronger. It is
established beyond argument, by official statistics, by the
experience of courts, and by the observation of enlightened
philanthropists, that the prevalence of intemperance in
every country is the standard by which its crimes may be
measured."

The charge against the liquor traffic and its use is, that

it does no good, but evil only, and that continually. The specifications under this charge, and which are claimed to have been proven beyond question or controversy, are the following:

1. That it occasions a waste and loss in the United States alone of over $1,800,000,000 annually.

2. That it works the destruction of the home.

3. That it is the parent of pauperism, with all its attendant suffering.

4. That it injures the public health, vitiates human stock, and destroys sixty thousand lives annually.

5. That it is the chief cause of crime.

6. That it is the universal ally of evil, the universal antagonist of good. What Charles Dickens said of the wine-shops of France may be said with equal truth of the liquor-saloons of this country: "The wine-shops are the colleges and chapels of the poor in France. History, morals, politics, jurisprudence, and literature in iniquitous forms are all taught in these colleges and chapels, where professors of evil continually deliver those lessons, and where hymns are sung nightly to the demon of demoralization. In these haunts of the poor, theft is taught as the morality of property, falsehood as speech, and assassination as the justice of the people. The wine-shops breed, in a physical atmosphere of malaria and a moral pestilence of envy and vengeance, the men of crime and revolution."

In our drinking-saloons burglaries, thefts, robberies, and other crimes are planned; to them the fruits of crime are brought; and there the perpetrators find a friendly welcome and protection after the commission of their crimes.

That strong drink acts as a poison when taken into the human system, and is capable of producing death, is a fact established beyond controversy by scientific observation. Dr. Hargreaves, in "Alcohol and Science," says, "The diseases produced by intoxicating drinks are legion. Thousands, aye, tens of thousands, die annually whose deaths are ascribed to diseases that would not seriously have affected them, or proved fatal, if alcohol had not laid the foundation of the disease by lowering the tone of the system, undermining the vital forces and the conservative energies of the system." Dr. Hargreaves and other eminent physicians, who had the opportunity to examine the stomach, liver, kidneys, and other organs of drinkers of wine, beer, and distilled liquors, give illustrations showing the frightful effects which they produce upon these organs. They show us the condition of the human stomach in a healthy state; the condition of that organ produced by moderate drinking, with the beautiful net-work of blood-vessels, which was invisible in the healthy stomach, dilated and distended with blood; the condition of that of the confirmed drunkard, with the blood-vessels of the inner coat so fully gorged as to render the most minute branches visible to the eye, like the rum-blossoms on the drunkard's face, thickening and softening the mucous coat, and often resulting in ulceration. Other illustrations show the ulcerated condition of the drunkard's stomach after a long debauch, and also where *delirium tremens*, resulting in death, has intervened, and the cancerous condition of the same organ. Other illustrations are given showing the disastrous effects of alcoholic drinks upon the liver and kidneys, and it is our firm conviction that if our liquor laws were so amended as to require every retail dealer in strong drinks to have an enlarged copy of these illustrations hung up by the side of his license certificate, in a conspicuous place in his saloon or bar-room, and he were required in every case, before selling or giving a drink to a customer, to direct his attention to them, the effect would not fail to be salutary, though it might tend to reduce the profits of his business.

Paralysis, paraplegia, insanity, epilepsy, disease of the

heart, and other nervous diseases are shown to be the natural effects of alcohol.

Dr. Hargreaves says that, "if only a small portion of the truth respecting alcohol as a predisposing and exciting cause of disease were known, our people would be dismayed; but as it is, hundreds are daily dying by it, and no cry is raised, no horror expressed."

Mr. Richmond says that "the grog-shop is not known among savages, and is not tolerated among Mahomedans or any of the half-civilized nations of the earth. It is only under the banner of the cross, where modern Christian enlightenment has shed its benign rays over the country, that such institutions can flourish."

Under this head of "Intemperance as a Cause of Crime" may properly be included the use of some other poisonous drugs that are used habitually by millions of people, both in enlightened, civilized, semi-civilized, and barbarous nations. Of these, that which is the most extensively used is *tobacco*.

The Bureau of Statistics, Department of Agriculture, through Mr. J. D. Dodge, statistician, furnishes an estimate of the area, product, and value of the tobacco crops in the United States and Territories from 1868 to 1883, inclusive, embracing a period of sixteen years. From the statements so furnished it appears that during that period the product amounted to 7,359,703,213 pounds, or an average of about 460,000,000 pounds a year, and that the average quantity of land annually used in producing this crop was over 650,000 acres, or over one thousand square miles. The average value to the producer of the annual yield, estimated at ten cents per pound, was $46,000,000, and the total value to the producer for the sixteen years embraced in the estimate was over $735,000,000.

After being manufactured into chewing and smoking tobacco, cigars, cigarettes, and snuff, its cost to the consumer has probably been not less than an average of one dollar per pound. According to this estimate the whole cost to the consumer of tobacco during the above-named period of sixteen years, was $7,359,703,213, or nearly $46,-000,000 annually.

To the direct and immediate cost of the drug must be added the expenses and losses of time from diseases originating in its use, and other incidental losses resulting from the same cause. We have no statistics from which any estimate of these expenses and losses can be made. Common observation, and the testimony of many eminent physicians who have given attention to this subject, offer abundant evidence that the total amount must have been several millions of dollars annually. The entire cost of tobacco in this country, to the consumer and those directly and indirectly affected by its production, manufacture, and consumption, has been estimated at the enormous sum of $600,000,000 annually, and from the best consideration we have been able to give of the evidence upon this subject, we are not prepared to say that this estimate is too large. This would make the entire cost of tobacco to the nation during the above-named period of sixteen years, $9,600,000,-000, a sum so enormous that the mind shrinks from any effort to realize it.

But if we assume that all the loss and injury resulting from the use of this drug, excepting the direct cost to the consumer, is in some way compensated for by its use, yet the estimates made from reliable statistics above referred to show the actual cost to the consumer during that period to have been over $7,350,000,000. This sum distributed equally among five millions of worthy wage-workers, would furnish to each of them a home and surroundings of the value of $1470, or ten millions with each a cottage and grounds worth $735. In the hands of the government, this sum would fortify our sea-coasts and frontiers and create the strongest navy in the world for national defence and protection.  Such an amount drawn at once from the resources of the most powerful nation would render it bankrupt and helpless.  Add to this the expenses of the nation's liquor bill, estimated at over $900,000,000 for the year 1883, and the amount of benefit it would be capable of conferring upon our people, if judiciously applied, would be incalculable.  It should not be forgotten, in this connection, that the production, sale, and use of intoxicating liquors and tobacco are among the means by which the rich are made richer and the poor are made poorer.

Scientific analysis of the properties of tobacco fails to show that it has any available food quality.  Its value, if any, must therefore consist in its physiological effects.  Analysis shows that the active principle of this drug is a substance called nicotine.

Vauquelin, in his analysis, gives the following ingredients in tobacco : the acrid, the volatile principle, nicotine, acetic acid, a soluble red matter, supermulate of lime, chlorophyl, nitrate of potash and chloride of potassium, sal-ammoniac, and water.  The strongest tobacco contains from six to seven per cent. of nicotine, "which," says "Appleton's Cyclopædia," "possesses an exceedingly acrid, burning taste, even when largely diluted.  Its vapor is exceedingly powerful and irritant to the nostrils, that arising from a single drop being sufficient to render the whole atmosphere of a room insupportable.  It is one of the most virulent poisons known, a drop of the concentrated solution being sufficient to kill a dog, and its vapor destroying birds."  Dr. Hobart A. Hare, of the University of Pennsylvania, says, " Recently, M. Le Bon announces, after long research, that he has obtained from tobacco-smoke a notable quantity of prussic acid ; a new alkaloid of very agreeable odor, but as poisonous as nicotine, the fiftieth of a drop being sufficient to produce paralysis and death.  Whatever value may be found in the ingredients of tobacco as a therapeutic agent, when applied under the direction of learned and skilful doctors of medicine, can afford no ground for concluding that its common use, either in chewing, smoking, or snuffing, is beneficial. Strichnine, arsenic, and chloral are all used as medicinal agents by physicians in diluted forms, and some, if not all, of them are habitually used for their soporific or narcotic effects by those who become slaves to their seductive influence, while probably none are more sensible of their injurious effects upon the human system than some of the victims of such unfortunate habits themselves; and every practising physician can attest their deplorable consequences, both physically and mentally.

"Tobacco, in its ordinary use, when introduced into the system in small quantities, by chewing, smoking, or snuffing, acts as a narcotic, and produces, for the time, a calm feeling of mind and body, a state of mild stupor and repose. This condition changes by reaction to one of nervous restlessness and a general feeling of muscular weakness when its habitual use is temporarily interrupted. In this condition the body and mind feel in need of stimulation, and there is danger that a resort to alcohol may be had. The use of alcohol is frequently induced by that of tobacco. Indeed, it is hard to find an inebriate who does not use tobacco; and probably the statement that in nine out of ten inebriates the tobacco-habit was first formed is not an exaggeration. Its influence deranges the nervous system and initiates a tremor which suggests to the morbid taste of the user the soothing, sedative action of alcohol, and thus the allied poisons unite in forging the chains that bind them more closely to the use of both.

"Botanically, tobacco belongs to the genus *nicotiana* and natural order *solanaceæ*, and is the near kin to stramonium, henbane, and the deadly nightshade. It is characterized in the 'Encyclopædia Americana' as 'a nauseous and poison-

6

ous weed, of an acrid taste and disagreeable odor,'—in short, whose only properties are deleterious.

"If tobacco is a poison it ought to act as such, and it may be safely affirmed that it has no other action,—no use in medicine except to depress vitality. Thus it nauseates, it paralyzes the nerve-centres, producing relaxation of the muscular system and such dreadful prostration that medical literature is full of warning, and abounds with reported cases of poisoning, both from ingesting it into the stomach and from applying it externally."

Medical testimony is abundant and emphatic to its deleterious effects. Dr. Alcott says that "even a small quantity introduced in the form of tea to relieve spasms has been known repeatedly to destroy life." Dr. Marshall Hall says, "The smoker cannot escape the poison of tobacco; it gets into his blood, travels the whole round of the system, interferes with the heart's action and the general circulation, and affects every organ and fibre of the frame." Dr. Solly says, "I scarcely meet a friend who does not bear testimony to the mischief to which he has been the witness, in his own case or that of some friend, from tobacco." Says Dr. Waterhouse, "I never observed such pallid faces and so many marks of declining health, nor ever knew so many hectical habits and consumptive affections as of late years, and I trace this alarming inroad upon *young constitutions* principally to the pernicious custom of smoking cigars." Even the organ of the tobacco trade says, "Few things could be more pernicious for boys, growing youths, and persons of unformed constitution than the use of tobacco in any of its forms."

"Tobacco," says Dr. H. Gibbons, "impairs digestion, poisons the blood, depresses the vital powers, causes the limbs to tremble, and weakens and otherwise disorders the heart." "I believe," says Dr. Fergus Ferguson, "that no one who smokes tobacco before the bodily powers are developed can make a strong, vigorous man."

A British surgeon examined thirty boy smokers between the ages of nine and fifteen years, and found serious disorders begun in twenty-two, with a more or less marked taste for strong drink, generated by the habit of smoking.

Dr. Johnson says, " For one inveterate smoker, who will bear testimony favorable to the practice of smoking, ninety-nine are found to declare their belief that this practice is injurious; and I scarcely ever met with one habitual smoker who did not, in his candid moments, regret his commencement of the habit."

Seventeen medical properties are ascribed to this drug; but medical men note many more diseases resulting from the tobacco habit than there are properties in the drug itself. Of the diseases and infirmities which frequently result from the habit are mentioned cancer, especially of the lip and tongue, dimness of vision, deafness, loss of the sense of smell, perverted taste, dyspepsia, bronchitis, consumption, acne, hemorrhoids, palpitation, spinal weakness, chronic tonsillitis, anorexia, amorosis, caries of the teeth, coryza, ozæna, epilepsy, hypochondriasis, paralysis, impotency, apoplexy, tremors, delirium, insanity. Rev. Edward P. Thwing, in his essay entitled " Facts about Tobacco," cites numerous authenticated cases of disease and suffering arising from the baneful effects of this drug, and, among others, those of clergymen and zealous advocates of temperance, who, failing to see the inconsistency involved in their professions and practices, or being made conscious of it, either broke the chains that enslaved them by a desperate effort, or sank under the burden that they could not throw off. Some of these cases are intensely dramatic and others in a high degree tragic, and all of them are deeply interesting and instructive, and the reading of the entire essay will well repay the " lover of the weed" for giving it a careful perusal.

It is not assumed that all those who have given attention

to the subject, and who are presumably qualified to judge
of the effects of tobacco upon the human system, are
entirely agreed in regard to its effects; and we fully recognize and appreciate the truth of the proposition that no
cause, however good in its aims and purposes, can be
essentially benefited by any exaggeration or perversion of
facts, or any strained deductions from admitted facts. Zeal
without knowledge, earnestness without candor and fairness,
are not only vain and futile to accomplish the good that may
be intended, but often bring contempt upon the advocates
of a good cause and reproach to the cause itself. We have
stated the opinions and observations of eminent physicians
and scientists for the purpose of showing the deleterious
effects of tobacco as commonly used, and they are such as
accord with our own experience and the limited observation
we have had opportunity for making. Having chewed the
weed for a period of about twenty-one years (from 1832 to
1853), and struggled with the appetite that was stronger
than we until compelled to choose between its continued indulgence and the prospect of a premature demise or such
an exertion of the will as to overcome the habit, we can
well understand what has been its effects upon others, and
know how to sympathize with those who have acquired an
insatiable appetite for a stimulant or narcotic. That tobacco
and alcohol and the other poisonous substances we have
referred to may be used for beneficial purposes, we have no
doubt, nor can we doubt that the habitual use of any such
substance is injurious in its effects upon the human system,
and tends to the destruction of body and mind and of life
itself.

Dr. Hare, of the University of Pennsylvania, in his late
dissertation on the " Physiological and Pathological Effects
of Tobacco," says, " When we consider the vast number
of the human race who use tobacco, and the enormous
quantity which they consume, we can hardly avoid coming

to the same conclusion as Dr. Anstie, that while the use of tobacco is in some cases highly injurious, in others it has very little effect. To the young, especially, tobacco is a perfect curse, stunting their development, injuring irreparably their general physique and growth, and often entirely altering their dispositions by bringing on a state of constant irritability. Its use is to be condemned in those of a sanguine and nervous temperament, and to be at least winked at, if not approved of, in those whose temperament is more phlegmatic and less easily disturbed." This writer even goes further than this, and asserts that "to the aged, who by long use have become accustomed to the drug, it is an actual necessity for health or happiness. Withdraw for one day the accustomed smokes of an old man, and see how miserable he becomes." "This," says Dr. Hare, "is not entirely a feeling brought about by mental desire for the drug, but because his system must have its accustomed dose of tobacco." And he adds, "The writer knows an old man personally, who after being out for a few hours will come into his house pale, feeble, and exhausted, so nervous, too, that he can hardly articulate, but who becomes quiet and comfortable after a few draws at his well-beloved pipe." We do not doubt the literal truth of this statement of Dr. Hare. But we also personally know an old man (now in his eightieth year) who thirty-three years ago was in nearly a like condition, who not only had no mental desire for the drug, but a strong mental aversion to its use, but whose whole system had become so tobacconized by chewing it moderately for a few years that its disuse for a few hours would produce pallor, dizziness, and a feeling of exhaustion, which could only be quieted by a quid of the filthy weed. This last-mentioned old man, after having the tobacco expurgated from his system and recovering from most of its deleterious effects, has not felt the need of any new supply of the narcotic to render him quiet and comfortable, and

*e* 6*

most firmly believes that by discontinuing its use he has extended the duration of his life for perhaps a decade, if not a score of years. Dr. Hare expresses the opinion that to the laborer, or the man whose avocation keeps him out of doors, it is probable that tobacco rarely does harm, and that in cases of great physical fatigue it is often of use, calming the restlessness so often present after a hard day's tramp in the open air; but that to the man of business who is confined to an office and desk all day, to the hard student or the sickly, tobacco is decidedly harmful.

"After all," says Dr. Hare, "the whole question of tobacco use depends upon the quantity consumed, and the user of tobacco must gauge his use of 'the weed' not by the amount another man can stand without harm, but by the power which he finds the drug can exercise in his own person. Moderation is not the use of a small quantity of tobacco, but the use of such a small quantity that its results are not serious." Dr. Hare further says, "Certainly opium and hasheesh, and tobacco too, for that matter, are capable of producing great evils if they are used in excess, but not if moderation of a strict type be adhered to. After all, tobacco is only one of the numerous luxuries with which mankind enjoy themselves, and coffee and tea have probably produced an equal number of victims."

Dr. Hare says that he "considers that the enormous use of tobacco is probably the instinctive desire for some article which will retard tissue-waste. Indeed, all drugs which prevent the excretion of nitrogenous material have been sought after since the earliest history of man, and we can be pretty sure that a drug which is used everywhere, and by everybody, is one which helps a man to stand the jar and worry of business or other pursuits. Tobacco, coffee, alcohol, all retard tissue-waste, and therefore men, women, and children long for them, and, from using them instinctively and for a purpose, they soon use them in excess and as a luxury."

The brute is guided by instinct to reject the poison that would injure or destroy and to use the food which is adapted to its well-being; while the human being has been compelled to determine by experiment what was useful for food and what was hurtful, and was endowed with the faculties of reason and memory to enable him to choose what experience taught him was good and to reject what was injurious. That "men, women, and children long" for "tobacco, coffee, and alcohol, and use them instinctively for a purpose," as stated by Dr. Hare, is a startling proposition, and appears to us to be a very extravagant and unwarrantable one; but that they soon learn to use them in excess and as a luxury, when the natural repugnance to their use is overcome and an appetite for them is acquired, is a fact of general observation, and forcibly suggests to every candid mind the exceeding danger in using them at all. Coffee and tea have their victims; but as a beverage or narcotic, alcohol, opium, and tobacco probably destroy thousands where coffee and tea destroy hundreds. But even if the coffee were equally injurious, that fact would not detract one iota from the force of the argument against the use of alcohol, tobacco, or any other poisonous substance.

In closing our discussion of "Intemperance as a cause of Crime," it seems proper to remind the reader that we have not undertaken to write a dissertation upon the uses and abuses of alcoholic drinks or of poisonous drugs. We have only stated such facts in regard to them, as they are commonly used, as tended to prove that intemperance in the use of intoxicating drinks has been one of the most fruitful causes of crime, and that tobacco and other drugs in common use are deleterious and lead to the intemperate use of strong drinks, and thus indirectly to crime.

# CHAPTER V.

## IGNORANCE A CAUSE OF CRIME.

" Learn to live, and live to learn,
Ignorance like a fire doth burn."
BAYARD TAYLOR.

" First upon his path stood Ignorance,
Hideous in his brutal might."

IGNORANCE is rather a negative than an active source of crime. By ignorance in this relation we do not mean the want of such intellectual training alone as the schools afford, but a want of that physical and ethical training and culture which are necessary in order to prepare men and women to be good citizens, and to fit them for usefulness to themselves and others in all the relations of public and private life; ignorance of the interest which all have in abstaining from evil and learning to do well; ignorance of the value of character and a pure life; ignorance of those high aims and purposes which elevate men in the scale of being and raise them above the dominion of appetite, passion, and sensual indulgence, and make them masters of themselves and the governors of their impulses.

Intellectual attainments are in themselves neither good nor bad. Knowledge and wisdom are not the same. " Knowledge and wisdom, far from being one, have ofttimes no connection." The former is a perception of that which exists, or of truth and fact; learning; illumination of mind; skill. Wisdom is the right use or exercise of knowledge; the choice of laudable ends, and of the best means to accomplish them. As a faculty of the mind it is the faculty of discerning or judging what is most just, beneficent, useful; and considered as an acquirement it is the knowledge and *use* of what is best, most just, most proper, most conducive to prosperity or happiness. "Wisdom," says the proverb, "is the principal thing; therefore get wisdom; and with all thy getting get understanding." "Happy is the man that findeth wisdom, and the man that getteth understanding. She is more precious than rubies: and all the things thou canst desire are not to be compared unto her." Not that wisdom which consists of the craft and artifices of men in promoting their selfish ends, not quickness of intellect and dexterity of execution alone; not a knowledge of arts, sciences, and literature merely, but that higher and more enlightened wisdom which applies knowledge to the attainment of what is best and most useful.

That "ignorance is the parent of many vices" has long since passed into a proverb. No man with a clear perception of what is right and just, and of what is wrong, and of the duty which he owes to himself and others, and of the ultimate consequences of his actions, can ever choose to commit a wrong. It is that ignorance, therefore, which is the antithesis of wisdom, that is the cause of crime. This ignorance results mainly either from a false education or the want of a proper education of youth. The proposition that the welfare of the State depends upon the proper education of its citizens, and that it is therefore its duty to provide for such education of all the children and youths within its jurisdiction as is calculated to make them intelligent, peaceable, and useful citizens, is fully recognized as true in most of the Commonwealths of the Union, and, as far as its powers extend, by the government of the United States; but our methods for the attainment of so great and noble a purpose have been and are sadly defective, and for obvious reasons must continue so for a considerable time to come.

Free schools are established and supported by assessments upon the taxable property of the country, and school-houses and teachers are provided in every neighborhood, as well as books for those whose parents or guardians are unable to furnish them, and free libraries are supported at public expense in every city and township. All the elementary branches of knowledge are taught in the primary schools, and arts, science, and literature in our high-schools and colleges; but all these may leave the man ignorant of the nature and requirements of his physical organism, and the means of securing and perpetuating physical health and soundness of body, without which the highest degree of mental and moral soundness may not be expected to exist. This ignorance is the cause of those "errors of youth" which are so prevalent in civilized communities, and which undermine the physical and mental constitution, and often result in insanity, moral pollution, and premature death.

Physiologists and medical writers tell us that those "secret vices" are practised more extensively among pupils in schools than elsewhere. This is due to the fault of parents and teachers, who, from their own ignorance or false notions of delicacy, fail to instruct those under their care in regard to the nature and uses of those delicate and sensitive organs upon the healthful condition of which the welfare of the individual depends, and to guard them against those abuses which are inevitably disastrous to health and happiness, and whose consequences may become a sad inheritance of weakness and imbecility to their descendants.

Man is endowed with a physical, a mental, and a moral constitution, and each of these requires to be developed and carefully trained by his teachers. The education of the schools is directed mainly to the cultivation of the intellect, and may leave the student who has graduated with the highest honors ignorant of the practical duties of life, and of his obligations to himself and to others in the various relations, domestic, social and political, in which he is to exist. The education of his moral perceptions and faculties may have been entirely neglected, and his ethical nature—the most important of all—left to become a barren waste. If he has failed to learn that manhood and character are better than knowledge, he may possess great intellectual power and extensive learning, but may be neither a good or useful citizen. On the contrary, his great intellectual strength may be directed solely to the gratification of selfish and unholy ambitions, or of sensual appetites and passions, involving himself and others in crime and consequent ruin. History affords us hundreds of examples of such men in all ages of the world since knowledge became an object of pursuit for the sake of the power which it gives to its possessor over his weaker brothers. During our brief history as a people, our own country has furnished striking examples of men of extraordinary intellectual vigor and extensive knowledge who were habitually guilty of great vices, and some of whose characters were stained with great crimes. Not only the great good that such men might have done, had their moral nature been properly cultivated and developed, is lost to the world, but their pernicious example and evil conduct have caused the ruin of many. They die, and better men eulogize them for their brilliant mental endowments and achievements, but shrink from allusion to their vices and crimes, charitably preferring to leave them to such judgment as the mysteries of death and the hereafter may have in reserve for them.

There are in every city a large number of idle boys, apparently running wild and neglected, who not only receive little or no moral instruction, but who live in an atmosphere of vice, and whose teaching is in the direction of mischief leading to crime. They are, in general, the children of criminals, or of ignorant and degraded or drunken parents, who make no effort to secure for them moral or industrial education, without which they are likely to become a disgrace to humanity and a burden and curse to the community. The condition of their lives has a natural tendency to create an aversion to labor or any steady application to industrial pursuits, while these afford the only means by which they can become self-supporting and useful citizens. The State has an especial interest in the welfare of these unfortunate youths, and cannot afford to ignore the duty it owes to the whole body politic to provide for the control and proper instruction and training of this class of boys in the ways of honesty, sobriety, and industry, instead of leaving them to become a bane and terror to her orderly and peaceable citizens.

Mr. A. B. Richmond, in " Leaves from the Diary of an Old Lawyer," gives the following graphic description of the " hoodlums and street Arabs" in a large commercial town. Mr. Richmond says, " At the usual terms of our court, after the sentences have been passed upon the old and grave offenders of the law, the sheriff ushers into the court-room a number of small boys from ten to fifteen years of age. All dirty and unkempt they come. Precocious in vice, they seem to be the very embodiment of the genius of original sin. Young and hardy plants of transgression and crime, they need no hot-house or gardener's care to fully develop them into house-breakers, thieves, and robbers. They are the natural and spontaneous growth of the soil, the weeds and thistle-plants of society, scattered by fate along the by-ways of life. Born of drunken and vicious parents in the purlieus of vice, from the hour of their birth they have been surrounded by every bad and corrupting influence. The thieves' vocabulary their mother-tongue, the oath profane, the ribald song of the low drinking-houses have been familiar to their ears since infancy. A mother's love they never knew. A father's care they never had. They are the 'hoodlums' and street Arabs, begotten of drunkenness and debauchery. It is no fault of theirs that they have been thrust into this world to suffer cold and hunger, and

compelled by the unfortunate surroundings of their childhood to steal or starve. Accustomed to sleep under the
wharves and bridges, or in empty hogsheads and dry-goods
boxes, gleaning their miserable food from the garbage-
barrels in the streets, the prison to them a palace, and the
plain, wholesome prison food a feast of good things they
may have 'dreamed of but not enjoyed,' what wonder is it
that they are what they are, that grave and learned judges
are at a loss to know how to deal with them, and that they
are a part of our social system yet unsolved! . . . Many
of them are bright and intelligent, with innate capacities for
great good or evil; with proper care and education they
may be made useful men and good citizens. Yes, in that
group of ragged, dirty outcasts there may be, perhaps,

> 'Some mute inglorious Milton, or
> Some Cromwell guiltless of his country's blood.' "

"The child's the father of the man." He comes into the
light of this world the most ignorant and helpless of all
animals that are born. His existence is to the wisest a
great mystery. The only evidence he gives that he is conscious of his own being is the instinctive cry for sustenance
which he craves in common with the young of all other
animals. A few months ago he was not, but to-day he is.
He has not chosen to be, nor from what parentage he
should spring, nor what should be his surroundings in infancy or in youth. He is a creature of circumstances over
which he had and has no control. His infant veins may
contain the seeds of scrofula, consumption, or any other of
the physical diseases to which his ancestors were subject,
even to the third or fourth of the genealogical line. The
germs of vice and crime may have been implanted in his
moral nature. He may have inherited an uncontrollable
appetite for strong drink, or a disposition to steal and defraud, or to rob and murder.

D 7

As his physical and mental faculties are developed he finds himself and all things that exist subject to inexorable laws, and discovers that unless his life and actions are in harmony with these laws, and conformable to their demands, a fearful retribution awaits him.   There is but one straight and narrow path in which he can walk with safety, which few, if any, have ever found; and however weak or blind or burdened with the consequences of others' sins he may be, he must find it and pursue it at his peril, and if he fail to do so the law, which he is bound to know but does not, will grind him to powder.  *Ignorantia lex non excusat* is a maxim which admits of no exceptions in the operations of nature.   Fire will burn him, cold will freeze him, and poison destroy his health or extinguish his life.   And when his moral perceptions are opened he also finds a law of his moral nature equally exacting, and whose sanctions are equally certain and terrible.   This law declares to him that "though hand join in hand, the wicked shall not be un- punished," and this declaration ever has been, is now, and ever will be, true, and none can ever possibly evade or be exempted from it.   "The soul that sinneth, it shall die," and no saviour that does not save from its commission can save it from the consequences of sin.

Fortunate are they who have inherited a good physical constitution and such mental and moral qualities as make it natural for them to walk in the ways of wisdom, and to love mercy, justice, and right, and whose surroundings are favor- able to the development of the good and the suppression of the evil towards which their natures would otherwise tend.

Whatever qualities he may possess, he is a part of the universe, a creature of infinite possibilities, and is related to everything that exists.   His life may influence the lives of thousands for good or for evil.   The world has an interest in every child that is born into it, and it is the interest and duty of the State to see that every child has the instruction

and training necessary to develop his capabilities for usefulness and right living in accordance with the laws of his
physical, mental, and moral being.

> " Mysterious oft it seems to me
> How I a being come to be,
> Since through the myriad years gone by
> Suns rose and set, but lived not I."
>
> RICHARD HOWITT.

---

# CHAPTER VI.

### IDLENESS AS A CAUSE OF CRIME.

IDLENESS is nearly related to ignorance and leads to many
vices and crimes.  The diligent pursuit of some useful
labor, business, or calling is as necessary to the growth and
development of manhood and self-respect as wholesome
food is to the growth and health of the physical frame.
The idle youth naturally falls into association with the
street Arabs and hoodlums, and imbibes their contempt of
labor and good morals, and is likely to become a tramp or
vagrant, and, like him, seek to live upon the fruits of others'
labor without giving any equivalent for what he lives on.

" Nay," says Carlyle, " I will thank the great God that
He has said, in whatever fearful ways and just wrath against
us, ' Idleness shall be no more.'"   " Idleness ?   The
awakened soul of man, all but the asphyxied soul of man,
turns from it as from worse than death.   It is the life-in-
death of Poet Coleridge."

To be idle, as the term is here used, is to be unemployed
in any useful occupation.   "To be idle," says Dr. Johnson,
" is to be vicious."   This may be illustrated in many ways,
and such illustrations will be found in the following chapters
in connection with the subjects of education and employment
in industrial pursuits.

## CHAPTER VII.

### AVARICE, CUPIDITY, AND PERSONAL AMBITION AS CAUSES OF CRIME.

"Avarice sheds a blasting influence on the finest affections and sweetest comforts of mankind."—BUCKMINSTER.

WE have embraced in our definition of crime not only those wrongs which the laws of the State denounce and punish as such, but also all those great wrongs which men commit against individuals or the public for selfish ends, against conscience, and against right and justice, for which the laws of the land provide no punishment by fine and imprisonment, but which must in some way be fully and fearfully avenged, according to the inexorable principles of the higher law of righteousness and equity.

The desire to accumulate property by fair and honest means, and for the purpose of using it to benefit those whom it may be our duty to provide for or aid in the struggle for subsistence, is not only natural and salutary in itself, but is called into exercise by the law of kindness and brotherly love, and that sense of moral obligation which an enlightened conscience enjoins upon all who possess the ability to labor for their own and others' good. The mental and physical labor which such a desire stimulates to the performance of, tend to ennoble and elevate manhood, and afford the highest satisfaction to the mind and heart of the man who justly appreciates the blessings that such labor can procure. It embraces the elements of unselfish generosity, philanthropy, sacrifice, and good will, and commands the unqualified approbation of the wise and good everywhere, and in all time.

But when we consider the quality of *avarice,* or the in-
ordinate desire of gaining and possessing wealth for ignoble
and selfish ends, and the wrong and injustice which it impels
its possessor to commit, we find it the source of grave offences against the rights of humanity. It is the greed of
gain that adulterates or assimilates a large portion of our
daily food and sells it to us under the names of pure unadulterated articles. Some of the substances used for this
purpose are poisonous and injurious to health, and all of
them of little or no intrinsic value, when not positively
hurtful. They are mingled with food substances for purposes of fraud and deceit, and are such as cannot be easily
detected without chemical analysis. The report of the
Michigan State Board of Health for 1882 contains an article
on food adulterations by Dr. Prescott, in which he treats of
the office and purpose of food. He says, " It is the substance which builds the fibre of muscle and of bone ; it is
the force that supports the steady work of the heart, the
even movement of the lungs, the full power of the brain,
the quiet steadiness of the nerves. If a horse is to be
trained, careful attention is given to his food. The human
body requires more fine and sturdy material than the body
of a horse. The forces of physical life in man demand a
more generous substance than the forces of life in an animal.
Food modifies manhood and influences national characteristics."

" Opposite to food is poison. We fear to be poisoned
more than to be starved. Animals are given instinct to find
their food, with rejection of poison ; man does the same by
reason and observation. Tests of skill are demanded, and
safety requires that the invention of the analyst shall keep
pace with the invention of the manufacturer. But it is not
for poison alone that scrutiny must be devoted to food. In
the failure of good faith a thousand tamperings may occur.
A poorer article is substituted for a better one, a cheap

7*

thing is colored to imitate one of more value, an article
of good quality is diluted for greater weight or volume.
Foods are purchased and used under the name and upon
the reputation of articles belonging to another hemisphere.
A man proceeds to select suitable food for his family, and is
robbed of his privilege of choice by the unrestricted circulation of counterfeits.  As is said, in the bitter voice of a
poet not often bitter,—

> "Chalk and alum and plaster are sold to the poor for bread,
> And the spirit of murder works in the very means of life."

Dr. Prescott says, "One of the most stupendous substitutions ever accomplished is now in the height of a brief
career in this country.  It is the annual manufacture of as
much as a third of a million tons of corn-starch sugar, all
of which steals its way through the avenues of trade under
the guise of ordinary cane-sugar.  The solid sugar, called
grape-sugar at the factories, is mostly mixed with cane-
sugar.  The syrups, called glucose, require but little mix-
ture of cane-sugar to fit them for the market.  While real
cane-sugars have been carried through the course of trade
at slight and insufficient profit, the consumer of this article
probably pays from three hundred to eight hundred per
cent. above its cost.  It is stated that the factories could sell
it at one and a half to two cents per pound, and do sell it at
three or four cents per pound.  It is sold at as good prices
as other sugars, but it is not sold at all to consumers under
its own name, so far as can be learned.  An article of un-
mixed grape-sugar pressed in cubes is sold as cut sugar."

These "stupendous substitutions" appear to be without
abatement, and bid fair to have a long career unless suppressed or regulated under efficient legislative intervention.
"Another manufacture of extensive proportions," says Dr.
Prescott, "is that of purified beef-tallow, prepared for table

use, and colored to resemble butter. Under the name of oleomargarine the public has been well advised that, though it may be wholesome nourishment, it is not butter, and under this adopted name, which seems to distinguish the article, though it is a misnomer, the presentation to the public is wholly legitimate. As a digestible food it will probably be found to rank much below butter. This article is made to resemble butter so nearly, in appearance and taste, that it is difficult, if not impossible, to distinguish it from butter without chemical analysis. The fraud consists in selling it under a false name and as a substance which it is not."

Numerous other fraudulent adulterations of foods and drinks are generally known, such as of tea, coffee, wines, and other liquors, pepper, ginger, cloves, and other ground spices. Most cruel, perhaps, and disastrous of all to the denizens of our large cities is the sale of adulterated or otherwise unwholesome milk. If it were only used by adults in connection with other foods which are sufficient for the support of life, it would be a fraud and a crime; but when it is considered that the milk of the cow is the only food of thousands of infant children, whose mothers cannot or will not give them their natural sustenance, from the time of their birth until they are able to digest stronger food, and that in consequence of the impurity of the milk furnished the death-rate of children in cities under five years of age amounts to forty-five per cent. of the entire number of deaths among the population, the criminality of those who are instrumental in bringing about this " slaughter of the innocents" is calculated to shock the feelings and excite the indignation of every humane person. Can the unhallowed greed of gain inspire the commission of acts more cruel and inhuman? Those who supply the impure or diluted article to the consumers do not deliberately intend to be instrumental in causing disease or death, and are perhaps ignorant of the consequences of the fraud they commit. But will not an awakened and more enlightened conscience some time cause them to see the evil they have wrought, and visit them with the just retribution due to their reckless disregard of others' rights in order to gratify their covetous desires and selfish ambitions?

The importance of the proper selection of appropriate food can hardly be over-estimated. Says Dr. V. C. Vaughan, "Certainly it cannot be denied that the kind of food influences greatly the physical condition of nations. With the potato the Irishman lived, and when this crop failed he died. . . . When the potato was almost the only food, scrofula and its kindred diseases visited the Emerald Island every year; but since the introduction of corn into the country the people have become less susceptible to disease. We have another lesson by the study of the gradual rise of the people of England. In that country the type of disease has changed radically, and there has been a corresponding change in the food of the people. During the fourteenth, fifteenth, and sixteenth centuries the Englishman was more brutal than human. This was partly due to his food and partly to other conditions. The ancient baron consumed flesh almost with the same eagerness that the king of the forest consumed his prey. A well-known historian says, 'Bloodshed and robbery were universal. Two-thirds of the country were moor, forest, or vast swamps; the houses were small and squalid, built of wood and thatched with straw, without chimneys or other conveniences; the floors without boards or bricks, and covered with straw or hay, which remained for months saturated with reeking filth; the streets of London were narrow, unpaved, and filled with refuse of all kinds; the towns and many of the individual houses were surrounded by ditches which were filled with filth.' Take such surroundings as these, and then load the man's stomach with the poisons—urea, uric acid, etc.—

arising from the excessive consumption of flesh, and you make him more of a brute than a man."

Incontestable facts show that not only the physical well-being of an individual or a nation depends very largely upon the kind and quality of the food consumed, but also that the moral character and constitution are greatly influenced by the physical health. If food adulterations are poisonous, they engender disease; if not poisonous, but merely innutritious, their effect is to defraud the human organism of the sustenance it needs and deprive it of the energy and vigor which unadulterated food of the proper kind would supply.

We have laws upon our statute-books intended to prevent and punish these frauds and abuses, but these laws are not enforced, and seem to be entirely disregarded by dealers in food material everywhere to accumulate money and gratify the spirit of avarice. Money still is power, and men have learned that

> " Friends, beauty, birth, fair fame,
> These are the gifts of money. . . .
> Be but a moneyed man, persuasion tips
> Your tongue and Venus settles on your lips.
> Get money still,
> And then let Virtue follow—if she will."

It is avarice that prompts the dealer or trader in goods to misrepresent the quality and value of his wares, and to take advantage of the ignorance or necessities of purchasers and defraud them by delusive and false pretences. Goods are every day advertised to be sold at the purchaser's own price, at cost, or at twenty-five or fifty per cent. below cost, at special prices, or with a gift or a lottery-ticket, etc. Several in the same line of trade advertise the best goods at the lowest prices of any dealer in the town or State. Goods are offered as all wool, all linen, or silk, which the advertiser knows are largely composed of cotton; or as

*f*

French or Italian stuffs of certain quality which were never within two thousand miles of France or Italy. The goods *may* be sold at as low a price as they can be afforded for, and the purchaser *may* get the worth of his money; or he may (understanding the custom of dealers to overrate and misrepresent their goods) fully understand that he is not getting what they are represented to be, and thus not be deceived thereby. The merchant, too, knowing that purchasers generally understand it to be the universal custom and usage of trade for the seller to represent all articles of sale as something better than they really are, as well as for the buyer to say "It is naught," finds reason for believing that, if he represents them honestly and truly as he knows them to be, his customers would be few and his profits small, and justifies himself in adhering to the common usage. Travellers represent the wild Arabs of the desert to be such liars that no reliance can be placed on their statements. Are we also such falsifiers of facts that our statements are not to be relied upon, but must be taken as untrue whenever self-interest and truth are opposed to each other? Taking the most lenient and charitable view we can of the dealings of men in the purchase and sale or exchange of property as they occur daily with millions of our people, and comparing the standard of moral principles which if adopted and acted upon, with that simple rule of right and justice which requires that a man shall love his neighbor as himself, and shall do unto others as he would that others should in like circumstances do unto him, and the contrast indicates that our condition in the scale of moral progression requires to be greatly elevated and improved before our dealings with each other can be justly regarded as fair and honest.

The covetous man takes advantage of the wants or necessities of his less fortunate brother, and exacts from him exorbitant rates of interest, and does not hesitate to take the property given in pledge as his security at a tithe of its value. He it is that "devours widows' houses, and for a pretence makes long prayers," or prays only to mammon.

All betting and gaming are unlawful and iniquitous, yet in all our large cities, and many smaller ones, and at all places of resort for purposes of amusement or recreation, gaming and betting upon the result of all kinds of races, fights, or trials of skill, strength, or agility by man or other animals are constantly practised, and generally with entire impunity. Their corrupting influence would not be questioned by one in a thousand of our citizens, nor is it probable that one in ten thousand would vote for a repeal of the laws which forbid these practices. Yet they are only enforced spasmodically, if at all. Lotteries and the sale or advertising of lottery tickets are forbidden, but all sorts of schemes involving the same principle are concocted and put in operation, appealing to the cupidity of such as may be tempted to invest in them with the hope of gaining what they give no adequate consideration for, and where all gain arises from others' loss.

Our statutes for preserving the purity of elections not only forbid all betting upon the result, but provide punishment for using any means to unduly influence the action of any elector in casting his ballot. But when has an election of a President of the United States or of State officers or members of Congress occurred, during the last quarter of a century, when immense sums of money have not been "put up" and "changed hands" in consequence of the result? And when has a general election been held within the same period when vast amounts of money have not been raised and used by the candidates and their political party friends for the avowed purpose of unduly influencing votes by deceiving some and tempting the cupidity or ambition of others, and pandering to the depraved appetites of many? The means habitually resorted to for these purposes are

well known ; and it is well understood that in every district
where the result is considered at all doubtful, the candidates
themselves are expected to, and generally do, contribute a
round sum to the fund known as "the election fund," and
popularly and very appropriately designated "election corruption fund."

During the excitement of an important election, when
party feeling runs high and so many are struggling for
victory, the desire for success is the dominant and controlling impulse, and the character of the means employed to
secure it is little thought of, and the fact that large bets
have been made tend to stimulate men to adopt any
available means to insure success, however questionable
or clearly unlawful.

The man who secretly takes my property with intent to
deprive me of it, or who is intrusted with my money and
embezzles it, is held to be guilty of larceny; and if the
value of the thing stolen is twenty-five dollars or more, or
is taken from the person, the crime is a felony.  Why should
not he be deemed equally guilty who deliberately, by trick
or artifice, or superior skill or judgment, or by taking advantage of my weakness or incapacity, possesses himself of
my property, giving me no equivalent for the same ?  The
wrong is the same, and the means of its accomplishment
more cowardly than those by which the thief or burglar
seeks to secure the fruits of his wrong-doing, and why
should not the *animus* of such wrong-doer be deemed
equally criminal ?  Avarice seeks its own gratification, and
is never satisfied.  It is unscrupulous in regard to the means
by which its ends are accomplished, and centres all its motives in self, regardless of consequences to others.  It seeks
to accumulate wealth by absorbing what justly belongs to
others.  The bulls and the bears manipulate the market in
our great commercial centres, each striving to accomplish
what may be the other's ruin.  Corners in stocks, in bread-

stuffs, and other products of human industry and skill, the
watering of stocks of great railroad and other corporations,
the buying and selling of margins at the "bucket shops,"
dealing in "puts and calls" and "futures," lotteries, and
other like gambling operations are all of the same character.
Those who have most have the most power, and, with
shrewdness and sharpness, they are the winners. Wealth
is not increased by gambling or speculation, but is turned
into the hands of those who are the most unscrupulous and
least worthy.

Four or five centuries ago our Anglo-Saxon ancestors
lived largely by the violent plundering of their neighbors
and of each other, and each feudal lord supported a band
of armed retainers for this purpose. We are accustomed
to read the history of their deeds of violence, robbery, and
bloodshed with feelings of horror, and to congratulate ourselves that the times of such sanguinary deeds of rapine
and terror have passed away, and that we are living in an
era of civilization and enlightenment, wherein the just rights
of all are respected and protected by laws which are enforced by the government and generally respected and
obeyed. If any candid man of ordinary intelligence should
say, as many anarchists in the old world and some in our
own country are saying, thàt all accumulation of property
is robbery, and that the social and political condition of the
people is no better than it was during those periods of
turbulence and lawlessness, we should not hesitate to pronounce such an one insane. But when we contemplate the
innumerable wrongs that are constantly being committed
by the strong against the weak, the sharp against the
simple, the powerful against those who are helpless, some
of them against law, and many of them tolerated and even
encouraged and protected by law, and all proceeding from the
promptings of avarice or personal selfish ambition, we may
well ask how much less of wrong and outrage are perpe-

trated in these days of intellectual enlightenment than during those periods which we are accustomed to refer to as " the dark ages ?"

Computed by numbers, the wrongs of the present age probably equal, and perhaps exceed, those of preceding ages ; but in their character and consequences those of the present age, in general, bear no comparison to those of the past. The power of the savage and barbarian is mainly in the physical. In civilized society it is mainly in the mental and moral. A body of civilized men, seeking only the gratification of their sensuous natures, restrained by no sense of moral right or obligation, inspire universal terror and apprehension by the depredations they commit in the pursuit of their objects. Acts of violence in civilized communities, where education is general and knowledge diffused among the people, are comparatively few, and, excepting in cases of rebellion against the government, or attempted revolution, or war between nations, which are usually of short duration, excite no general alarm or disquietude.

Most of the wrongs which proceed from avarice and ambition are committed quietly, the perpetrator and the victim, in many cases, each striving to victimize the other, as in betting and gaming. Generosity, benevolence, conscientiousness, are the opposites of avarice and cupidity. These restrain men from invading the just rights of others. The just man holds what he possesses as a trust to be administered (1) for the promotion of his own physical health and the development of his intellectual and moral faculties, in order that his capacity to benefit others may be increased ; (2) to make suitable provision for the comfort and mental and moral culture of those immediately dependent upon him ; and (3) for promoting the happiness and welfare of others in general, and especially for assisting those whose misfortunes call for friendly aid and encouragement.

Avarice is not the sole cause of the frauds that are perpetrated and the crimes that are committed for pecuniary gain.
There are many men of sharp intellect, but whose moral
faculties have not been developed, who, though capable of
earning an honest living, instead of engaging in some useful occupation, prefer to acquire the means of living by the
habitual practice of fraud, deception, and humbuggery, and
making dupes of the credulous, some for the purpose of
acquiring riches, and more, perhaps, for the purpose of
obtaining the means of gratifying their sensual appetites
and passions than for hoarding wealth. This class of men
are generally irresponsible, having no fixed habitation, no
good name to defend or protect, but assuming many different names and characters, and advertising their pretended
business as located in various places, and under as many
high-sounding firm-names and styles as may suit their purposes and enable them to evade police scrutiny and interference.

Some of them are roving in their habits, and sometimes
hunt in couples, and sometimes singly, as the game they
are seeking may require. One advertises in the guise of a
retired physician or clergyman, whose sands of life are
nearly run out, and who has been snatched from the jaws
of death by some remedy, the secret of which he will reveal
to those similarly afflicted on receipt of a few postage-
stamps. One is the distinguished Dr. J. P. M., who, to re-
cruit his shattered health, which has been ruined by his
former laborious practice, penetrated to the very heart of
Africa, and there, by reason of the privileges accorded him
by King Munza, discovered a remedy for disease such as
the civilized world had never seen or heard of, and which he
is ready to dispense for the healing of his afflicted fellow-
creatures, under the name of " Monbutto coca compound,"
for an adequate consideration. How this shattered invalid
penetrated to the very heart of Africa, and how he got

away with sufficient Monbutto coca for the healing of the nations, when Livingstone, Stanley, and other African explorers, with retinues of armed retainers and abundant resources, have encountered the greatest difficulties and numerous disasters in attempting to reach the interior of that "Dark Continent," the doctor modestly refrains from informing us. But the doctor expects that many will take his statement for the truth and purchase his nostrum, and no doubt many will do so, and he may become as rich as the proprietor of Warner's Safe Cures, and own islands in the Saginaw Bay, and boldly apply to Congress to confirm to him and his heirs a large tract of land adjacent thereto as an accretion, without being indignantly repulsed by that honorable body, for

"Wealth makes the man, the want of it the fellow."

And when Dr. J. P. M. becomes wealthy he can subsidize the public press and fill its columns with sensational accounts of marvellous cures of other doctors, clergymen, and other prominent citizens by the use of his compound.

Another, more humble, advertises "A cure for the borer in trees," which he will send to any address for fifty cents (which is found to be a small parcel of hard soap worth two cents), with directions to place it in the crotch of a tree where the rains will dissolve it, and with the assurance that it will permeate the wood and destroy the insect.

Numbers of unscrupulous fellows visit the farming communities, professing to represent the great "Crawford, Henry & Williams County Seed Store" (C. H. Brassington, Secretary) or some other great seed store, and sell what they call the Bohemian Oats at one hundred dollars for ten bushels, under an agreement, to which the name and style of Brassington are attached, to sell twenty bushels of the product for the purchaser in the following year for two hundred dollars, neither the company nor its secretary or agent ever being found to respond in damages for a breach of the contract.

One, assuming the name of " The Tunquery Crayon Portrait Society," advertises to furnish from a photograph to be sent to the firm a crayon portrait free of charge, on condition that an order be given them for framing it."

Another advertises a " Sure cure for deafness," which he will furnish on receipt of ten dollars, fifteen dollars more to be paid when the cure is effected; no reference being had to the cause of the deafness, and no inquiry ever being made as to whether a cure had been effected.

Captain Smith, proposing to leave the salt water and retire upon a farm, calls upon a farmer and gets his price, is satisfied, and proposes to pay fifty dollars down to bind the bargain and return in a week to consummate the purchase, exhibits a roll of one hundred-dollar bills, and the farmer changes one of them, giving the captain fifty dollars in honest money, and finds, too late, that his hundred-dollar bill is counterfeit.

A stranger calls upon a farmer and enters into a contract to purchase his farm and pay four thousand dollars for it, which is all the farmer values it at. Another stranger soon puts in an appearance, wants to buy the farm, and offers six thousand dollars for the same place, if the contract of sale can be cancelled. The farmer seeks the man he contracted with and induces him to give up his contract upon the payment of one thousand dollars. Strangers disappear and divide the plunder, and the farmer deplores his misplaced confidence.

The lightning-rod man; the bogus tree peddler; the pretended son of an old friend; the advertiser of large profits on small investments; of fascinating employments for ladies at their own homes; of large estates in England belonging to heirs in this country, who are called upon to contribute for paying agents and attorneys for investigating their claims and securing the money or property inherited; stock in joint-stock live-stock companies, or prospecting and improvement companies, with fabulous accounts of increase and accumulations of wealth; valuable packages to be sent on receipt of a few cents; some liquid that will give skimmed milk a genuine creamy color; a new systematic method of railroad stock speculation; information by an old merchant as to stocks that will positively advance, yielding large profits to the investor; writing to be done at home, applicants to send ten cents in postage-stamps; information how to obtain immediate employment on receipt of a few stamps; the freight dodge and the confidence games, are a few of the thousand humbugs that have been ventilated and exposed from month to month during a quarter of a century in the columns of the *American Agriculturist*, under the head of "Sundry Humbugs."

If the pecuniary losses of the victims of these and other like frauds were all the injury growing out of them, that alone would be sufficient to stamp the perpetrators as enemies to humanity and fit subjects for the discipline of a prison; but a greater injury arises from the tendency of such wrongs to destroy confidence in the general integrity of mankind, and to provoke resentment and retaliatory acts on the part of those who suffer the wrong.

Many who would not deliberately have entertained the thought of committing an unjust act, on being deceived and swindled by one who has abused their confidence, smarting under the sense of injury, will be prompted to punish the wrong-doer by resorting to means equally reprehensible, and thus themselves become wrong-doers. As a small spark may kindle a large conflagration, so a wrong done to a single individual may be the cause of innumerable other wrongs; and this is a lesson which should be indelibly impressed upon the mind of every child by its parents and teachers, as soon as it is old enough to distinguish between good and evil conduct.

The wrongs we have been treating of as proceeding from avarice and cupidity are such as are perpetrated against individuals, and only affect the community indirectly. They tend to the corruption of the public morals and the increase of vice and crime, and the general disregard of truth and honesty, and infect the whole body politic with their baneful influence, until the moral sense of the great mass of society has been so obscured as to tolerate the most stupendous evils, which in a morally healthy condition of society might be at once and forever abolished. The great majority of our citizens who have the power to do this, if they would unitedly exert that power, and who are conscious of, and really deplore the existence of, such evils, are wanting in that moral courage and energy which are necessary to impel them to act according to their convictions. If any attempt to do so, they find a demoralized public opinion operating against their efforts, which are thus rendered futile for the time. There are too many who, though they see the right, are not deeply impressed with its importance, or are diverted from it by interests and associations that they are not disposed to surrender for the public good. Those whose pockets would be affected by a reform that would destroy their occupation constitute a strong and influential body, who are associated for mutual protection and defence of what they claim as their rights, and politicians and legislators and aspirants to public office are not willing to offend them, or lose the weight of their influence at the election polls. The spirit of avarice is narrow and selfish. It stimulates the lower and represses the higher and nobler qualities of the soul, and belittles instead of enlarging and elevating manhood. It coils its slimy folds around the image of Deity, and infuses into it the poison that destroys all that was Godlike in man's nature. Its insidious influence

enslaves not only men in the ranks of common life, corrupting the courses of trade and commerce, but it subjugates
and brings under its power men of large intellectual attainments, occupying high positions in the professions, in the
X  halls of legislation, and other public positions of trust and
responsibility, and strikes at the integrity, if not the very
existence, of government itself.

During the first half-century after our ancestors had, by
the most heroic and self-sacrificing efforts, achieved independence and established a republican form of government
based upon the principle of equal rights and equal protection to all, public opinion required that those who were to
have any share in public affairs should be men of sufficient
ability, and of the most undoubted integrity of character.
Selfish ambition and the seeking of public office for private
ends were frowned upon, and very few instances of abuse of
the trust confided to them occurred among those who held
public positions.   When one was proposed for appointment
to a place in the service of the government, the inquiry was,
" Is he honest?   Is he capable?"   And unless this inquiry
could be satisfactorily answered, he was not considered
worthy of the place.   Office-seeking was considered as
despicable.   Those who were deemed the fittest were called
into the service, and the best and ablest men were those
selected to exercise the functions of government.   Great
economy and severe simplicity characterized the government in all its relations, both foreign and domestic, and
every species of extravagance in the public expenditures
was discountenanced.   The application of Emerson's idea
of the sovereignty of ethics was held applicable to politics
as well as to the common affairs of men, and if a man was
not just and upright as a citizen he was not deemed a fit or
safe man in any public position.   Public office was deemed
an honor, not because it made the individual more worthy,
but because it was regarded as evidence of honorable char-

acter and superior attainments. But as our country has
increased in population, and grown in wealth and power,
there has come to be a very prevalent and increasing feeling
that it has become politically corrupt,—that there is a deep-
seated disease in political affairs which demands heroic
remedies, and not a few of our most thoughtful citizens are
disposed to take a pessimistic view of the future of our
country, and to despair of any remedy; and there are certain dark facts apparent to all which may well awaken the
most serious apprehensions as to what that future is to be.
We have already alluded to some of the means which are
habitually resorted to for the purpose of influencing votes
at the elections. The enormous amounts of money placed
under the control of the general committees chosen by the
respective political parties to manage their affairs in all
general elections are used not only to procure the printing
and circulation of articles intended to mislead and deceive,
and to compensate the most unscrupulous and reckless men
for misrepresenting the motives, acts, and intentions of their
respective opponents, but to subsidize those who minister to
the depraved appetites of the lovers of strong drink, or more
directly to bribe voters by gifts of money.

Nominations of candidates for political offices do not
proceed from the spontaneous wishes or preferences of the
electors because of their fitness for the positions assigned
to them. Personal ambition, cupidity, or the promotion of
some measure or scheme of individual or class aggrandizement, or the protection of some nefarious traffic opposed to
the general welfare of the people, are often, if not generally,
the motives which control the action of those who are actively engaged in politics. The caucus system of nominations, as practised by the several political parties, is adapted
to, and would seem to have been devised for, the purpose
of putting the administration of public affairs into the hands
of incompetent and unscrupulous men. No man can faith-

fully and truly perform the duties of a public trust, unless he can feel that he is free to act in accordance with the public interest alone according to his best judgment, and that he is bound to do so. But how many of our legislators and other public functionaries elected by the people understand that they were nominated and elected to act solely for the public good? Public opinion, based upon apparently indubitable evidence, certainly favors the conclusion that there are comparatively few in such positions who so understand their duties and obligations, and so act. "Private greed, petty personal ambitions, the selfish aims, passions, and conveniences of powerful political cliques, have more weight with many legislators than the public good. Hence the fatal facility with which bad measures get enacted and the extreme difficulty and tedious slowness with which good legislation is accomplished." When the sources of power become corrupted, its channels will be corrupt from the least to the greatest. When nominations are secured by bargaining and intrigue, and elections by bribing and deception, it is folly to expect devotion to the public interests from those who obtain power by such corrupt means. Through the machinery of the caucus, and bargaining, and the use of money in the elections, small, popular, "smart" men of wealth and personally ambitious men secure their nominations and election and pollute the halls of legislation. The result is that the public interests are postponed or lost sight of in the struggle for the attainment of personal and selfish ends.

One of the most damning facts in our national history is the feeling, generally prevailing and freely expressed, that the law-makers, who should be above suspicion of corruption, are mercenary and venal, and that the votes and influence of many of them can be bought with money, and that in cases of private claims or local matters requiring legislation in which individuals have an interest, however meritorious, favorable action cannot be secured without first purchasing the influence of members of the legislative body; and that private claims, however baseless, and schemes of plunder having only the merest semblance of merit are recognized and provided for through the corrupting power of money.

The United States Congress, the State Legislatures, and municipal bodies having legislative powers are all become subject to distrust and suspicion, and the investigation and public exposure of astounding crimes and frauds perpetrated in the corrupt and flagrant abuse of legislative power have become so frequent as scarcely to excite surprise in the public mind.

We do not assume that the great body of American citizens are politically corrupt, nor that the majority of those who are intrusted with power are disposed to abuse it or prostitute it for selfish purposes; but the great body of our citizens are too careless with regard to these dangerous political symptoms as they appear in an active minority who control the action of the primary meetings and, through this action, the general politics of the country.

The following from a New York newspaper of a late date, on the subject of "Money in Politics," discloses some startling facts:

"Money in politics is becoming one of the evils that threaten the body politic. The condition of politics in New York City is one of the best arguments in support of a truth that is becoming more apparent every campaign. City Chamberlain W. M. Ivins, of New York, . . . delivered an address . . . on the subject of political assessments. He began by stating that important offices of honor, profit, and trust are either put up at auction or raffled away. He argued that if such a state of affairs was allowed to continue it would end in the complete corruption of the city government. Mr. Ivins gave it as his opinion that from 1880 to

1886 there was never less than $100,000 or $250,000 raised
by Tammany and the County Democracy every campaign
during those years. 'As far back as 1876,' he said, 'Tammany Hall raised $165,000 for the campaign. In 1883, John
Reilly was assessed $50,000 for the nomination as register.
Judicial nominations were bought for as high as $30,000.
The nomination for district attorney commanded $10,000
or $15,000. The mayoralty assessment cost as high as
$35,000.' According to Ivins, the election expenses in New
York City in 1886, official and unofficial, reached the sum
of $700,000. He thought $1,000,000 would not cover the
amount expended in that city for the expenses of the Presidential election in 1884. He said that fully twenty out of
every hundred voters are under pay, official or unofficial, on
election day. The members of the club looked surprised
when Mr. Ivins said that the men who were connected with
the Tweed ring, and the false counting of votes of those
days, were now holding important offices in this city. He
laid stress on the hiring of political workers at the polls,
saying that it was only a species of bribery. Mr. Ivins
claimed that if a man was as great as Cæsar or Napoleon
or as good as St. Paul, he could never, under the present
management of our politics, be nominated for mayor unless
he had $15,000 or $30,000 to put up for the expenses of
his election. Mr. Ivins said that he had been told that
candidates for the State Senate had to spend as high as
$50,000 to be elected. In 1885 the cost of one senatorial
fight amounted to $39,000. He knew that it had cost one
Republican $6000 to be elected to the Assembly, where the
salary is only $1800 a year. A Democrat who had been
elected to the State Senate twice told him that his first
fight cost him $8000 and his second contest $12,000. Mr.
Ivins closed by saying that he favored a law for printing the
ballots of candidates at the expense of the people and to
limit the campaign expenditures of candidates."

The corrupting influences of such practices are too obvious, and their tendency too deplorable, to be contemplated without the most serious apprehensions and alarm for the future welfare of our country, and it will require great wisdom and consummate statesmanship on the part of legislators to counteract or prevent them.

----

# CHAPTER VIII.

## THE CONFLICT BETWEEN CAPITAL AND LABOR AS A CAUSE OF CRIME.

IT would perhaps be more strictly correct to designate the conflict which is now so prevalent, and which has been going on and intensifying during the last few years between employers and employés, the one investing capital in business enterprises and the other performing the necessary labor for certain stipulated wages, as the conflict between capitalists and laborers.

There is no necessary conflict between capital and labor, nor any necessary hostility of the laborer to the capitalist or of the capitalist to the laborer, for their interests are each . dependent upon the other, and, if rightly understood, mutual, and equity and justice are the interests of both. Capital, which is produced by labor, would be valueless if it could not be converted into labor, and labor would find no employment if capital did not supply it. The great mass of our citizens, and probably the happiest and best-conditioned, are those who are at the same time their own capitalists and employés. The owner of a small farm, or vegetable garden, or a shop for some mechanical trade or business which he carries on mainly or wholly by his own labor and skill, finds no antagonism between his capital and labor, but under-

stands the relative value of both and the mutual depend-
ence of each upon the other. In all those branches of
business which are carried on with a comparatively small
amount of capital, and in which the employer and employé
work side by side in the field or the shop, each feels more
interest in the other's welfare; social distinctions are not
marked between them, and their relations are generally
satisfactory and mutually beneficial.

Those of us who can look back through an active life
experience of seven decades and remember the condition
of the people in the New England and Middle States, and
their modes of living at that time, and who have observed
the vast changes that have taken place through the progress
of science, arts, economic inventions, and improvements
during that period, may discern in these some of the causes
of dissatisfaction on the part of the wage-workers which
now so generally prevails.

Seventy years ago there were very few men in this country
whose estates were worth a million of dollars, very few corporations or other associations for manufacturing or other
business enterprises which required the consolidation of
large capital. There were no railroads, steamboats, nor
steam-mills in existence, or perhaps thought of. No
mowers, reapers, or threshers operated by horse-power, no
iron or steel ploughs or cultivators had been invented. The
Erie Canal had no existence except in the brain of its projector, who was jeered as a visionary dreamer. The telegraph, the telephone, photography, and the electric light are
discoveries of a later period.

The spinning-jenny, invented and improved by Hargreaves and Arkwright, and perfected by Crampton, was
not in successful operation in this country until the beginning of the present century, and the mule-jenny and the
power-loom had not yet displaced the domestic spinning-
wheel and weaving-loom.

Farming and all mechanical operations were slow and laborious, and the tools used in them were clumsy and unwieldy compared with those in modern use. All land transportation was performed by animal power, and the stage-coach was the common vehicle for public travel. The flax and the wool for clothing were raised and prepared by the farmer and spun and woven and made up into garments by the female members of his family. Life was toilsome, simple, and frugal, and general contentment and friendship prevailed.

But few new discoveries or inventions had occurred during the preceding century to disturb or interfere with the settled course of affairs. The habits, customs, and opinions of ancestors were held in reverence, and what was good enough for them was considered good enough for their posterity. They had no Knights of Labor or other labor organizations exercising any general influence, nor ever dreamed of striking or boycotting as a remedy for existing evils. Political parties existed under the names of Federals and Democrats, and political party feeling sometimes waxed warm and disturbed the social harmony of neighbors, but the people had confidence in the integrity of their legislators and other public functionaries, and the trust reposed in them was seldom betrayed. Syndicates, credit mobiliers, and other like combinations for the purpose of corrupting legislators and defrauding governments and peoples had not yet been formed in this country, and the absence of strong temptations made it comparatively easy for the public servants to act honestly in the discharge of their public duties.

The Great West was then a howling wilderness and its inland seas a solitude. A large portion of it, now occupied with active, thriving populations, was supposed to be uninhabitable. Michigan at a later period was reported as a swamp, and its lands not worth surveying, while the vast plains east of the Rocky Mountains, now known to be fertile and capable of being made productive, were described in the early school geographies and designated on the maps as a barren desert like that of Sahara in Africa.

If, to one who has personally observed the inception, progress, and consummation of the discoveries, inventions, and vast enterprises and improvements which have character- ized the history of the last seventy years, their magnitude and the changes they have wrought appear astonishing, what language could express the amazement of one who, having been familiar with the old order of things, should be suddenly introduced into the new without the knowledge or experience of the intervening transitionary conditions and events from and through which the present has been evolved? If he had been educated in the schools of the olden time, and were now introduced into the primary and high schools and colleges of the present day, he would find none of the old text-books nor of the old modes of instruc- tion. All would be strange and unfamiliar to him, and the grammar of his native language, as now taught, even the learned author of Murray's English Grammar would hardly be able to understand. Place him upon a well-conducted farm, where the modern improvements in farm implements are used, and show him the mowing and raking and thresh- ing and separating machines, propelled by horse-power, the steel plough, horse hoe, and cultivator, which have super- seded the hand scythe and rake, the flail and hand fan, the wooden plough and the hand hoe, and by the use of which two men are able to perform the labor of ten in the old ways, and with more efficiency and less exhaustion of strength, and he could hardly believe in their reality. Show him the great manufactories of cotton and woollen fabrics, propelled by steam- or water-power, and requiring millions of capital, whose machinery enables one man to perform the labor which would have required ten or perhaps twenty according to the old modes of manufacture; introduce him into the great furnaces, rolling-mills, and manufactories of all kinds of iron and steel machinery, tools, and implements, from a knife to a ponderous locomotive railroad engine; let him take a survey of the vast net-work of railroads, extending from the Atlantic to the Pacific Ocean and from the Gulf of Mexico to Oregon, and penetrating every part of the country where commerce and travel invite enterprise and promise a return for capital invested; direct him to the telephone, and tell him to converse through it with parties a hundred miles away; and finally, let him read in the daily newspapers the telegraphic reports from all parts of the world, giving accounts of all the important and thousands of unimportant occurrences of yesterday, and what sensations would all these, and the thousand other changes and transformations which would attract his attention, be calculated to produce? Would not he then be impressed with the thought that he had been translated into a world of enchantment, which was subject to be changed at will by the waving of the enchanter's wand?

When persuaded that all is real and substantial, and that it is the old world with nothing lost that was worth saving, but advanced, progressed, and improved through the intellectual force of the human mind, freed from the domination of ancient traditions, superstitions, and ignorance, and left free to work out its great inherent capabilities without fear of offending the majesty of heaven, or of being supposed to be in league with the powers of darkness, he would be forced to exclaim, "Surely the old things are passed away, and behold, all things have become new."

While he was becoming familiarized with the new conditions thus wrought by the power of mind, through the aid of science, art, and the treasured knowledge of the ages, he observes that yet new inventions and discoveries are constantly occurring to supersede and displace those now in existence, as they have displaced those that preceded them, and finds *change, improvement, progress* written over all the works of men's hands. And of all the wonderful products of human skill, invention, and enterprise, he dare not lay his hand upon any and say, " This is perfect, and must therefore be enduring." Must he therefore conclude that there is nothing subject to his cognition that is stable, fixed, and immutable, never failing or disappointing to those who earnestly seek after the good and the true? Back of, underlying, and controlling all things is *the law*, which we recognize as the law of nature, because it inheres in all things,—the law of God, " without variableness or shadow of turning," a law perfect in its operation alike in the physical world and in the mental and moral constitution of man ; a law of blessing to those who conform to its requirements, and of destruction to everything which resists its authority. In the domain of the physical none question its supremacy, or hope to escape the penalty imposed for its violation. In the domain of the moral and spiritual its operation is less clearly discerned, because its penalties are not so obvious to the senses, and some hope to escape the just consequences of its infraction by the imputation of their sins to a sinless Mediator, who is supposed to have paid the penalty in advance, and imputing to them His righteousness, whereby they are to secure all the benefits of obedience. Others denounce the law itself as unjust, and can see no good or justice in a law under the operation of which the world is filled with misery and woe, and human hearts are wrung with anguish on account of acts and events over which they have no control, and which they have no power to avert.

It is not our purpose to discuss matters of religious or irreligious belief or opinion any further than they are immediately connected with our present theme. But all experience has shown that men's beliefs, as well in regard to moral and religious as to political and other subjects, have constantly influenced or controlled human action, and that men in a great degree measure and determine their duties and obligations in all their public and private, social and domestic relations according to their several beliefs. Hence it is an old proverb that "As a man thinketh, so is he." It is equally for the interest of all to accept and believe what is true and to reject what is false; but what appears to one to be true to another is false, and where all are confessedly ignorant, it behooves us to be modest and charitable and candid with ourselves and others, and to refrain from dogmatism where demonstration is impossible. The controversy between some of the ablest and most learned scientists and philosophers as to whether things have a real objective existence as they appear to the senses, or whether they exist only as ideas in our consciousness, and without such consciousness have no existence, may teach those who claim no distinction as scientists or philosophers a useful lesson. The objectist says, "I see a mountain, a dwelling-house, a horse, or a man." The idealist replies, "These are mere phenomena, shadowy forms, deceptive and illusive." The common mind apprehends the real existence of objects corresponding to man's consciousness of them; while the idealist, by a process of metaphysical reasoning and assumption, proves to his own satisfaction, and convinces others, that the old sophists were right in repudiating the evidence of the senses and proclaiming the non-existence of material objects.

Religious opinions assume similar antagonisms. In reason, and according to the common apprehension of mankind, justice requires that he who violates the law, and not another, shall suffer the consequences of his sin, and the idea that the innocent shall be deemed guilty, and the guilty innocent, would be too abhorrent to *human reason* to be accepted. But by a process of theological metaphysics, assumed to be *above reason*, and treating reason as its foe,

millions have been persuaded to accept the belief, and
millions do profess to believe, that under the administration
of a perfect law by an all-wise and all-powerful and good
Creator, this doctrine of imputed sin and imputed righteousness is true, and that the consequences of rejecting it may
extend to all eternity.

That the opinions of our people in regard to morals and
religion have had a very large influence in bringing about
the changes we have referred to in their physical condition
during the last six or seven decades there can be no doubt.
Under a theocratic government the people could not be
allowed the free exercise of their reasoning faculties in
searching after truth, for all truth was supposed to be communicated by a mystical revelation of the divine will,
through the appointed and divinely-authorized agents of
Deity, and whatever thought or discovery was not so revealed was held to be error, and the thinker or discoverer
was liable to be put to death for heresy.

" The powers that be are ordained of God," was proclaimed
by the Prophet of Nazareth, and his disciples for eighteen
hundred years have held his words to be the expression of
absolute truth, and whenever they have had the power have
visited the rejection of this doctrine with condign punishment.    From the time of the Jewish hierarchy to the beginning of the nineteenth century every civilized nation was
practically, as some of them still are, under hierarchal dominion or influence, and free thought was hedged about and
restrained by religious dogmatism.    As, however, the religious world became divided up into many sects holding
divers opinions, each assuming the right to determine its
own religious belief, and no sect having the power to dictate
the belief of the others, religious toleration came to be established; and when freedom of thought in religious matters
was once recognized and protected by the State, an impetus
was given to free-thinking on all subjects which could not

be suppressed, and its quickening influence upon character and intellect is apparent in the wonderful changes and vast progress in the means of making life enjoyable and in elevating humanity, mentally, socially, and morally. Whether the means thus afforded us of reaching and sustaining a more elevated manhood shall be made available for that purpose must depend largely upon the wisdom of those who may have the direction of public affairs, but perhaps more largely upon the intelligence and appreciation of right and justice of the capitalists on the one hand and the laborers on the other. In the exercise of a broad and enlightened philanthropy which recognizes the highest benefit to each in the universal happiness and prosperity of all rests our only hope of so adjusting the relations between employer and employé, or capitalist and laborer, that both shall have reason to be satisfied with what it produces.

In looking over the history of the present century, and observing the changes we have referred to in every department of business and human enterprise, by means of new inventions and discoveries, we see an exemplification of that inexorable law which declares that in all the departments of life and of nature the fittest shall survive and that which is unfit shall cease to exist. This is a law of sacrifice, but it is the law of progress; a law of destruction, but of substitution of better things in the place of those destroyed. When the Erie Canal was constructed, in the early part of this century, it was strenuously opposed by those engaged in the carrying trade by wagon through the region traversed by it, as destructive to their business. And so it was; but it cheapened transportation and benefited thousands for every one it injured. The spinning and weaving of cotton and woollen goods by machinery was as bitterly opposed by the spinners and weavers of that day, and it was not without great difficulty that the new machinery could be saved from destruction. Had it been perfected at its first introduction as it now is, enabling one man to do the work which had required twenty, it would not have been allowed to exist. Its invention and use caused sacrifice to thousands and suffering to many, but it has reduced the expense of clothing material to a fraction of what it would have cost if manufactured by the former methods. Railroads and steam navigation have cheapened transportation and travel, and rendered it practicable to transport the products of the soil and the manufactory for long distances at small expense and with tenfold speed. Our railroads bring the cattle and the grains of the far West to the markets of the East! They bring the fruits and vegetables of California and of Florida and the West India Islands, and fish from the seas, fresh as when gathered or caught, and distribute them to every town and hamlet throughout the country. Travel is made easy, rapid, and comfortable, without increasing its dangers, and thus time, often so precious, is saved, and fatigue and exposure are avoided. But these new modes of transportation and travel have superseded and destroyed the old methods and caused loss and disaster to those who were engaged in those pursuits; and while they have opened new avenues of trade and commerce, and extended the fields of human industry and enterprise, they, with other great innovations upon previously existing orders of things, have been attended by evils of great magnitude, which have intensified the conflict between labor and capital,—a conflict which has assumed such an alarming aspect and such large proportions within the last few years as to create the deepest anxiety in the mind of every one who has the best interests of his country and its people at heart.

It is apparent to every man of intelligence and observation that while the means of production have been increased tenfold by the new and improved methods invented and brought into use during the present century, and the wealth of the country has been proportionately increased, this increased wealth has not been distributed according to the requirements of natural justice and equity, so that all should receive a share of the benefits it was capable of conferring upon them, and so that few, if any, should be compelled to suffer for the want of means of comfortable subsistence; but has gone largely to the building up of great fortunes in the hands of the comparatively few, who have gathered where others have sown, and luxuriate upon what others have earned.

The eminent statesmen who laid the foundations of our government had before them the example of the wealthy nations of Europe, in which the privileged few were the owners of the land and controlled its products, and the many labored for a mere subsistence, and thousands were compelled to suffer extreme poverty and destitution, and they attributed those unjust inequalities of condition to their false theories of government and political economy.

In monarchial governments the sovereign power is in the hands of a single individual, who is assumed to exercise supreme authority by a divine right, and to be the source of all honor and authority in the State, and the fountain of justice. The Prophet of Nazareth enjoined upon his followers obedience to such authority, declaring to them that "the powers that be are ordained of God;" hence those Christians who oppose liberty and resistance to tyranny by the constituted authorities are entirely consistent with the letter, if not the spirit, of the teachings by which they profess to be guided. The great charter of British liberty, called the English Constitution, was a concession from the king to his subjects, and not a declaration of rights emanating from or inherent in the people. Under that form of government the few whom the king favored were endowed with great authority and great wealth, while the many were born to be their servants. But ideas of liberty and political rights and justice had taken root and become diffused among all classes of people, especially among the sturdy denizens of this new world; and when the people of the colonies, through their representatives, determined to sever their connection with Great Britain and form a new government for themselves, they were prepared to put forth to the world a declaration of principles wherein the people were declared to be the source of all political power. They declared that all men are created equal, and that they are endowed by their Creator with certain inalienable rights ; and that among these rights are life, liberty, and the pursuit of happiness ; and that to secure these rights governments are instituted among men, deriving their just powers from the consent of the governed. The new government was based upon the idea that it was to be a government *by the people*, *for the people*, and that its blessings should be participated in alike by all. None were entitled to exclusive privileges, nor to any monopoly of trade, business, position, or peculiar advantages. Those intrusted with the exercise of authority under the constitution and the laws were to be the *servants of the people*, whose will they were to obey, and not their masters.

The history of the ancient republics and empires which had risen to great power and opulence and then declined and fallen into decay through the corruptions, weakness, and effeminacy consequent upon the accumulation of great wealth and the concentration of power in the hands of the few, while the masses were kept in ignorance and a condition of enforced servitude, was one of warning, indicating the dangers which ought to be avoided and provided against in establishing a new republic.

Under monarchial and aristocratic governments the common people had no voice and were not recognized as having any interest in governmental affairs, but were assumed to have been born to be governed and to serve their superiors, and in their ignorance of the powers and possibilities with which nature had endowed them, and a superstitious reverence for the knowledge and wisdom attributed to those who exercised authority over them, consisted the safety and stability of the State. The essence and spirit of kingly government was expressed by Louis XIV. of France, when he said, " I am the state." Even now, where, as in England, but little except the name of monarchy remains, all governmental acts are done in the name of, and are supposed to emanate from, the queen, to whose name is affixed, as the source of her authority, the term " *Dei Gratia Regina*" (By the Grace of God, Queen).

Assuming the converse of the proposition that one or a few have been divinely appointed and constituted the fountain of all honor and authority in the state, " the government of the United States," says Chancellor Kent, in his " Commentaries on American Law," " was erected by the free voice and joint will of the people of America, for their common defence and general welfare." All the State constitutions are framed and adopted by the free voice and joint will of the people of the respective States, and have for their object the health, peace, and prosperity of every person within their several jurisdictions. In order to maintain the stability and purity of governments based upon the suffrages of the people, it was necessary that the education, culture, and enlightenment of the whole people, intellectually, morally, and physically, should be made an object of primary concern; and hence it has been the policy, both of the State and United States governments, to make provision for the education of children and youth, and to encourage the acquisition of useful knowledge in every department of learning. Thus, in the ordinance for the government of the territory of the United States northwest of the Ohio River, among the articles which it was declared should be considered as articles of compact between the original States and the

people and States in said territory, and which should forever remain unalterable, unless by common consent, the
Congress of the United States declared that " Religion,
morality, and knowledge, being necessary to good government and the happiness of mankind, schools and the means
of education shall forever be encouraged." Ordinance of
1787, Article III.

For the support of universities, colleges, and schools,
Congress has, from time to time, appropriated lands of immense value; and the State Legislatures have adopted
systems of education, and made provision for their maintenance, in order to qualify the people for the exercise of
sovereignty and self-government.

It was the design of those who represented the voice of
the people in laying the foundations of the new government,
to establish it upon principles so rational, so broad and comprehensive, and so clearly just, that they should forever commend it to the approval and the affections of all, through all
coming time; and that, with such changes only as experience
might prove to be necessary to secure more effectually the
happiness of the people, it should be perpetual.  Did they,
in their earnest zeal for securing civil and religious liberty
to all, fail to provide for securing that *equality* which they
acknowledged to be the birthright of all men?  The declaration of independence asserted great general principles, not
with the force and effect of a statute, but as an expression
of the highest conception of the combined wisdom of the
representatives of the people, of their rights, and the duty
of the government to secure such rights.  At the time this
declaration was solemnly adopted by the Congress of the
confederated colonies, slavery existed in all, or nearly all,
of them, and the slave-trade was prosecuted with New
England capital, and large fortunes were being made by the
traffic in human flesh and blood, and chattel slavery continued to exist under the protection of the government of

the United States until within the last quarter of a century, and after a fierce and bloody conflict waged in its defence by the Southern against the Northern States of the Union, when it was abolished. The children of the slaves were born slaves, and had no recognized political or civil rights under the laws. But by force of circumstances not then foreseen, after a long period of oppression and injustice entirely opposed to the declared principles of our government, the colored race have come to be legally equal with the white race in their right to life, liberty, and the pursuit of happiness, and to be secured and protected by the government in the exercise of these inalienable rights. But while every male citizen above the age of twenty-one years—the most ignorant and depraved equally with the most intelligent and worthy—is allowed an equal voice in public affairs, an unjust and, we think, a very unwise discrimination is made against women, who are denied equality of political rights with men on the ground of sex alone. Upon the abolition of slavery of the colored race, and the recognition of their political rights without education or reference to character or other qualification for the exercise of such rights, the injustice and impolicy of refusing to recognize the same equal rights in women seems too plain to be seriously disputed. But it is only a question of time when this wrong will be righted, and that time cannot be far distant. There are some other palpable deviations from the principles upon which our republican States were declared to be founded, which are still allowed to pass without correction, but which require to be, and eventually must be, corrected by appropriate legislation.

The ordinance of 1787 was adopted by a Congress of representatives who well understood the spirit of the Declaration of Independence and of the popular will, and they declared that the fundamental principles of civil and religious liberty formed the basis whereon these republics, their laws , and constitutions, were erected, and that in the new States to be organized out of the territory of the United States northwest of the Ohio River, no person demeaning himself in a peaceable and orderly manner should ever be molested on account of his mode of worship or religious sentiments. The Constitution of the United States, by an amendment proposed in 1789, declares that Congress shall make no law respecting an establishment of religion, or prohibiting the free exercise thereof; and in article VI. of the original Constitution, adopted in 1787, it is declared that no religious test shall ever be required as a qualification to any office or public trust under the United States. The constitution of Michigan prohibits the Legislature from passing any law to prevent any person from worshipping God according to the dictates of his own conscience, or to compel any person to attend, erect, or support any place of religious worship, or to pay tithes, taxes, or other rates for the support of any minister of the gospel or teacher of religion; and provides that no money shall be appropriated or drawn from the treasury for the benefit of any religious sect or society, theological or religious seminary; and that it shall not diminish nor enlarge the civil or political rights, privileges, and capacities of any person on account of his opinion or belief concerning matters of religion. These provisions are followed by another, which is a natural and necessary sequence of the former, which declares that no law shall ever be passed to restrain or abridge the liberty of speech. Most of the State constitutions contain similar provisions. Yet the laws exempting church property from taxation, because it is devoted to religious uses, remain upon the statute books and are enforced, and thus every property holder is indirectly taxed for the benefit of religious sects and societies. On this subject the warnings of some of our most eminent statesmen should not remain unheeded. President Garfield, in Congress, January 21, 1874, said: "The divorce between church and state ought to be absolute. It ought to be so absolute that no church property anywhere, in any State or in the nation, should be exempt from equal taxation, for if you exempt the property of any church organization, to that extent you impose a tax upon the whole community."

President Grant, in his message in 1875, said: "I would call your attention to the importance of correcting an evil that, if permitted to continue, will probably lead to great trouble in our land before the close of the nineteenth century. It is the acquisition of vast amounts of untaxed church property. By 1900, without check, it is safe to say this property will reach a sum exceeding three billion dollars. So vast a sum, receiving all the protection and benefits of government, without bearing its proportion of the burdens and expenses of the same, will not be looked upon acquiescently by those who have to pay the taxes. In a growing country where real estate enhances so rapidly with time as in the United States, there is scarcely a limit to the wealth that may be acquired by corporations, religious or otherwise, if allowed to retain real estate without taxation, and may lead to sequestration without constitutional authority and through blood. I would suggest the taxation of all property equally."

The laws also invest the first day of the week, known as the Christian Sabbath, with a religious sanctity, which they require all persons to observe. All labor and business on that day are prohibited, except works of necessity and charity, and no one is allowed to be present at any dancing or public diversion, show or entertainment, however moral or instructive it may be, nor to take part in any sport, game, or play on that day, under a certain penalty for each offence. And it is also made an offence to be present on the evening of that day at any game, sport, play, or public diversion, or to resort to any public assembly, excepting meetings for religious worship, or moral instruction, or concerts of sacred

*h*                    10*

music. Exceptions are made in some of the States in favor of those who conscientiously believe that the seventh day of the week ought to be observed as the Sabbath, and such persons are allowed to perform secular labor on Sunday, provided they abstain from secular business on Saturday. So, too, notwithstanding the provision which forbids the legislature passing any law to restrain or abridge the liberty of speech, yet laws punishing what are called blasphemy and profanity are still held to be in force, and are occasionally, though now very rarely, invoked for the purpose of preventing the public expression of opinions which are obnoxious to some religious sects. The harmonizing of the laws relating to these subjects, and conforming them to the principles of civil and religious liberty, and the true spirit of rational freedom, will be effected through the mental and moral education and enlightenment of the people. Numerous modifications of the laws on these subjects have been made within the last few years, and other modifications will continue to be adopted until they are made to harmonize with the spirit of the constitution; and our descendants, if not ourselves, will realize that although the government is purely secular, yet it is based upon the highest and noblest principles of the universal religion of humanity, and interferes with no special belief or form of religious opinion or worship.

So far as political economy has come within the scope of legislation in the American Republic, the policy has been to place as few restrictions upon internal trade and commerce, and the accumulation and transfer of property, as were consistent with the safety and good order of the community, and to encourage every kind of useful invention and enterprise for developing and utilizing the resources of the country, and increasing the national wealth and individual and corporate prosperity.

Our people, as British colonists, had been subject to the

code of rules known as the Common Law of England; and the municipal laws of that country, excepting as modified by the Colonial Assemblies under authority conferred by the Crown, controlled private rights. This common law, which consists of a collection of principles to be found in the opinions of sages, or deduced from universal and immemorial usage, and progressively receiving the sanction of courts, so far as it was applicable to our situation and government, has been expressly recognized and adopted by the constitutions of several of the States, and has been assumed by the courts of justice, or declared by statute, with the like modifications, as the law of the land in nearly every State of the Union.

In the formation of a republican government, under which all were to be considered equal, and none could be recognized as entitled to or allowed exclusive privileges, and under which all monopolies were intended to be prevented, there could remain no class distinctions. Hence it was provided by the Constitution of 1787 that no title of nobility should be granted by the United States, and that no person holding any office of profit or trust under them should, without the consent of Congress, accept of any present, emolument, office, or title of any kind whatever, from any king, prince, or foreign state; and it was further provided that no State should grant any title of nobility.

The laws of primogeniture and the entailment of estates, being equally repugnant to the principles of free republican government, have been abolished. Many other changes and modifications of the laws as they existed when our Constitution was framed and adopted have been made, for the purpose of conforming them to the principles enunciated in the declaration of independence. These changes have been made progressively as their necessity became apparent, or as public opinion demanded, and many of them were of so radical a character as to occasion serious alarm to the

more conservative of our people, and to evoke the most
strenuous opposition.  Among these have been the exten-
sion of the elective franchise; the abolition of imprisonment for debt; the recognition of the equal rights of married
women to control and dispose of their own property, independently of the husband; the exemption of the homestead
from forced sale, together with sufficient provisions and other
personal property to protect the family from immediate want
in case of financial misfortune or disaster; and the distribution of intestate estates to the children or next of kin, males
and females alike.

The legislation in favor of greater liberty and more perfect equality of political and social rights than those previously recognized has proceeded slowly but surely from the
basic idea of a government of the people, by the people, and
for the greatest benefit of the whole people.

A century of unexampled national prosperity has elapsed
since the government was organized.  Our resources are unlimited, and our national wealth is beyond computation.  Our
people are the freest upon the earth, and claim to be among
the most enlightened.  They possess abundant means to
satisfy all the rational needs of every soul within our borders,
and to educate and provide for the physical comfort and
moral and intellectual improvement of all.  But notwithstanding all our wealth and enlightenment, and the abun-
dance of our resources, there are to-day many thousands of
our fellow-citizens living in a state of destitution and squalor,
and who are feeling the " wants that pinch the poor" without the hope of adequate relief; and there are many thousands more who are dissatisfied with their condition and
feel that they are deprived of their just share of the wealth
which their labor, united with capital, has produced, and the
struggle for subsistence by the great masses of our citizens,
who are obliged to rely upon the products of their daily
labor for support, is constantly becoming more intense,

while the number of employés, in comparison with that of employers, has been constantly increasing, and their condition becoming more and more unsatisfactory.

It has been the policy of the government to protect and encourage manufactures, the invention and construction of every kind of useful and labor-saving machinery, the construction and operation of railroads and other means of transportation, and every other kind of business enterprises which were calculated to develop the resources and increase the wealth of the country. Home industries and productions are protected by a tax upon importations from foreign countries, and a large portion of the public domain has been given to corporations to aid in the construction of railroads.

These great enterprises have necessitated the concentration of large amounts of capital, and the organization of capitalists into companies and corporate bodies, and these have been vested with special powers and privileges, upon the assumption that the public good required them. These artificial bodies, under such restrictions and regulations as the legislature has seen fit to impose or prescribe, now monopolize and control nearly the entire business of the country, and by means of their wealth and political influence in a large degree control its legislation.

They have become the principal employers of labor, and by combination they are enabled not only to prevent competition among themselves and control the prices of their own productions or services, but to determine the compensation to be paid for the labor and services which they require.

Those who are employed as officers and agents or managers of such corporations are, in general, amply, and many of them munificently, compensated for their services and the skill and ability which they bring into the service of their employers. But laborers of inferior grade, who furnish much of the skill, and perform the work without which railroads could not exist, nor manufactories, ships, or vessels be built or operated, complain that their just share of the wealth their toil produces is withheld from them, and hence discontent exists among them, and organized resistance to what they denounce as the organized tyranny of wealth. It has been computed that " fully ten thousand trades unions, farmers' alliances, Knights of Labor assemblies, and kindred organizations appear arrayed against employers, for purposes of change in the laws and conditions affecting the laboring classes, or in self-defence. All over the land strikes of workmen are of daily occurrence, and lock-outs are little less frequent. Mines are covered, factories closed, work-shops abandoned; those who could labor either refusing or not permitted to do so, while over one million of unemployed men and an equal number of destitute and helpless women make a standing army of witnesses against some terrible error in our social system, or some injustice perpetrated by legislation."

In a country where perfect freedom of speech and of the press exist by the fundamental law, and the means of education are extended to all; where knowledge is diffused with the speed of lightning to every nook and corner of the land, and all are legally free to choose their own occupation in life, and to aspire to any position in society or under the government, no sort of mental or physical slavery can continue to exist, and all social and political injustice will eventually be resented and opposed or avenged by the people. In such a country, and with such means of elevation and growth, the dignity of labor and the just rights of the laboring man must eventually find universal recognition and just appreciation. Slowly and through many centuries, and against the strongest prejudices and most powerful influences, has the idea of equality of rights in all men been advancing. The ruins of Egypt, Assyria, Carthagenia, and Rome, and those of other ancient peoples, attest that their rulers were task-masters and the people slaves; and the republics of the succeeding era, while they made vast contributions to human knowledge, did not arrive at a comprehension of this great truth, now declared to be self-evident, that all men are created equal and are entitled to equal rights. Plato and Aristotle, who were deemed to be wise above all the other philosophers of antiquity, taught that the occupations of artisans degrade those who engage in them; that they were base mercenaries, excluded by their condition from political rights; and that tradesmen, accustomed to lie and deceive, should be suffered in a community only as a necessary evil. In Rome the masses were laborers, and all laborers were slaves; and even Cicero, the most gentle and liberal statesman of his time, affirmed that all artisans were engaged in a degrading profession. The old civilizations began and ended without a thought of the dignity of labor or the just rights of the masses of the people either to participate in the affairs of government or to demand a share of the wealth which their labor produced. To us who view their course by the clear light of history their doom appears to have been inevitable. The luxury, extravagance, effeminacy, and corruption of the wealthy and powerful on the one hand, and the ignorance, poverty, and degradation of the masses on the other, could not fail to result in their destruction.

These facts of history suggest to us questions of the gravest and most momentous import,—namely, have we, as a people, arisen to a true comprehension of the dignity of humanity in all its conditions, employments, and occupations; and have we the wisdom and virtue necessary to carry into practical effect the great fundamental principles of government, declared to be vital, and upon which alone the perpetuity of a free state can be maintained? Have we made the great mistake of placing no restrictions or limitations upon the increase and accumulation of wealth by individuals and private corporations, and of granting special privileges and encouragement and protection to capital by legislation, without affording adequate encouragement or protection to the workers who are equally worthy, but without capital? If capital had not been organized under charters from the government, with powers, privileges, and immunities secured to the corporations which the non-capitalist does not and cannot possess, it could never have wielded the immense influence it now has, and the inequalities that now exist would have been impossible.

It has been the policy of the national and State governments to encourage every kind of enterprise that would be likely to increase the wealth and prosperity of the country and the products of our national industries. But great national wealth may be a great curse or a great blessing to a people. If it is controlled by the comparatively few, it becomes an engine of oppression ; its influence is corrupting, and its tendency is towards national disease and dissolution. If wealth is diffused so that all may share the benefits it is capable of producing, it may be a blessing to all, and its influence be everywhere felt as a power for the development of healthy, vigorous manhood and the elevation of the whole people into higher and nobler conditions.

A small army of well-armed and disciplined men, organized and controlled by a skilful commander, may subjugate and enslave a million of unarmed and undisciplined people, and this has been done a thousand times in the history of the world. So a few men, absorbing the wealth of a country, and organized for its protection, may practically enslave and hold in subjection to their will the millions of laborers who must live by their daily toil, or seek a subsistence at the hands of charity, or else starve. When Ahasuerus had, at the instigation of a vain and cruel minister, decreed the destruction of the unarmed and helpless Jews within his dominions at an appointed time by his armed soldiers, and afterwards repented of the great crime, it was too late for him to revoke the decree he had made; but he then warned the intended victims of their impending doom, and furnished them the weapons with which they were able to defend themselves, and we commend this ancient king for this act of justice. If the policy of our government has been such as to build up and establish a force that is capable of subjugating the many to the power and control of the few, does not justice demand that these shall either be protected by the government, or armed with the power to protect themselves against such a force? It is claimed by many earnest, intelligent thinkers that the plain duty of the government is either to disarm capital of the special powers and privileges it has conferred upon it, and withhold its special protection and encouragement to capital in the future, and thus leave a fair field for the battle of life to all, or, if it is too late to do this, that it should by a counter-policy invest the laboring man with powers and privileges equal to those conferred upon capitalists, by means of which he can protect himself.

The most powerful monopolies that have grown up within the last half-century have been the railroad corporations. These have a nominal capital of upward of seven thousand millions of dollars in the United States, but the actual cost of all the roads and their equipments has probably not been much if any more than half that amount, the balance being what is known in Wall Street as "water," a part of which represents the avails of either stock or bonds, which have gone into the pockets of the directors or stockholders, and a part being only nominal stock; and this fictitious capital demands and receives its share of the earnings of the roads, which the workingman has to pay.

These mammoth properties are conducted by their managers solely with the purpose of making them yield the largest possible profits to the corporators, and their financial success is exhibited in the railroad reports of 1884, which show a net profit for that year of over three hundred millions of dollars.

The great manufacturing corporations conduct their affairs upon the same principle, and the census returns of 1880 show that one hundred thousand manufacturers, all of whom are incorporated, received returns on their capital of thirty-seven per cent. A combination of companies wielding thirty millions of capital controls the steel product of this country. Others control the oil, the coal, the iron, and other leading articles of consumption, and what they do not monopolize is covered by combinations of dealers, so that there is scarcely anything, from a steam-engine to a lucifer-match, the price of which is not fixed by a corporation.

Land monopoly, when permitted, has always been, and always will be, an injury to the workingman, and a means of enslaving the poor. There is probably no country at this time where this monopoly is more oppressive and disastrous to the people than in Ireland. The population of that island is a little over 5,100,000, and it contains about 20,000,000 acres of land, of which one-half is owned by less than seven hundred and fifty proprietors, each holding upward of 50,000 acres. Three proprietors hold over 100,000 acres each, fourteen over 50,000 each, and ninety over 20,000 each. One hundred and ten landlords hold among them over 4,000,000 acres, or one-fifth of the soil of the whole country. The whole civilized world is familiar with the history of the Irish people since their union with Great Britain, and know of the hopeless poverty, misery, and degradation which has been brought upon them by their vicious system of land monopoly.

Of the people of the British Islands, it is said that thirty thousand men have legal power to expel five-sixths of their population, and that the vast majority of the British people have no right to their native land, save to walk the streets and trudge the roads. The condition of the English laborers, too, is everywhere known. With all her wealth, England maintains over one million paupers on official charity.

The history of Rome illustrates the disastrous effect of land monopoly. In the time of Cicero only two thousand citizens of Rome owned real estate, and with it they possessed legions of slaves. While Tiberius Gracchus was a Tribune of the Roman people, he addressed to them this memorable language: *"Men of Rome, you are called the lords of the world, yet have no right to a square foot of the soil. The wild beasts have their dens, but the soldiers of Italy have only air and water."*

In this country, whatever danger there may be from land monopoly in the future, its effects have not been seriously felt in the past, and are not so perceptible as to create any special alarm in the present. Our public domains have been so broad, and such vast portions of our territory constantly open to purchase and settlement in large or small tracts, at a moderate price, or to homestead entry, that it has always been in the power of those who desired to become the owners of land and tillers of their own soil, to acquire and possess it. But is there no danger that, without any limitations or restrictions upon the purchase of government lands, whether by citizens or foreigners, large portions of them may be monopolized by wealthy individuals or associations, and eventually held under a system of landlordism similar to that which prevails in Ireland and England, with a tenantry equally in the power of the great land-owners?

The *Kansas City Times* recently published a list of the leading foreign corporations that own land in the United States, showing an aggregate of 20,740,000 acres, equal to more than one-half of England, and more than one-fourth of the United Kingdom of Great Britain and Ireland. Other foreign associations and wealthy individuals have become large real-estate owners in the Territories and new States, and many of our own citizens have acquired titles to hundreds of thousands of acres, either for purposes of speculation or occupancy. The general government has the power to impose such restrictions upon the purchase and uses of its own lands as it shall deem necessary for the best interests of the people, and the State governments can, by wise legislation, counteract the tendency which exists to the accumulation of large estates in lands by individuals or associations.

Power is always and everywhere liable to abuse, and whether it arise from the possession of wealth, or other fortuitous circumstances or conditions, its tendency, when not duly restrained or controlled, is to the aggrandizement of its possessor and the oppression of those who are subject to its influence.

> " Ill fares the land, to hastening ills a prey,
>    Where wealth accumulates, and men decay."

Legislators have enacted laws for controlling, in many respects, the power which wealth gives to the capitalist, and to protect those of small means, or who are dependent upon the labor of their hands for support, against the grasping cupidity of the monopolist. They have limited the rate of interest upon the loan of money; fixed the number of hours which shall constitute a day's work; abolished the right which the creditor formerly exercised to incarcerate his debtor in a prison; exempted the homestead from a forced sale, together with the clothing, furniture, provisions, etc., necessary for immediate use by the debtor and his family, and sufficient tools, implements, and stock to enable him to carry on his business; and in other respects provided for his protection, and securing to him the means of earning a comfortable subsistence, educating his children, and acquiring the knowledge which is indispensable to good citizenship.

These legislative changes have occurred during the present century, and they indicate a corresponding change in the views, feelings, and sentiments of the entire people, and are the result of a prevailing and constantly growing conviction among the most intelligent and enlightened thinkers of the age, that they are promotive of the best interests of all, the wealthy as well as the poor, the strong as well as the weak and the simple. They are, so far as they extend, a practical recognition of the common interest and brotherhood of man, and the equal right of all to share the blessings of a higher and nobler civilization towards which we are progressing.

But many evils still remain to be remedied. General intelligence has advanced, and the knowledge by which existing evils are discerned has increased more rapidly than the wisdom of the legislature or the people has been able to devise means for their cure; and those upon whom they bear most heavily become restless and impatient. These are the wage-workers, who are obliged to depend upon the avails of their daily labor for subsistence, who have no accumulated stores to draw upon in case of enforced idleness, sickness, or other misfortune; with whom the struggle for life grows fiercer as the chances of profitable employment become more uncertain.

They see improved machinery, which capital only can purchase and control, doing the work which they and their ancestors were accustomed to perform by muscular power, and performing it with such celerity that fewer and fewer human hands are needed to perform the work, and when displaced and compelled to seek other employment, they are again liable to be displaced by some new invention. Statistics gathered and carefully collated under the direction of the Commissioner of Labor at Washington, in 1886, show the displacement of muscular labor in various branches of industry by the use of machinery to be as follows :

In the manufacture of wall-paper, 99 in 100 are displaced ; in silk (weaving), 95 in 100; in paper-making, 94½ in 100; in woollen manufactures, 94$\frac{2}{17}$ in 100; in silk (winding), 90 in 100; in hats (stiff), 88$\frac{4}{5}$ in 100; in tobacco manufactures, 87½ in 100; in manufacture of glass jars, 83½ in 100; in manufacture of brooms, 80 in 100; in manufacture of boots and shoes, 80 in 100; in farm labor, 80 in 100; in manufacture of flour, 75 in 100; in cotton manufacture, 66⅔ in 100; in hats (medium), 66⅔ in 100; in wooden-ware, 66⅔ in 100; in manufacture of carriages, 65$\frac{4}{5}$ in 100; in manufacture of saws, 60 in 100; in manufacture of furniture, 50 in 100; in railroad supplies, 50 in 100; in rubber boots and shoes, 50 in 100; in manufacture of soap, 50 in 100; in manufacture of fire-bricks, 40 in 100; in general silk manufacture, 40 in 100.

A sewing-machine does the work of twelve women. A "Boston bootmaker" will enable a workman to make three hundred pairs of boots daily. Glen's California reaper will cut, thresh, winnow, and put in bags, the wheat of sixty acres in twenty-four hours. The Hercules ditcher, Michigan, removes seven hundred and fifty cubic yards, or seven hundred tons of clay per hour. (Story of Labor, p. 706.)

These statements show that in the several industries named, 650 men, by the use of machinery, accomplish the work which it would require 2300 to perform by muscular labor, and that for every 650 thus employed, 1650 have been displaced.

To illustrate the effect of steam- and water-power, and labor-saving machinery upon the industries of the country, the Commissioner of Labor, in his annual report of March, 1886 (pp. 87, 89), makes the following statements :

" The mechanical industries of the United States carried on by steam- and water-power, represent, in round numbers,

3,500,000 horse-power, each horse-power equalling the muscular labor of six men ; that is to say, if men were employed
to furnish the power to carry on the industries of this country,
it would require 21,000,000 men, and 21,000,000 represent
a population, according to the ratio of the census of 1880,
of 105,000,000. The industries are now carried on by
4,000,000 persons, in round numbers, representing a popu-
tion of 20,000,000 only. There are in the United States
28,600 locomotives. To do the work of these locomotives
upon the existing common roads of the country, and the
equivalent of that which has been done upon the railroads
the past year, would require, in round numbers, 54,000,000
horses, and 13,500,000 men. The work is now done, so far
as men are concerned, by 250,000, representing a population
of 1,200,000, while the population required for the number
of men necessary to do the work with horses would be
67,500,000. To do the work, then, now accomplished by
power and power-machinery in our mechanical industries
and upon our railroads, would require men representing a
population of 172,500,000 in addition to the present population of the country of 55,000,000, or a total population with
hand-processes and with horse-power, of 227,500,000, which
population would be obliged to subsist on present means.
In an economic view the cost to the country would be
enormous. The present cost of operating the railroads of
the country with steam-power is, in round numbers, $502,-
600,000 per annum ; but to carry on the same amount of
work with men and horses would cost the country $11,308,-
500,000."

In view of these facts, and the influx of great numbers of
laboring men from Europe who are competing with our
laborers for employment, and of the aggregation and rapid
accumulation of wealth by corporations and individuals, and
the enforced idleness of large numbers who are willing to
labor, by reason of the existing state of affairs, many of

whom are in destitute conditions, notwithstanding our unexampled national prosperity, it is not unnatural that a
feeling of dissatisfaction and alarm, and more or less of
resentment, should exist among laboring men ; nor that the
unequal distribution of the joint products of capital and
labor and skill should produce a sense of wrong and oppression, and provoke retaliation.

By a natural instinct all men are prompted to resist, and
endeavor to avert evil to themselves.   Self-defence has been
denominated the first law of nature, and until men have
become so cultivated and enlightened as to be elevated
above the desire to seek revenge for wrongs inflicted, they
will be disposed to render evil for evil to those they deem
to be the cause of, or responsible for, the injuries they suffer.
Hence the law of retaliation, though repudiated by all wise
men and all enlightened nations in theory, is still acted
upon, and this savage principle is so ingrained into the
constitution of man, that it will probably be the last to be
eradicated under a higher civilization, and a new system of
education in which the culture of the moral faculties and
perceptions shall be treated as of the highest importance.

The vices, corruptions and oppressions, and overbearing
arrogances of the wealthy and powerful in Europe, have
produced the anarchists, nihilists and kindred associations,
who are the resolute and determined enemies of social order
and government, and who, but for lack of power, would
destroy every existing organized government, and reduce
society to a chaotic mass, to be reorganized, if at all, upon
some idea of equality, in which there shall be neither rich
nor poor, high nor low, nor any responsibility under fixed
laws.   These orders, by reason of their secret organizations
and the desperate character of the principles they advocate,
and the revengeful and destructive means to which they
resort for accomplishing their purposes, have become a
terror to the community against which they have proven

themselves capable of committing the most horrible crimes without remorse, and facing the penalty of death for such deeds without fear or any expression of regret. Some of the most desperate anarchists have been driven out of European governments, and transplanted to our own country, where they have shown themselves to be equally the enemies of a free republican government; and while claiming the protection of our laws which secure the right of all to freely express their thoughts and advocate their opinions, they abuse that right by denouncing all government and all law, and counselling the most atrocious acts of villany and crime.

"It would not be easy to exaggerate," says Mr. J. W. Chadwick (Index of April 29, 1886), "the amount of irritation and unrest that characterize the interests of labor at the present time. These elements confront us, turn which way we will: strikes east and west here in America, in Belgium worse and worse; Ireland waiting in agonized suspense for the response of England to her cry for justice; a multitude of books and pamphlets, hundreds of articles, thousands of editorials directed to this question of questions; men of enormous force and genius, like Lassalle and Marx, giving their splendid energies to the most daring speculations; such brilliant theorists as George and Geonlund bringing fresh fuel to the dancing flames; every variety of socialism, communism, and co-operation advocated with supreme self-confidence; the nihilist and anarchist hopeless of any polity that is not built upon the levelled ruins of the present structure of industrial and social life. Where there is so much restlessness and fever there is surely something wrong. A million of men out of employment in the United States for the year 1885. A loss of wages equal to $300,-000,000. The something wrong is not merely a few years of depression and collapse, succeeding to a few of generous expanse. Prosperity may come again after five years of

*i*

depression, as it came in 1879 after the much more gloomy period from 1873, and with it prosperity may cause some temporary abatement of the stress of labor agitation. But it will not wholly cease, because the principal cause of it is a great deal deeper than the immediate depression or collapse. It is the immense and steadily increasing disproportion that exists between the condition of the rich and poor. It is not true, as frequently insisted, that the rich are growing richer and the poor are growing poorer all the time; it is true that the rich are growing *relatively* richer and the poor are growing *relatively* poorer. Here is the dreadful fact that, corresponding to the enormous increase of the general wealth, there has been no corresponding increase of the wage-earner's wages. From 1850 to 1880, the net product of American manufactures increased four hundred per cent., the wages of labor forty per cent. That is to say, the advantage which the manufacturer has derived from the improvement of machinery and other methods of production has been ten times as great as that derived from this improvement to the wage-earners. The industrial statistics of every European government show a similar result, which is the efficient cause of all that is most fundamental to the industrial agitation of to-day."

For the purpose of counteracting this tendency and securing to labor a more just distribution of the profits derived from capital and labor combined, numerous associations of laboring men have been formed. Craft guilds, originally instituted in Rome by the Emperor Numa, as related by Plutarch, that they might be more easily governed, made rapid progress under the republic, and became protecting bulwarks of the various trades, and kept a vigilant watch on the rights of the members. The guilds gradually extended over Europe, and attained to a high degree of prosperity. After their decadence as labor organizations, which commenced in the fourteenth century, numerous voluntary combinations were formed, now generally known as trades-unions. These were organized for the purposes of mutual aid, and promoting the interest of those of their respective crafts, and many such organizations have continued to exist, and are still existing, both in Europe and America.

Their history has been one of struggle against the power of wealth and the advantages which capital affords its possessors to control not only the prices of labor, but also the price the laborer shall pay for the means of subsistence. In their numerous conflicts with their employers they have sometimes been successful in securing a recognition of the justice of their claims, but more generally have been defeated with loss and suffering to themselves in their attempts to cause a compliance with their demands.

These labor unions have been formed by those of the same craft or trade. Such are the Typographical Unions; the Hat-makers' and Hat-finishers' Associations; the Iron-moulders' Union; the Glass-blowers' League; the Grand International Brotherhood of Locomotive Engineers; the Order of Railroad Conductors; the International Cigar-makers' Union; the Bricklayers' and Stone-masons' International Union of America; the Patrons of Husbandry; the Knights of St. Crispin; and many others of similar character.

In 1869 a labor organization was formed upon a new principle, known since 1871 as "The Knights of Labor," which it is said now numbers over one million in the United States, and three hundred thousand more in Canada. This is not a trades-union, nor an assemblage of trades-unions. It accepts the unskilled workman as well as the skilled artisan. The cardinal principle of their constitution is that of a union of all wage-workers, irrespective of race, color, or creed, and it is understood to have been the first organization ever attempted based upon the broad principle of uniting all laborers and wage-workers in one order, with a common centre of power for its direction and government. It is a society for mutual defence and united attack, and is now the strongest combination ever formed for promoting the interests of wage-earners.

By their constitution persons who either sell, or make a living, or any part of it, by the sale of, intoxicating drink, lawyers, bankers, professional gamblers, and stock-brokers are excluded from membership in the order.

When any grievance requiring adjustment is reported to the proper officers of the assembly, they are required to take the matter into full consideration, and use every effort to avoid a conflict. If negotiation fails to secure a settlement of the difficulty, and arbitration is refused, and the grievance is deemed of such a character as to require a resort to coercive measures, the weapons used are strikes or boycotts, the latter, however, being generally discountenanced by those who have the general direction of the affairs of the order.

Strikes have been the most common means resorted to by all kinds of labor organizations to compel the employers of wage-labor to recognize the rights claimed by the employed, or to redress their grievances, when other means have failed to secure their adjustment. Strikes are not in themselves unlawful, and may be justifiable upon the same principle that war by one nation against another may under certain conditions be justified,—that is to say, when waged in self-defence. But as war for the purpose of conquest, national aggrandizement, or revenge is condemned by every principle of justice and humanity, so strikes are hostile proceedings that can be approved only as a necessary means of self-defence. Any individual laborer, or any number of laborers combined, may refuse to serve any other individual or corporation, or to engage in any particular employment, if he or they cannot secure an adequate compensation for the service rendered, or if the terms and conditions of the employment are unreasonable or otherwise unjust, and any number of associations may combine to act together in concert, and to aid each other in securing and defending the just rights of their members in all lawful and proper ways. The strikes which have been organized by some of the strongest of the trades-unions, and by the Knights of Labor during the last decade, have been numerous, and some of them far-reaching in their effects, paralyzing or obstructing the business of large districts of country, and attended by immense pecuniary losses, both to the strikers and their former employers, and injuriously affecting the interests of millions of others whose occupations and means of subsistence depended upon the uninterrupted carrying on of the business suspended by the strike. Rioting and the wanton destruction of life and property, preventing those who would labor in their places from doing so by threats and violence, compelling other laborers to join them and quit their employment against their will through fear of violence, are acts of lawlessness and brutality which have frequently occurred, and been resorted to as a means of making the strike successful,—means justified by no law, but condemned by every principle which ought to govern the motives and guide the actions of men. The sudden withdrawal of thousands of men from employment in a business upon the continuance of which depends the commercial, manufacturing, and other business of hundreds of thousands of others, who are forced to depend upon its continuance for success as the means of support, by the mere fiat of an executive committee or master-workman, is in itself an act of fearful import, and the exercise of a despotic power which should not be allowed to exist, even by the voluntary consent of those who are subject to it, unless its existence can be justified by conditions that imperiously demand it. It is said that none of the outrages referred to are directed or sanctioned by the order, but are deprecated by the members

generally.   And this is undoubtedly the fact.   But these
orders include amongst them men who are ever ready, when
a pretext is afforded them, to engage in turbulent and
disorderly conduct; and that they will do so under the
excitement of a conflict with their employers, making that
a pretext for such conduct, the history of strikes, both in
this and some European countries, proves to be inevitable;
and knowing this fact, are not the orders to which they
belong to be justly regarded as morally responsible for the
crimes they commit?

The most important and fiercely-contested strikes have
been those of railroad employés.   That which occurred in
1886 by the Knights of Labor against the Missouri Pacific
and the Texas Pacific Railroad Companies and their con-
necting roads in the southwest, known as the Gould system,
commencing the 1st of March and continuing a little over
two months, has been characterized as the most fierce fight
of the century between organized capital and organized
labor.   It cost the Knights of Labor one million dollars in
loss of wages, seriously curtailed the financial resources of
the railroads, and caused much suffering and incalculable
losses to trades-people in all branches of industry and business throughout the immense region of country traversed
by, or dependent upon, this system of roads.   The strikers
in several places were turbulent and riotous to such a degree
that it became necessary to call out the military forces of
the States, and employ great numbers of police-officers for
the protection of property, and especially to protect the
lives of such men as were employed to fill the places vacated
by the strikers.   These men, like those who were engaged
in rebuilding the walls of Jerusalem under the direction of
the prophet, were furnished with weapons for their defence
in case of attack, and while earning their bread by the labor
of their hands, were obliged to keep their weapons of defence
constantly within their reach.   Among the desperate acts of

the strikers was that of waylaying a freight-train near Fort Worth, firing upon the new men who were operating it and those who had been assigned to their protection, wounding four of the marshals, and two of them fatally, some of the strikers also being wounded in the skirmish that ensued. Another was that of two hundred strikers, on the 7th of April, going the rounds of the freight-yards in East St. Louis, and ordering the men there employed to quit work and fall into line with themselves. On the 9th of April some of the men who had accepted service under the Louisville and Nashville Railroad, and had been supplied with arms, either with murderous intent or from sudden panic, fired into the crowds of people in East Louis, and killed seven men and one woman. Acts of violence and lawlessness were of daily occurrence during the continuance of the strike. Engines were "killed," freight-trains ditched, and other property injured or destroyed. Aside from the wrongs committed against individuals and corporations in consequence of this strike, the effect of such a warfare, carried on for so long a time, with such asperity and bitterness of feeling, and attended by such circumstances as we have described, upon the public morals of the people can never be estimated.

The authors of the "Story of Manual Labor," whose sympathies are strongly with the laboring men, after treating of the history of the Knights of Labor, and giving a brief account of this strike and the incidents connected with it, remark as follows: " The first serious check which the order received was in the great railroad strike of 1886. . . . Mistakes were made which will hardly be repeated, and as we have endeavored to show in other parts of this book, it is only by their mistakes that the workingmen of the world have been able to find out, painfully and with great losses, the right path to the position which labor, in a free country like America, ought to assume. Strikes will not win. Violence simply invites counter-violence. If it come to the test, capital would secure more dynamite than labor, and could apply it more successfully. The only road out of the wilderness is to be won by careful organization and peaceful and constitutional remedies."

The general characteristics of all the railroad strikes that have occurred in this country are the same, and the pretexts for their institution in some instances appear to have been frivolous or trivial, in view of the grave consequences necessarily resulting from the measures adopted for redress. In the case of the great strike of 1886, the Texas and Pacific Railroad Company had discharged from their employment C. A. Hall, foreman of the wood-workers in their car-shops at Marshall, and after a struggle of eight and a half weeks to compel his reinstatement, by the whole force of the order, the strike was ended by an unconditional submission, without accomplishing the purpose for which it was ostensibly instituted. The real purpose of the managers of the order seems to have been to make such a demonstration of their power as would compel the corporations involved to submit to such terms as they should dictate, which they believed themselves strong enough at that time to accomplish. Had they succeeded in bringing these great corporations to their feet, they would have demonstrated the fact, which some of them then assumed and threatened to put into practical effect, that they had the power to stop every wheel in the United States. Every sound political economist, however strong his sympathies may have been in favor of the laboring men of the country, would equally deprecate any assumption of right on the part of organized labor to dictate to capitalists the manner and terms of conducting their business, and the assumption of any such right by the capitalist to dictate to labor the terms upon which it shall be employed. The exercise of any such power by either would destroy the other, and establish a tyranny that would result in anarchy. The solution of the question lies in the recognition of the supreme law which declares that the interests of capital and labor are mutual, and so blended that neither can prosper without the other, and neither should ever be allowed to subvert the rights of the other.

Almost every manufacturing town and mining district in the country has, within the last few years, been the scene of strikes by labor organizations, and their extent and frequency have been such as to seriously obstruct and unsettle the course of business. Pursuant to a previous understanding among the trade associations, a demand was made on the 1st of May, 1886, that eight hours should be accepted by the employers as a day's work. The refusal of most of the employers of labor to accede to this demand was followed by strikes in all the principal cities of the Northern States, and extending to St. Louis in the southwest. New York and Chicago were among those which suffered the greatest losses in their business, and it was in these cities, especially the latter, where the anarchist element was made prominent in the conflict by demonstrations of ferocious malignity towards the friends and defenders of social order, which sent a thrill of horror through the civilized world. The tragic events resulting from that strike in Chicago, as the world now knows, culminated in the conviction of seven leading anarchists of that city of murder of the first degree, and the sentencing of all of them to be hung, the self-murder of one of them, and the judicial murder, under the laws of the State of Illinois, of four, and commutation of the sentence of two of them to imprisonment for life.

The question of pecuniary loss to employers and employed, growing out of these strikes for fewer hours of labor, is one of minor importance compared with the wrongs and crimes of which they were the efficient cause; but it has been computed that these losses, including wages, loss in current business, and the stopping of new business, amounted to nearly or quite thirty millions of dollars.

The design of every strike by a labor combination is to do injury, by crippling the business of those against whom it is instituted. The motive for doing such injury is to enforce a compliance with their demands by inspiring a fear of further injury in case of non-compliance. The principle upon which such acts and motives are sought to be justified, if generally approved and acted upon, would reverse the stream of progress and set back the wheels of civilization perhaps for centuries. That such a course should be persisted in as a remedy for the evils of which laboring men complain seems incredible, and we believe the good sense and cooler judgments of the great majority of them will soon check the rashness and impatience of the more impulsive and inconsiderate, until they shall discover and unitedly pursue the path that will lead them, by peaceful and lawful methods, to that elevated and secure position which the laborers in a free country ought to, and must eventually, occupy.

Most, if not all, the most disastrous strikes that have occurred, might have been avoided by the exercise of a little more patience and moderation, and taking more ample time for discussion and negotiation, and the exhibition of a conciliatory spirit. It should not be forgotten that while a strike of the employés of a railroad, or system of roads, is directed primarily against the corporations, and is intended to injure them by interrupting their business, a vastly greater amount of injury is done to others who are in no wise responsible for the grievances complained of, and that among those who suffer most are brother laborers, thrown out of employment by the enforced suspension of the business in which they are employed. But above all, the demoralizing effect of large and powerful bodies of men associated together and acting under the directions of a central directory of their own creation, under no sanction of law, to redress, by forcible and violent means, assumed wrongs for which the laws of the country afford a peaceful remedy where the act complained of is unlawful, or which if lawful is not to be regarded as a wrong until declared so by the legislature, can hardly be estimated. Such exhibitions of power, directed to such purposes, afford opportunities and encouragement to the most desperate and vicious to mingle in the strife for the purpose of gratifying their criminal propensities with better chances of escaping the consequences of their acts. Every such demonstration has in it an element of anarchism, which attracts to it the open and pronounced, as well as the secret enemies of social order, and of a government which protects the rights of property.

Men are justly held to contemplate and intend the natural consequence of their acts, and such as usually flow from those of a similar character. The wilful killing of a human being with malice aforethought is murder, and those who conspire with such as commit the act to compass the death, are held to be equally guilty. How much less guilty are those who deliberately, without some overmastering necessity, institute and carry into effect measures of .retaliation which all previous experience has shown are likely to, and probably will, cause the commission of this highest crime known to the law (treason excepted), together with innumerable smaller crimes and offences?

The taking of the property of another, with intent to deprive the owner of his property, is theft, and subjects the offender to imprisonment in a county jail or State penitentiary, and in England, but a few years ago, was punishable with death. How much less guilty, morally, are they who deliberately deprive hundreds of thousands of their fellow-citizens of millions of money or of property, by forcibly obstructing the trade or business in which they are engaged?

The great strike of 1886 in the southwest interfered with or suspended the business of a population estimated at five millions, who were dependent upon the working of the Gould system of railroads.   The strike of the engineers and firemen of the Burlington and Quincy system, embracing six thousand miles of railroad, now on foot, if long continued, may be equally disastrous to the business of the country.   A circular just issued by the chief of the Brotherhood of Engineers and grand master of the firemen engaged in the strike contains the following announcement: " Five days have elapsed since the great strike was inaugurated upon the Burlington, and from end to end the system is paralyzed and unable to move." / The strike on the Reading Railroad system in Pennsylvania by the Knights of Labor, which is still pending (March 3, 1888), is attended with similar effects, while the issue as between the strikers and employers is problematical, but the results of the conflict will certainly be vastly injurious, with no compensating benefits likely to follow.   It is said with truth that laboring men have grievances of which they may justly complain; that wealth has been accumulated largely by speculation and fraud, and by withholding the just rewards of labor, and that its power has been used to oppress the poor.   But all these facts do not justify or excuse any resort to violent or criminal means of redress.   It is also true that many millions of wealth are freely given every year for the benefit of laborers and the improvement of their condition.

When we come to treat of the prevention of crime in a subsequent article, we hope to be able to indicate a better way of adjusting the rights of labor, and preventing future conflict between labor and capital.   It presents a question of momentous importance, and the best minds of the civilized world are occupied in its consideration, and endeavoring to find a way of solving it which will be satisfactory and beneficial to all.

## CHAPTER IX.

### OTHER CAUSES OF CRIME.

AMONG the many other causes of crime is the debasing influence of a demoralized newspaper press. A sound thinker and keen observer of events, their causes and effects, writes on the subject as follows: "There is no end of prating of the power of the press, and no one can truthfully deny its incalculable influence; but that it approximates even to the degree of greatest usefulness would be an unfounded claim. In its eagerness for news, in catering to an unrefined and vulgar taste, the press has become prostituted and debased; and, with the facilities of telephone and telegraph, is a sewer into which is poured the effeteness, rottenness, degradation, imbecility, villany, moral disease, profligacy, and corruption of the whole world, in a seething mass of unutterable abomination. The great metropolitan journals, with world-wide facilities, take the lead in the gossip of villany and prurient rascality, and the smaller fry of town and village closely imitate, like hounds in a well-trained pack. Special correspondents are sent, regardless of distance or expense, to report murders, robberies, debaucheries, hangings, and numberless crimes. The taste of the public is not only catered to, but cultivated in this direction, and the evil intensifies with the morbid feeling it creates for moral and social carrion; and when the actual fails in supply, the ready pen and debased fancy of the reporter pour forth the reeking column. The 'mirror of the times' has no surface for the reflection of good deeds or kind acts. It is sensitive only to the reverse. Its face is red with crime, and foul with corruption.

The literary taste of the people is degraded and vulgarized, instead of being improved and elevated. The glowing narratives of robberies, murders, prize-fights, assignations, elopements, and nameless deviltry, instead of preventing by example, stimulate to imitation and engender the thirst for crime. The leading news journals are too unclean to enter the family circle and be read by children. The *Police Gazette* excels them only by its illustrations." *

The histories of Captain Kidd, Jack Cade, and other noted outlaws of all ages, their daring deeds and their cunning, adroitness, and success in securing the fruits of their crimes, and the stratagems by which they evaded arrest, or escaped from prison when incarcerated, especially when spiced with some romantic love affair or account of devoted friendship, inflame the minds of thousands of youthful readers, and inspire in them a yearning for wild adventure and reckless daring, leading to crime; and thus the nobler impulses and aspirations which, if properly cultivated and directed, would have made them good and true men, are perverted and drawn into the paths which lead to disgrace and ignominy.

The great mass of cheap sensational literature which gets into the hands of the young of both sexes, and fascinates the youthful mind, is mischievous in its tendency. It unduly excites the imagination, inculcates false views of life, misleads the judgment, vitiates the taste, and unfits its votaries for the sober realities and duties of ordinary life. If it does not directly lead to the commission of crime, it stimulates hopes and ambitions that are never to be realized, and induces a mental condition that undermines or perverts

---

* Hudson Tuttle, in *Index* of December 24, 1885.

the moral sense, and renders the allurements of sin more enticing, while it weakens the power of the will to resist temptation. Works of fiction are not objectionable merely because the events they describe are not real. Many such inculcate great moral truths in an impressive and forcible manner, and may be read with profit. Allegory and parable were the favorite modes among the ancient peoples of illustrating and enforcing great moral truths, and impressing them upon the mind, and many a fable contains a lesson of inestimable value. The parables uttered by the prophet of Nazareth will be read, remembered, and their meaning discussed as long as man exists upon the earth. The quality of every work of fiction is determined by its character and the influence it is calculated to exert upon the mind and heart.

There is another class of literature so vile and pernicious in its character that its importation, publication, or circulation is denounced as criminal, and made punishable by fine and imprisonment. Yet the large profits derived from its publication and sale stimulate the cupidity of unprincipled dealers, and it is secretly thrust into the hands of children and inexperienced youth who are not aware of its poisonous character, and by them eagerly devoured. This consists of obscene books, pamphlets, prints, and pictures, tending to the corruption of their morals by inciting prurient desires and inflaming the animal passions, causing their abnormal or premature development. Self-abuse, libertinism, and criminal assaults for the gratification of passion upon females of tender age by adult men are some of the natural results of this nefarious traffic.

Evil example and association with the corrupt and vicious are pregnant sources of vice and crime. Their insidious effect is described by Pope, the English poet, in the following stanza, which it were well for every youth to commit to memory :

> " Vice is a monster of such frightful mien,
> As, to be hated, needs but to be seen;
> But seen too oft, familiar with her face,
> We first endure, then pity, then embrace."

Vice, says the Rambler, begins in mistake and ends in ignominy.

The "street Arabs" described in a preceding chapter, and who are too numerous in all our large cities, are always ready to impart to other idle rovers about the streets all they know of mischief and crime, and to initiate the unsophisticated into the mysteries of the craft by which they manage to sustain a miserable existence without honest labor. Thousands of parents who have allowed their boys to live in idleness, or without proper supervision and control, and to be upon the streets at night, confident that they were incapable of engaging in any wrong-doing, have been suddenly surprised and humiliated by the information that they have been led astray and been guilty of acts that called for judicial intervention. Not only the children of the poor, who are obliged to neglect them in order to earn bread for their families, are thus exposed to ruin, but many parents with sufficient means and opportunities to protect their children from such danger fail in the performance of that duty, and reap the bitter fruits of their folly when it is too late to retrieve their error, or avert the direful consequences of neglected parental duty.

Many of our jails and other prisons are nurseries of crime. Wherever those who are detained awaiting examination or trial are mixed up with professional burglars, thieves, and other hardened criminals, the prison becomes a school of crime, where those who have only been suspected of an offence, or under the influence of circumstances of strong temptation have for the first time violated the law, are taught the vocabulary of crime and villany. No truth is more surely verified by the experience of mankind than that "Evil communications corrupt good manners." The duty of separating the different classes of prisoners, and of isolating those who have not become addicted to crime, is generally acknowledged, but its importance has not been so generally appreciated, and hence the proper arrangements have not been provided for keeping the different classes separate from each other.

On this subject Hon. Levi L. Barber, a member of the Michigan Board of Corrections and Charities in 1884, in a paper read at a convention of the county agents of the Board, says, " In jail a prisoner is either teaching, learning, or plotting mischief. If he chances to be an old offender, he loves to recount his dangers, escapes, and successes, tell stories of magnificent crimes perpetrated by himself or his acquaintances ; how they were accomplished, and the allurements connected with them in glowing colors. How many a young man, arrested as a tramp or for some petty misdemeanor, through such influence is lured on to a life of crime !" General Brinkerhoof, of the Ohio Board of Corrections and Charities, says, " In every jail of a dozen inmates there are at least two or three who have made crime a profession, spent years in its practice, and are adepts in all its arts and appliances. To them nothing is more delightful than to communicate their knowledge to others less experienced than themselves, and the leisure and opportunity for this congenial work in our ordinary jails they never fail to realize to the utmost."

Judge Walker, then president of the Michigan State Board of Charities, made a report to the Board in which he says, " The prisoners have no work, no instruction, nothing to do but to amuse themselves as best they can. Here are to be found, in intimate association, the old offender and the wayward youth, the former relating his exploits, glorying in his crimes, and inspiring the latter with a desire for similar adventures. In the very nature of things imprisonment without labor, and the unrestrained association of different grades, must have the effect to increase rather than diminish the number of criminals. Any fair-minded man, on an examination of our jails, must be satisfied that, as generally conducted, they are simply training-schools to make adepts in crime."

Our jails are for the confinement of the following classes of persons: 1. Persons arrested for crime and held for examination; 2. Prisoners awaiting trial; 3. Convicts awaiting sentence, or removal to a State prison or reformatory; 4. Prisoners convicted and sentenced to a term in jail; 5. Prisoners bound over to keep the peace; 6. Fraudulent debtors, and such as are subject to imprisonment upon execution in civil actions; 7. Witnesses in criminal prosecutions; 8. Persons convicted of contempt of court; 9. Persons who are insane, and awaiting removal to an asylum.

The grinding slavery of fashion,—the envy, jealousy, hatred, desire of revenge, and all the other evil passions of men and women are familiar sources of crime which need no illustration here, for "every day's report of wrong and outrage" attests their power to destroy happiness and entail misery upon our race.

Religious fanaticism in former ages was one of the most terrible sources of atrocity which the world has ever witnessed. It destroyed the noblest and best, and deprived the world of all that they would have accomplished for the advancement of mankind in wisdom and knowledge. Let us pray that the history of religious intolerance and persecution may not be repeated in this or any future age.

# ARTICLE III.

## TREATMENT OF CRIME.

" God gave to earth a gift; a child,
Weak, innocent, and undefiled,
Opened its ignorant eyes and smiled.

It lay so helpless, so forlorn,
Earth took it coldly and in scorn,
Cursing the day when it was born.

She gave it first a tarnished name,
For heritage a tainted fame,
Then cradled it in want and shame.

\* \* \* \* \* \* \*

God gave to earth a gift; a child,
Weak, innocent, and undefiled,
Opened its ignorant eyes and smiled.

And earth received the gift and cried
Her joy and triumph far and wide,
Till echo answered to her pride.

She blest the hour when first he came
To take the crown of pride and fame,
Wreathed through long ages for his name.

\* \* \* \* \* \* \* \*

O world, both gifts were pure and bright,
Holy and sacred in God's sight;
God will judge them and thee aright."

ADELAIDE PROCTOR.

147

# CHAPTER I.

## TREATMENT OF CRIME PRIOR TO THE PRESENT CENTURY.

THE progress of the human race towards civilization and enlightenment has been slow and very unequal. Thus, while some of their faculties have been developed and cultivated in the direction of a higher and nobler manhood, others have been neglected, and hence both the individual and society have presented incongruities of character which they were not at the time capable of understanding or appreciating, but which are revealed to them by a gradually dawning light as the ages roll on, and men are prepared for a new revelation, and capable of comprehending and applying truths of which the older civilizations scarcely had any conception.

This light is like the morning sun that first illumes the hill-tops and mountain peaks, and is reflected upon the expanse below, until its effulgence extends over plain and valley and casts a glimmer into the dark caves and recesses of the rock-ribbed mountains.

So the great truths of religion and morality, of justice, charity, and brotherhood, are first perceived by a few only who have progressed to higher conditions of life and live in an atmosphere of moral and spiritual purity, which renders them receptive to the light by which great truths are discovered and their application to the welfare and happiness of mankind is discerned.

As some become wise and great and good, while the masses remain in ignorance and mental and moral darkness, so some faculties of the individual are developed in a high degree, while others have remained in an unprogressed state ; and for the same reason it has occurred that as society has advanced and knowledge increased, and arts and sciences have progressed and been utilized for man's physical comfort and enjoyment, the perception of his moral obligations and duties and the higher interests involved in the cultivation of his moral faculties has been weak and confused, and circumscribed by selfishness and passion.

What is understood as science deals with the material and physical only. It discovers no soul in man, detects no spirit, and predicts no future state of conscious individual existence for him. It discovers whatever can be perceived through the exercise of the physical senses, takes cognizance of and collates the facts thus discovered, and deduces the laws and properties of matter, while it leaves the ethical and spiritual nature untouched, and relegates them to the domain of conjecture or speculation. Liberal provision has been made for the cultivation of the intellect and the stimulation of mental growth and activity. Knowledge has increased, and the secrets of nature have been explored and her most subtle forces and hidden stores subjected to the uses of man. From the bowels of the earth coal has been drawn forth for fuel, and oil and gas from great hidden reservoirs, both for heat and light, and the waters on the face of the earth have been made to yield, at his bidding, an unlimited force to carry man's burdens and perform for him a thousand toilsome labors. The lightning has been tamed and taught not only to carry his messages to the remotest parts of the world and return appropriate answers with almost inconceivable speed, but to supply a brilliant light for streets and factories, stores and dwellings by night, and to do many other wonderful things. New treasures and sources of wealth are constantly being discovered and made subservient to man's uses by the exercise of his intellectual powers.

A few sages and students of moral philosophy have, from age to age, for thousands of years, perceived and taught the

common brotherhood of the race as members of one universal family.  Confucius and Mencius, Socrates and Plato,
Cicero and Jesus, and a few others, have been able to rise
so far above the common level of thought and perception
around them, into the higher and purer atmosphere of
wisdom and love and truth, as to discern the great principles of righteousness, justice, and charity, by which alone
true happiness can be attained.  The maxims by which
these great principles have been illustrated and enforced
are among the most sublime utterances that ever fell from
human lips, and are worthy to be recorded and revered as
revelations of the Divine will and wisdom.  When Confucius was asked whether any one sentence could express
the conduct most fitting for one's whole life, he replied,
" Do not unto others what you would not have others do to
you."  " As ye would that men should do to you, do ye
also to them likewise," is the correlative of the same pre-
cept as rendered by the Seer of Nazareth.  Cicero, more
than two thousand years ago, taught that men ought to
seek the good of others, and that a man should do no
wrong, even if his act were forever hidden from both gods
and men.  " Love your enemies, and do good, and ye shall
be the children of the Highest, for he is kind unto the un-
thankful and the evil."  " Love your enemies, do good to
them which hate you, bless them that curse you, and pray
for them which despitefully use you."  " Render not evil
for evil."  These are among the sublime instructions of the
Great Teacher, whose professed followers are numbered by
many millions, and claim to be the most enlightened peoples
upon the face of the earth.

These exalted principles are opposed to all greed, all
selfishness, all hate, all retaliations for wrongs done, all
vindictiveness or desire for revenge towards any, however
vicious and degraded.  On the contrary, they demand that,
while we detest villany and crime, and hate all manner of

iniquity and vice, we allow no feeling of resentment to
exist in our hearts towards even the vilest of our fellow-men,
but rather that we seek to benefit them by teaching them
the way of salvation from sin, and how to obtain that
satisfaction which can be found only in doing good and
abstaining from evil.

Shall we love thieves, robbers, murderers, and those remorseless villains who have cast a blight worse than death
upon the innocent victims of their lusts? Shall we love
those hideous monsters, gross and repulsive in feature and
expression, reeking with filth and moral pollution from the
slums and dens of vice?

It is not in man's nature, however exalted in goodness
he may become, to entertain the same feeling of affection
or friendship for such that he can freely give, nay, cannot
help giving, to the pure and good, and especially to those
congenial souls among his kindred and friends whose
thoughts, feelings, and aspirations are a help and an inspiration to him in his upward progress, and whose characters
and conduct command his admiration and approval. It is
not impossible, nor contrary to man's better nature, that we
should love our enemies and those that hate us and use us
despitefully; but we are not required to admire nor approve
of their character or conduct. John (the lesser) was the beloved disciple of Jesus. His soul was attuned to celestial
harmony, and the gentle sweetness of his spirit was in
unison with that of the Great Teacher whom he called
master,—and all his tenderness and devotion were recipro-
cated. Peter and James, Thomas and Judas, and others
were chosen by Jesus to be his disciples and apostles of
the gospel of peace and good will; and Jesus loved them
all, but not in the same degree. He loved all mankind, and
sought to benefit the entire human race, but not with the
same personal affection which his beloved disciple inspired.
He regarded the poor, the unfortunate, the sin-sick, the

oppressor, and the oppressed with a love which impelled him to seek the redemption of the vilest, and raise them from their low estate into higher and better conditions.

It was the love of humanity which we denominate philanthropy that prompted John Howard, of England, in the last century, to spend a fortune in benefactions, and sacrifice his health and life in visiting the prisons, hospitals, and lazarettos of Europe, and in the endeavor to alleviate the miseries their inmates were subjected to, and whose public services were summed up by Edmund Burke in the following eloquent language: " He has visited all Europe, not to survey the sumptuousness of palaces, or the stateliness of temples ; not to make accurate measurements of the remains of ancient grandeur ; not to form a scale of the curiosity of modern art ; not to collate medals or collect manuscripts ; but to dive into the depths of dungeons ; to plunge into the infections of hospitals ; to survey the mansions of sorrow and pain ; to take the gauge and dimensions of misery ; to remember the forgotten, to attend to the neglected, to visit the forsaken, and to compare and collate the distresses of men in all countries." Howard's great soul was awakened to the miseries of those who were in prison by having himself been made a prisoner of war.

William Wilberforce, another English philanthropist and able statesman, actuated by the same love of humanity and high sense of justice and duty, after having first devoted his efforts to reform measures and secured a royal proclamation against vice and immorality, having his sympathies strongly interested in behalf of the colored race by his friend Clarkson, who had written a work on the slave-trade, commenced agitating the subject of its abolition in Parliament in 1787, and in 1807 secured the adoption of the measure by both Houses. Soon after this measure was adopted he commenced the advocacy of negro emancipation, and continued his labors to that end until just before his death in 1833, when this measure was also adopted, and negro slavery ceased to exist throughout the British dominions. Howard and Wilberforce devoted their lives and fortunes in practical and effective ways to the amelioration and improvement of the condition of the lowest and most degraded and ignorant of their species, and their names and characters are known and revered throughout the world. Not less worthy of honor and reverence are the names of Elizabeth Fry and Florence Nightingale, of England, the former having devoted her life to improving the condition of those confined in jails, houses of correction, and lunatic asylums, with eminent success, and the latter to ministering to the sick and inaugurating a system for securing an improved administration of hospital service. Many thousands of the sick and wounded in the hospitals at Bucharest during the Crimean war breathed the name of Florence Nightingale with emotions of deepest gratitude and affection.

Not less honored and beloved is the name of Dorothea L. Dix, of Massachusetts, who spent the mature years of her life in the service of the wretched in poor-houses, asylums, and prisons. These and other eminent reformers of the last half of the eighteenth century and the first half of the nineteenth, having imbibed the spirit of the gospel as taught in the precepts above cited, became evangelists and missionaries in the work of human improvement, and lived and labored at a period more propitious for the reception of the light of truth than had ever before existed since civilization began. This is the gospel of humanity that was preached to the poor more than eighteen hundred years ago in Galilee, which was then but little understood, and has been buried during the intervening centuries among the rubbish of theological dogmas, and amid the clashing of religious theories and speculations in regard to faith and doctrine, until good works came to be regarded by zealous controversialists as not only of no value, but as the most dangerous upon which the hope of favor with God could be based. The meaning of the words of Jesus, when he said, " He that believeth and is baptized shall be saved, and he that believeth not shall be damned," was taken as a declaration that faith alone, with baptism, was all that was required of his followers, disregarding the definition of pure and undefiled religion as given by John, and the declaration of James that " Faith, if it hath not works, is dead, being alone."

The condition of the prisons in Europe, and of those confined in them, was deplorable almost beyond the power of the imagination to conceive. Crime had been considered and treated as something which placed the perpetrator outside of all human sympathy, depriving him of all rights, and rendering him deserving only of hatred and contumely, and of any suffering which the brutality of his keepers might prompt them to inflict upon him. Most of the prisons were filthy and loathsome beyond description. Men and women were incarcerated in them for punishment, pure and simple, without any thought of reformation or improvement, or any benefit to the prisoners. They were confined in dens like ferocious wild beasts, and kept and fed like brute animals, without labor or opportunity for healthful exercise; and every cruel device was resorted to for the purpose of crushing out any remaining spark of manhood or self-repect. The appeals of Howard and those whom he interested to the British Parliament in behalf of the victims of public vengeance and private malice resulted in securing legislation intended to alleviate their suffering and improve their condition. One of the measures adopted was an " Act for preserving the health of prisoners," and another was an act which provided for the introducing of labor into prisons, both of which were most beneficent in their character. From that time to the present a steady progress has been made in prison reform, more especially during the last half-century.

But it requires a long period of time after a community
has become convinced of the existence of great wrongs that
have existed for ages before the appropriate remedies can
be devised and put in practical and successful operation.
Old established ways of thinking and acting, however unreasonable, are not readily given up, and it is often a long
time after the necessity for reform is everywhere admitted
before new principles will be adopted and acted upon. In
no department of human progress has this fact been more
strikingly illustrated than in that which relates to the treatment of offenders against criminal laws. For more than a
century the cruelty and injustice practised against persons
charged with or convicted of crime have been the subject
of discussion by the ablest jurists, and deprecated by all enlightened philanthropists. Sir William Blackstone, in his
Commentaries on the laws of England, published in 1765,
called the attention of the people and government of that
country to the melancholy fact that among the variety of
acts which men were daily liable to commit, no less than
one hundred and sixty had been declared by act of Parliament to be felonies without benefit of clergy; or, in other
words, to be worthy of instant death; and he remarks that
"so dreadful a list, instead of diminishing, increases the
number of offenders." It now seems almost incredible that,
in a country so enlightened as England, in the latter part
of the eighteenth century, it could have been a capital crime
to break down the mound of a fish pound whereby any fish
should escape; or to cut down a cherry-tree in an orchard;
or to be seen for one month in the company of persons who
call themselves, or are called, Egyptians; or to steal a hand-
kerchief above the value of twelve pence privately from the
person. But the Parliament of England declared these acts
to be felonies punishable with death, and although, as Blackstone observes, these outrageous penalties were seldom or
never inflicted, for the reasons which he states, yet their

existence upon the statute-books indicates the cruel and vindictive disposition manifested by the governing classes towards those who offended even in small and trivial matters. It is encouraging, however, to note the fact that this fearful list of capital offences in that country has been reduced by more recent legislation, so that only a few of the more heinous crimes are now punishable capitally.

The modes of punishment for offences not capital were, many of them, grossly cruel and barbarous, such as burning the cheek or hand, slitting the nose, cutting out or disabling the tongue, cutting off the hand or the ears, putting in the pillory or stocks, whipping upon the bare back, and other injuries and indignities to the person; and in capital cases, burning at the stake, disembowelling, drawing in quarters, etc. Referring to these modes of punishment, Mr. Blackstone says that, " disgusting as this category may seem, it will afford pleasure to an English reader, and do honor to English law, to compare it with that shocking apparatus of death and torment to be met with in the criminal codes of almost every other nation in Europe."

To those who, at this day, are better capable of understanding and appreciating the principles and motives which should control human action, as enunciated in the precepts recited in a former part of this article, as given by the greatest, wisest, and best of the world's benefactors, it appears surprising indeed that in the eighteenth century of the Christian era, in a country where the Christian religion was the recognized religion of the state, and declared to be a part of the common law of the realm, where it was a crime to use any contumelious or reproachful language of Christ, who is designated in the statute as " Our Saviour," and where all scoffing at the Holy Scripture, or exposing it to ridicule or contempt, was punishable by fine and imprisonment or other infamous corporal punishnent, such laws could be allowed to exist, contrary to the spirit of all the teaching and the example of Jesus, and to the principles of human right and justice.

The facts of this sad history of human weakness and depravity show how deeply rooted was the spirit of vindictiveness inherited from a savage ancestry, and how slow has been the growth and development of those gentler, nobler, and more rational principles of human love and kindness which are based upon a recognition of the Fatherhood of God and the universal brotherhood and unity of the human race. They show, too, how a nation or people may accept and professedly adopt a theory of right and justice, of obligation and duty, while, apparently unconscious of their inconsistency, their conduct and the motives which actuate them are in direct opposition to such theory.

The history of crime and its treatment in other European countries is a dismal record of cruelty and suffering which it would be no pleasing task to review. The guillotines and the instruments of torture, the rack, the thumb-screw, and the slow consuming fires, and other devices for inflicting the most exquisite pain and mortal agony, were not all of pagan invention.

Punishment by imprisonment in penal institutions was scarcely less terrible than death by the hand of the public executioner. Until the latter part of the last century the condition of these institutions, and of the persons confined in them, seems to have attracted little or no public attention in Europe, and but for an incident which occurred in the history of John Howard, in 1773, the same conditions might have continued indefinitely. Having accepted the office of sheriff of Bedfordshire in that year, upon the opening of the assizes for that county, he visited in his official capacity the Bedford town gaol, the same in which John Bunyan was confined for twelve years, and where he wrote his " Pilgrim's Progress." The filthy state of the building and the wretched condition of the prisoners made a deep impres-

sion upon him.    Here he found many innocent persons, who
had been detained for months, and some for years, from
their inability to pay their fees of jail delivery.    These things
shocked his sense of justice, and prompted him to enter
upon the great work which has rendered his name immortal.
Most fortunate was it for the world that he was a man of
wealth, and of great ability and influence, as well as a friend
of the poor, the wretched, and the sinful of his race.    The
accounts published by him of the condition of the prisoners
of Europe presented an appalling picture of the inhumanity
and terrible cruelty with which prisoners, whether innocent
or guilty of crime, were treated in all the principal jails and
penitentiaries.    He had heard "the groans of the weak,
sacrificed to the cruel ignorance and indolence of the powerful," and witnessed "the barbarous torments, lavished and
multiplied with useless severity, for crimes either not proven
or in their nature impossible," and "the filth and horrors of
the prisons," referred to by Beccaria in the introduction to
his essay on crime, and his report aroused a feeling which
has led to radical changes of the laws relating to crime on
both sides of the Atlantic.

During our colonial relations with Great Britain, and for
a considerable period after that relation was severed, our
prisons were in a no less deplorable condition than those of
England, and some of them were execrable almost beyond
description.    Mr. McMaster, in his " History of the People
of the United States," referring to the indignation and horror
expressed by our ancestors at the brutal treatment of their
captive countrymen in British prison-ships and hulks, says
that "even then the land was dotted with prisons where
deeds of cruelty were done, in comparison with which the
foulest acts committed in those hulks sink into insignificance.
For more than fifty years after the peace there was in Connecticut an underground prison which surpassed in horrors
the Black Hole of Calcutta.    This den, known as the New-

gate prison, was an old worked-out mine in the hills near Granby." He describes this den and the indignities practised there in the following graphic language: "The only entrance to it was by means of a ladder down a shaft which led to the caverns under ground. Here, in little pens of wood, from thirty to one hundred culprits were immured, their feet made fast to iron bars, and their necks chained to beams in the roof. The darkness was intense; the caves reeked with filth; vermin abounded; water trickled from the roof and oozed from the sides of the caverns; huge masses of earth were perpetually falling off. In the dampness and filth the clothing of the prisoners grew mouldy and rotted away, and their limbs became stiff with rheumatism." This writer adds: "The Newgate was perhaps the worst in the country, yet in every county were jails such as would now be thought unfit places for the habitation of the vilest and most loathsome of beasts.

" At Northampton the cells were scarce four feet high, and filled with the noxious gases of the privy vaults through which they were supposed to be ventilated. Light came in through chinks in the wall. At the Worcester prison were a number of like cells, four feet high by eleven long, without a window or chimney, or even a hole in the wall. Not a ray of light ever penetrated them. In other jails in Massachusetts the cells were so small that the prisoners were lodged in hammocks swung one over the other. In Philadelphia the keeps were eighteen feet by twenty feet, and so crowded that at night each prisoner had a space of six feet by two to lie down in. Into such pits and dungeons all classes of offenders, of both sexes, were indiscriminately thrust. It is not surprising, therefore, that they became seminaries of every conceivable form of vice, and centres of the most disgusting diseases. Prostitutes plied their calling openly in the presence of men and women of decent station, and guilty of no crime but the inability to pay their debts.

Men confined as witnesses were compelled to mingle with the forger besmeared with the filth of the pillory, and the fornicator streaming with blood from the whipping-post, while here and there among the throng were culprits whose ears had been cropped, or whose arms, fresh from the branding iron, emitted the stench of scorched flesh. The entire system of punishment was such as cannot be contemplated without mingled feelings of pity and disgust.

" Offences to which a more merciful generation has attached no higher penalty than imprisonment and fine stood upon the statute-books as capital crimes. Modes of punishment long since driven from the prisons with execrations, as worthy of an African kraal, were looked upon by society with profound indifference. The tread-mill was always going. The pillory and the stocks were never empty. The shears, the branding-iron, and the lash were never idle. In Philadelphia the wheelbarrow men still went about the streets in gangs, or appeared with huge clogs, and chains hung to their necks. In Delaware, which to this hour treats her citizens with the degrading scenes of the whipping-post, twenty crimes were punished with the loss of life. Burglary and rape, sodomy and witchcraft, were among them. In Massachusetts ten crimes were declared by the General Court to be punishable with death. There the man who, in a fit of anger, was heard cursing and swearing, or spreading evil reports of his neighbor, was first set in the stocks, and then carried off to the whipping-post and soundly flogged. . . . In Rhode Island a perpetual mark of shame was, for many offences, judged to be the most fitting punishment. There a counterfeiter was punished with the loss of part of his ear, and distinguished from all other criminals by a large ' C ' deeply branded on his forehead. A wretch so hardened as to be recommitted was branded on the arms. Keepers knew no other mode of silencing the ravings of a madman than tying him up by the thumbs and flogging him until he was too exhausted to utter a groan.

"The miseries of the unfortunate creatures cooped up in the cells, even of the most humanely kept prisons, surpassed in horror anything ever recorded in fiction. No attendance was provided for the sick. No clothes were distributed to the naked. Such a thing as a bed was rarely seen, and this soon became so foul with vermin that the owner dispensed with it gladly. Many of the inmates of the prisons passed years without so much as washing themselves. Their hair grew long. Their bodies were covered with scabs and lice, and emitted a horrible stench. Their clothing rotted from their backs and exposed their bodies, tormented with all manner of skin diseases, and a yellow flesh cracking open with filth. As if such torments were not enough to bear, others were added to the half-maddened prisoners. No sooner did a new comer enter the door of a cell than a rush was made for him by the inmates, who stripped him of his clothing and let him stand stark naked until it was re- deemed by what, in the peculiar jargon of the place, was known as drink-money.

"It sometimes happened that prisoners were in possession of a carefully preserved blanket. Then this ceremony, called 'garnishing,' was passed over for the yet more brutal one of blanketing. In spite of prayers and entrea- ties, the miserable stranger was bound and tossed until he was half dead, and ready to give his tormentors every super- fluous garment to sell for money. With the tolls thus ex- acted liquor was bought, a fiendish revel was had, and, when bad rum and tobacco had done their work, the few sober inmates of the cell witnessed such scenes as would be thought shocking in the dance-houses which cluster along the wharves of our great sea-board towns."

Without the most indubitable evidence, who can believe it possible that, in a period so near to the present, extending

over more than half a century after the Declaration of Independence was promulgated, and near to the middle of the
present century, such horrors could exist unchallenged, and
be regarded by the people with indifference?   The thought,
too, that such horrors, and more terrible ones if it were
possible to conceive them, had existed in all countries and
under all governments throughout the civilized world, is too
shocking for expression.   The few voices that had been
raised against the prevailing sentiments and practices in
regard to crime and the treatment of criminals, seemed to
make but little impression for the time upon governments
or the peoples.

In 1764, the Marquis of Beccaria, an Italian economist,
published "An Essay upon Crimes and Punishments," in
which existing systems were criticised and reforms suggested.   In this work the author touches upon some important problems in regard to the ethics of crime, lays down
principles of evidence, and discriminates the respective
spheres of judges and legislators, declares his opposition to
capital punishment, assigning some cogent reasons therefor,
and sums up his essay with the following theorem,—viz,
that "an act of punishment may not be an act of violence
of one or of many against a private member of society.
It should be public, immediate, and necessary; the least
possible in a given case, proportioned to the crime, and determined by the laws."   Of this book a writer in the "New
American Cyclopædia" says, "It invites notice as the first
work of its kind in modern times."   "Never did so small a
book," says the "Biographie Universale," "produce so great
an effect."

The opinions broached in this book produced a marked
impression upon the criminal jurisprudence of Europe.
Reforms of greater or less scope followed its publication in
Russia, Austria, Tuscany, and Denmark.

The Commentaries of Sir William Blackstone upon the

laws of England, though written mainly for a different purpose, contain hints and suggestions of reform in the criminal
code which had their effect in producing important modifications of the laws relating to crimes and punishments. The
works of these eminent men, being followed a few years
later by the publication of Howard's report on the condition
of the prisons of Europe, a profound sensation was produced
upon the public mind, and many of the more serious abuses
in prison management were remedied.

The attention of governments was first directed to the
graduation of the punishment due to crimes according to
the degree of turpitude evinced in their perpetration, and
then to the rights of persons accused of crime to have a
fair and impartial trial and a full opportunity for defence;
next, to abolishing needless cruelties in executing the judgments of courts upon the persons of culprits; and last of
all to the condition of the prisons and their inmates. Mr.
McMaster, in the chapter of his history relating to the condition of the American people in 1784, from which we have
quoted a description of the American prisons of that period,
remarks that "To a generation which has beheld great reform in the statutes of criminal law, and in the discipline of
prisons and jails; to a generation that knows but two crimes
worthy of death, that against the life of the individual and
that against the life of the State; which has expended fabulous sums in the erection of reformatories, asylums, and
penitentiaries, houses of correction, houses of refuge, and
houses of detention all over the land; which has furnished
every State prison with a library, with a hospital, and with
schools, the brutal scenes on which our ancestors looked
with indifference seem scarcely a reality." Our pious ancestors in the New England States were too much occupied
in prosecuting witches and heretics, and separating the
goats from the sheep, to visit those confined in the jails and
prisons and seeking to alleviate their sufferings, or minister

to their necessities.   They chose rather to leave them to be
devoured by the scornful wrath and righteous indignation
of God and man, as deserving of all the miseries to which
they were subjected in this life, and intenser miseries thereafter without end.   Nor, until within the last half-century,
does the idea of reforming criminals in any other way than
by the infliction of bodily and mental suffering, and by appealing to the fears and apprehensions of men, appear to
have been conceived of, even by the most prominent reformers.   Thus, Blackstone defines punishments as evils, or
inconveniences consequent upon crimes and misdemeanors.
As to the end or final cause of punishment he says:

"This is not by way of atonement or expiation for the
crime committed, for that must be left to the just determination of the Supreme Being, but as a precaution against
future offences of the same kind.   This," he says, "is
effected in three ways: either by the amendment of the
offender, for which purpose all corporal punishments, fines,
and temporary exile are inflicted" (and corporal punishments include whipping, putting in the stocks or the pillory,
cropping the ears, slitting the nose, and branding with hot
irons), "or by deterring others by the dread of his example
from offending in a like way, which gives rise to all igno-
minious punishments, and to such executions of judgments
as are open and public; or, lastly, depriving the party of
the power to do future mischief, which is effected either by
putting him to death or condemning him to perpetual confinement, slavery, or exile."

Beccaria says, "The end of punishment is no other than
to prevent the criminal from doing further injury to society,
and to prevent others from committing the like offence.
Such punishments, therefore, and such a mode of inflicting
them, ought to be chosen as will make the strongest and
most lasting impressions on the minds of others, with the
least torment to the criminal."

Both Blackstone and Beccaria emphasize the idea that punishment should be inflicted in such a manner that it will operate as an example to deter others from the commission of similar offences, by the impression of terror which it is calculated to make upon the mind, and both agree that torment for that purpose may properly be inflicted, though the latter says it should be done " with the least torment to the body of the criminal." Both these authors at the same time refer to historical facts which show that all public exhibitions of cruelty, or the infliction of torment by way of punishment for crime, instead of deterring others have had a contrary effect, and tended to increase the number of offences of the same kind; and both of them refer to this fact as an argument against the infliction of the penalty of death. Had they lived and written at a later period in the progress of ethical culture and philosophical thought, they would have discovered and promulgated the deeper and profounder truth, that no torment or pain inflicted upon an individual which is not calculated and intended to benefit the individual upon whom it is inflicted can ever, by any possibility, benefit the public or any other individual. Anything beyond this by way of punishment provokes a feeling of resentment, or tends to blunt the natural susceptibilities of men to human sympathy and pity for others' woes, and works evil instead of benefit to the community. The highest and most effectual example to others, in the treatment of crime under human laws, is that which is directed, first, to the reformation of the offender; and, if that is found to be impracticable, then by perpetual restraint and supervision, under such conditions as will secure the health of the offender, and render him useful by labor performed for the indemnity of the State. Such treatment is tinged with no cruelty, no vindictiveness, and no injustice. The preamble to what has been characterized as " the most admirable and excellent statute ever passed by the English legislature" (that of 1 Edw. VI., c. 12) contains the following beautiful and eloquent language: "Nothing is more godly, more sure, more to be wished and desired betwixt a prince, the supreme head and ruler, and the subject whose governor and head he is, than on the prince's part great clemency and indulgency, and rather too much forgiveness and remission of his royal power and just punishment, than exact severity and justice to be showed; and on the subjects' behalf that they should obey rather for love, and for the necessity and love of a king and prince, than for the fear of his straight and severe laws." This statute, therefore, repealed every act which had created any treason since the 25 Edw. III., st. 5, c. 2, and all and every act of Parliament concerning doctrine or matters of religion; every felony created by the legislature during the preceding long and cruel reign of Henry VIII., and other obnoxious statutes. The preamble to the statute 1 Mar. st. l., c. 1, also recites that "the state of every King consists more in the love of the subject than in the dread of laws made with rigorous pains, and that laws made for the preservation of the commonwealth without great penalties are more often obeyed and kept than laws made with extreme punishments." Happy would it have been for the nations if these great principles could have been recognized and acted upon by their legislatures in the enactment of all laws relating to crime. Appeals to the fears of men may, in some instances, deter them temporarily from committing crime; but they are degrading and brutalizing in their effects, and, as all experience has proven, lay the foundation of more numerous crimes in the future.

The enunciation of the great truths set forth in such strains of simple eloquence as we have recited above from the preambles of memorable English statutes were not accepted and applied according to the spirit and true import of the language in which they were expressed, and many needlessly cruel and inhuman punishments have been and still are inflicted under the laws of all civilized nations. They were not, however, barren of good results. The most flagrantly unjust laws were abolished or amended, and the most cruel modes of inflicting punishment upon criminals were abandoned, and during this nineteenth century they have been better understood, and the fears which our ancestors of 1784 and still later entertained, that a relaxation of the rigors of the law would render life and property less safe, have been proven by experience to have been groundless. The reforms in the criminal laws, and still greater reforms in the management and discipline of penal institutions, especially in England and in this country, within the last sixty years, have been truly wonderful, and most gratifying to the hearts of philanthropists. But there are still many and great reforms yet to be accomplished, and errors in principle and administration to be eliminated from our criminal codes, before the demands of justice to the evil, the poor, and the miserable of our race shall be satisfied. These will appear more clearly in a succeeding chapter, in which the principles that, in our opinion, should govern all action relative to crime will be discussed.

## CHAPTER II.

### TREATMENT OF CRIME AND CONDITION OF PRISONS AT THE PRESENT TIME.

FROM the extract which we made in the last chapter from McMaster's history of the American people, in regard to the present condition of our prisons, it is not to be inferred that they are all in a satisfactory condition, nor that the treatment of prisoners sentenced to our penitentiaries is in

all respects humane and just.   Each of the great family of
States comprising the Union has its own code of criminal
laws, and its own penal or reformatory institutions and
modes of treating or disposing of its prisoners, and these
are in some respects widely different.   There is no central
power for the establishment of a general system of prisons
and prison management as in England, which may in some
degree account for the fact that in that country they are
nearly half a century ahead of us in prison reform; and
that in none of the United States has the condition and
management of prisons been equal to that of the English
penal institutions during that period, and especially since
1787, when all local prisons were placed under government
control.                              .

Rev. John Horsley, a very intelligent and well-informed
writer, who has had a long experience as a prison official,
and has taken a deep interest in the treatment and discipline
of prisoners in his own and other countries, in his book
entitled " Jottings from Jails," after giving some account of
the condition of the English prisons and their management,
and the treatment of prisoners confined in them, discusses
briefly the subject of American prison reform.   On this
subject he says, " A feeling not merely of surprise, but of
consternation, will be produced in any English reader of the
Annual Report of the Prison Association of New York.
British patriotism is said sometimes to take the form of a
depreciation of English ways and institutions, and our respect for the progressiveness of our transatlantic cousins
may sometimes lead us to take excellence for granted where
none of the hampering traditions and vested interests of
feudalism exist.   A wholesome corrective would be supplied
by an investigation into the state of their prisons, which we
do not hesitate to say would reveal a state of things unknown
here, unless we unearthed the records of some sixty years
ago."   This writer does not give his English readers the

date of the "annual report" he refers to, which many of them would probably like to know. However that may be, it is of little importance to us. But he gives his readers some statements embraced in that report which demand our most serious attention, as indicating a state of things that still exists to a degree which calls for energetic and continued efforts for reform. Recognizing that the Prison Association of New York is, "on paper, perfect in its plan," and after stating that it combines the objects of the Howard Society of England, and various organizations for aiding discharged prisoners,—having standing committees on finance, on detention, on prison discipline, and on discharged convicts, and a female department in addition; and with no less than fifty local committees for the different counties of the State, which co-operate and correspond, and that it seems to have unlimited powers of visiting the various prisons, etc., Mr. Horsley makes the following remarks upon their report: "Given, then, this society which reports annually to the Senate, and given also an enlightened public opinion, we are hardly prepared to find them speaking of the 'monstrous evils connected with our county gaols' and pointing out that, in the face of statutes, classification and separation of prisoners is almost necessarily disregarded and neglected in many cases; and even 'the safeguard of security is not generally maintained.' . . . It is frankly admitted that the county jail, as distinct from the State prison, remains, in a vast number of cases, 'the same vicious and abominable institution that it was a century ago;' and the evidence of De Tocqueville, fifty years later, is quoted to the effect: 'The gaols of the United States are the worst I have ever seen;' while so recently as 1877, the Prison Reform Conference denounced the whole system as a disgrace to civilization, hopelessly, irremediably bad! This, they say, is thoroughly supported by the latest reports from various counties."

In regard to the sanitary condition of our prisons as

compared with that of English prisons, Mr. Horsly remarks:
"The alarmingly high and unnecessarily fluctuating rate of
mortality (77 per 1000 in some gaols as contrasted with our
average of 8.4) is said to be caused by the innutritious
quality as well as the scantiness of the amount of the diet,
and the fact (impossible in England) that the ordinary sleep-
ing-cells have no method of ventilation beyond the doors.
Those generalizations," he says, "are supported by reports
from local committees, and by some tables of great interest."
He then proceeds to cite from the reports numerous statements which seem to fully support his conclusions. The
closing paragraph of this paper on American Prison Reform,
as exhibited in the report of the Prison Association of New
York, contains a scathing and not undeserved rebuke, which
it were well that those would heed who are responsible for
the wretched condition of American jails.

It is as follows : " In fact, to read this report causes one
perpetually to be turning back to the title-page to be sure
one is not perusing John Howard's 'State of the Prisons,'
as point after point comes up on which he animadverted
with such success, and abuse after abuse is described from
which our prisons have long been free, even before the introduction of a uniform system, which public intelligence
mainly created before centralization was attempted.   Intelligence, humanity, the knowledge of what has been
achieved in other countries,—the report shows that these
are not wanting to the Association.  Has it utterly failed
during thirty-eight years to educate and move an enlightened nation, that these things are still possible ?"

That the prison system of Great Britain is superior in
almost every respect to that of any of the States of the
Union there can be no question.  Rev. Mr. Dana, at the
fourteenth annual session of the National Conference of
Charities and Corrections, held at Omaha, Nebraska, in 1887,
made the following remarks on this subject:

"It may be of interest to the people of Nebraska, so far as they care for the experience of the rest of the world, to know that at present Great Britain, by general admission, has the best prison system extant. Among the things they deem to be settled, and the principles they deem established, are (1) that penal institutions are no longer to be conducted with a view to making them pecuniarily profitable to the State; (2) that politics are never to be allowed to enter into, or in any way affect their administration; (3) that the State account system of labor is, all things considered, the best for the reformatory purposes always to be kept in view, and avoids most of the complications connected with the contract system. Further, let me add, in England, among pœnologists and prison reformers, the lessee system has been wholly repudiated, and is regarded as a relic of a barbarous age, a reminder of the brutal methods once in vogue in convict establishments. Under these accepted principles of management, crime in Great Britain has been of late years steadily diminishing, and the number of her prisons has fallen from one hundred and thirteen to fifty-nine, while uniformity, economy, and improved administration have at the same time been secured."

Under our system of government, it is evident that we can have no general system of prison management, and that entire uniformity is unattainable. Some approximation to this desirable end may eventually be secured through the efforts of the National Conference of Charities and Corrections, aided by the State Boards of the different States and the existing Prison Associations, and we may hope that some of the worst features of existing systems will be eliminated at no distant day, although the obstacles in the way of accomplishing reforms conceded to be necessary, and correcting abuses that are generally admitted, are formidable and not to be easily overcome. In several of the States the lessee system prevails. Under this system, the prisoners sentenced to the State penitentiary are leased out to individuals or corporations, to work in the fields, on railroads, or in the mines, for longer or shorter periods, at a stipulated price paid to the State, and they are taken from the prison, and the custody of the warden, and consigned over to the lessees, whose interest is to get the greatest possible amount of work from them, at the least possible expense to themselves.

In an editorial article upon the methods of punishment in a late number of the *Central Law Journal*, the writer says, "In some of the States the penitentiary is becoming a sort of receiving-ship, where convicts abide until they are sold into slavery, or farmed out, if that expression is preferred, to the highest bidder, or to favored contractors. In due season, if this course is persevered in, it is safe to predict that the worst horrors of the galley of the penal colonies, even of Norfolk Island and the Siberian mines, will be reproduced in our own country. . . . In its best estate, 'a prison is a house of care.' The horrors of prison-life have been described in prose by philanthropists who have striven to reform its abuses, and depicted with the embellishments of fancy in fiction and poetry, but we have never encountered a more revolting picture than that presented by the subterranean prison in which drudge, in dampness and darkness, the convicts who are farmed or sold to contractors. We can only compare it to that very notable prison described by Dante, over the entrance to which was the inscription, 'Abandon hope, ye who enter here.'"

Undoubtedly there are evils inherent in the lessee system which ought to cause it to be abandoned. In some of the States where this system prevails, an earnest effort is made to secure the health of the convicts, and protect them from abuse by means of State supervision, as explained by Mr. Hicks, warden of the penitentiary in Raleigh, N. C., at the conference of 1884. He says, in regard to the treatment of convicts in that State, "No convicts are sent on roads out-side of the prison that are not supervised and controlled by the State authorities. A supervisor is appointed, and under him overseers and guards. From them we get reports every month. There is a physician at each separate set of works. In addition to that, one of the board of directors visits the works every month, examining the condition of the men, getting information in every way as to the management, whether there has been any abuse, whether the men have been overworked, whether they have been properly fed, clothed, etc. It is a matter looked into very carefully." In that State the system is presented in its best aspect. As the writer in the *Central Law Journal* remarks, however, "It is merely idle to say that due precautions will be taken that the convicts will be protected against inhuman treat-ment by government officers specially appointed and paid for that purpose ; that nothing shall be required of convicts out of the penitentiary that would not be required of them within it. The fatal error in this matter is the admission of private interest, in any form whatever, into the public pun-ishment of crime. There arises at once a temptation, and it is always a mistake and a misfortune to subject official virtue to avoidable temptation."

This system seems to have two objects in view,—namely, punishment and pay. The reformation of the convicts, by moral instruction or otherwise, is not one of its aims. It protects the community from his acts while the criminal is held as a prisoner, and leaves him at the end of his term no better, and probably worse, than before his conviction.

Another system of prison management is known as the "contract system," under which the labor of the prisoners is contracted for at a certain price per day by manufacturers who furnish their own material, and work the convicts within the prison; a foreman or manager employed by the contractor directing the work in the shop or factory, while the warden and other officers and guards under him have the entire care, direction, and control of the prisoners in all other respects. This is the plan adopted, and which has been long practised in most of the State prisons in the Eastern and Middle, and some of the Western States. It is a system which may afford opportunity for some degree of education and moral improvement of the convicts when suitable provision is made for that purpose. Several objections are urged against this system, and it has been abolished and replaced by another in several of the States. Its advantages, as stated in the report of the Committee on Crimes and Penalties to the National Conference of Corrections and Charities at their session in 1883, are that "it relieves the State from risking public funds in the hands of public officers in manufacturing and commerce, simplifies the immediate management of prison and prisoners, and furnishes for the time a definite and reasonably reliable income easily estimated." On the other hand, the system is in several respects inherently defective, and in its spirit and practice not adapted to the accomplishment "of the high purpose for which the State maintains the penitentiaries,— namely, protection from crimes through the reformation of the offenders." The committee from whose report the above extracts are made, consisting of seven of the most able and prominent pœnologists in this country, including Mr. Brockway, of the Elmira Reformatory, concluded their remarks upon this system as follows: "It seems that the contract system must go; it certainly would go if the wisdom of the times could suggest a satisfactory system of labor to replace it. It is understood that the public outcry against the system is largely demagogic, and is as much against every system of prison labor as against this particular form of it; but there is little prospect that sober-minded citizens will consent to the cost, the corrupting effect, and the cruelty of maintaining the prisoners of our penitentiaries in idleness."

Of the system of prison labor on public account the committee say, " The public account plan—that is, where the State becomes the manufacturer, furnishing capital, conducting the manufactures, and disposing of the products in open market—has been tried with varied success, and is now the system in several short-term prisons at least, and in the State prisons of California." The points in its favor are pointed out in this report, as well as the objections to it, and these objections are assumed to be " so weighty as to prevent, probably, its general adoption." "There is," say the committee, " the monetary risk,—not so much the ordinary hazard of capital in manufactures and commerce, nor the extraordinary hazard of public money so invested and managed by officials who, of themselves, have no practical knowledge of the business they conduct, or personal liability in case of loss or failure, for these risks may be reduced to a minimum, but rather the risk arising from the fact that the industries must be really under the control of a popular legislature whose action may be affected by partisan or other considerations than those governing a business firm in the transaction of its business." . . . " The public account system, in form as we are considering it, is impolitic, because of the large amount of investment required and the popular suspicion when the public money is largely intrusted to individual investment and care. It is estimated that for plant, for material, for a stock of manufactured goods, and for cost of citizen experts, each operative or prisoner must represent one thousand dollars of capital. So that a prison of five hundred workers would require half a million of money for manufacturing, while for the State prisons of New York, upon this basis, three millions must be supplied by the tax-payers. It could hardly be expected that such an opportunity for patronage could long remain unused for partisan ends, or if by any means it should be kept strictly to its legitimate use, the necessary conflict to preserve it would of itself jeopard the general prison management. It is questionable, also, whether it is not wrong in principle for the government of a State or a nation to directly engage in manufacturing and commercial enterprise with funds forced by taxation from the pockets of the people." There is another plan, called the "piece-price plan," of which the committee say in their report, "There is a possible substitute for the contract and public account systems, wellnigh free from the objections named. It is the piece-price plan,—that is to say, the contractor shall supply the machinery, materials, and, perhaps, citizen expert instructors, receiving and disposing of the manufactured goods on his own account, of course. The State furnishes operatives (prisoners), whose services are to be paid for, not by the day, as now, but by the piece or process for work done to a given standard of perfection. By this system (1) the State is relieved from furnishing manufacturing capital; (2) the whole business of the prison governors is with the prisoners; (3) the control of the prisoners is unified; (4) the evil influence of the contract employers is abated, because the contractor gains nothing by extorting exorbitant tasks,—there is no motive for chicanery; (5) the State is most sure to receive the real value of the prisoners' labor, more or less, and the State alone is responsible for the amount the prisoner shall earn; (6) the piece-price plan best enables the prison government to place the prisoner in condition, as to labor and living, closely analogous to the natural social state in this regard, the prisoner may be made to live and enjoy whatever he can earn, but no more, and such a situation is more serviceable in training and testing under the remedial *régime ;* (7) since the piece-price plan is almost universally practised by private manufacturers, the fair rate per piece can be easily ascertained, and may by law, if thought best, be fixed at the average paid free laborers in the same locality for the same quality of work, thus to the nearest possible point equalizing the valuation of prison labor and free labor by which injurious competition here, if any exists, is removed."

The committee further say, " Contractors generally express themselves satisfied with such a system, because by it they are relieved from all anxiety and liability for the quantity of work the prisoners shall do or not do, being sure to get an equivalent for every dollar paid to the State for labor.

" The piece-price plan can be put in place of the contract or public account system easily and without injury; the present industries may be, and naturally would be, continued. The system of accounts required is simple, and may be fully guarded against fraud by the identity of interest in earnings between the State and the prisoner.

" Prison industries should always subserve conjointly three grand purposes, which are, when stated inversely as to their importance, income, discipline, rehabilitation. Believing the plan here proposed best meets this requirement, and quite removes any real or fancied ground of complaint from the mercantile or laboring classes, it is recommended that the piece-price plan be put in the place of the contract and public account system of employing prisoners."

It is to be remembered that the penitentiary system itself is of recent origin, and the various systems of management, and of the employment of prisoners in useful labor has been largely experimental. The committee from whose report we have made the foregoing extracts say that it originated almost within the present century, and that " it was not until the latter part of the eighteenth century that attention was much given to the horrors, abuses, and errors of the existing criminal codes and penalties. Yet, withal, too near the barbarism of the dark ages to be entirely rid of the errors it was intended to correct, the penitentiary treatment of criminals was the attempt to moderate some

*m*

punishments, and to abolish others repugnant to the public
sense, and to better adjust the punishment to the offence, in
the expectation that confinement, hard labor, and the pain
of imprisonment, with opportunity for meditation, would
produce penitence, the supposed precursor and condition
of self-restraint and moral reformation.   The principle of
pain inflicted for deterrence, and privations for penitence,
was preserved, and is to-day maintained.   It was in 1790
the State prison at Philadelphia was erected; the New York
penitentiary in 1796; other States following quickly, as
Massachusetts in 1800; Maryland in 1811; Vermont, 1808;
New Hampshire, 1812; and about the same time New Jersey,
Tennessee, and Kentucky moved in the matter.   The laws
providing for these prisons were accompanied usually with
the repeal of the death penalty for many crimes.   It was
soon apparent that the penitentiary system was no preventive of crimes, and as early as 1822 the question was
carefully and seriously canvassed of abandoning it altogether,
with a return to the old sanguinary punishments.   It was
concluded finally that, notwithstanding the penitentiary
system was wellnigh a failure, it must be preserved, because corporal punishments and the death penalty for
crimes generally would not be again approved by the sentiment of the American people, and transportation for crime
was impracticable.   The real obstacle to the success of the
system was the same sixty years ago as it is to-day.   It is
believed to be the vain reliance upon *punishment* to prevent
crimes.   The projectors of the penitentiary system seemed
not to perceive it, and now we are marvellously slow in
learning it.   Can there be any doubt that had the penitentiary system at its inception been pervaded with the principle
of reformation, and the alternative of *incapacitation*, the indeterminate sentence principle, . . . there would have been
better results reached and greater progress attained in the
treatment of criminals and the prevention of crime?"

The committee, in the last three sentences above recited, have struck the key-note to all progression towards the proper treatment of criminals and the prevention of crime, and enunciated the principle which lies at the foundation of all upward progress in social ethics and practical religion, and inspires all wise and intelligent efforts for the elevation and improvement of mankind.

We may safely assume, in view of the progressive spirit of this age in all humanitarian and economic affairs, that the system of prison management best calculated to promote the welfare of both the prisoners and of society will be adopted at no very distant day. But in this country, so long as the policy of the great political parties continues to be what it has been for the last half-century, whatever system may be determined upon as the best, there will continue to exist a serious obstacle in the way of making it successful.

The difficulty alluded to arises from its conflict with another system which has been established for many years, and has become so deeply rooted that it resists all the efforts of philanthropists and friends of public right and justice to abolish it. This is familiarly known as "the spoils system," which demands that as often as a change takes place in the national or State government, all appointive offices shall be filled by the friends of the "new administration," regardless of the fitness or experience of those thereby displaced. When it was first announced in Congress, between fifty and sixty years ago, as a political axiom, that "to the victor belong the spoils," it was denounced as corrupting in its tendency, and injurious to the public interests in its operation; but however much the principle was disclaimed and denounced at the time, it was soon adopted, and has ever since been acted upon by both the great political parties into which the population was divided, and has been a principal cause of the bribery, corruption, and fraud which have attended our elections and are a shame and disgrace to our country. Its demoralizing effects have been everywhere felt, and have extended throughout the social, political, and business circles, and it has lowered the standard of character and morals among our people. It imports that all is fair in politics, as in war, and, as war ever produces a new flood of crime, so do our election contests, which are waged upon the same principle as a war for conquest and spoils.

But what, it may be asked, has all this to do with pœnology, and the management of our prisons? The answer is plain, and has freqently been given by those who have written and spoken upon the comparative advantages of the different systems of management. In order to successfully carry on a manufacturing business, employing five or six hundred men, business experience and capacity of a high order and approved integrity, as well as tact and special adaptation to the position, are indispensable qualifications of the warden and manager, and, when these have been secured, no change can safely be made on account of political opinions or party affiliations or policy. But the executive and legislative departments of the State government are changed every year or second year, and on the accession of a new party, or of a new executive and legislature of the same party, the clamor for rotation in office, or for a distribution of the spoils among the victors, is irresistible; and no matter how faithful and capable a warden may have been, he is liable to be displaced in order to make room for one who perhaps has no other claim to, or fitness for, the position than his ability to render effective service to the party in power.

With all these difficulties in the way of progress and the adoption of practical and wise methods for the treatment of the convicts in our prisons, it is no matter of wonder that crime increases, instead of being diminished, in this country, nor that it is to-day considered as a debatable question whether, as a people, we are really becoming better or worse. That few, if any, of our jails or prisons are in a satisfactory condition is conclusively shown by the reports of the various Boards of Charities and Corrections; and that a large majority of them are in such a bad condition, and so improperly conducted as to be nurseries of crime and schools of vice, appears to be equally true. It is humiliating to a citizen of the American Republic, whose government has so long been the boast of its orators and leading statesmen as "the best government on the earth," to be obliged to confess these disagreeable facts, while we have the example of Great Britain, under a monarchial government, reducing the number of her prisons by nearly one-half in half a century, and diminishing the number of crimes committed in nearly the same proportion, and by enlightened legislation having established the best prison system now existing. Are we as a people so weak, and blind to our national and individual interests, and so corrupted by our conditions and selfish aims and pursuits that we have become or remain indifferent to the principles of humanity and the calls of duty to our fellow-men; that we allow these great public evils to continue?

While these dark clouds are still hanging over us, and the turbid waters of a vicious and corrupt political system are dashing upon us and percolating through all the veins of our whole social and political fabric, it is gratifying to observe the interest that has been awakened within the last few years in the work of attempting the reformation of criminals, and especially juvenile offenders, and preventing crime by taking care of and educating the neglected and dependent children, and such as are surrounded by evil influences that would be likely to lead them into lives of infamy and shame, and securing suitable homes for them in good families. The institutions and associations created or formed for these and kindred objects will be referred to hereafter.

16

# CHAPTER III.

### OF THE PRINCIPLES WHICH SHOULD GOVERN ALL ACTION RELATIVE TO CRIME.

WHEN we lay it down as an axiom, that *all crime should be treated as a disease*, we are stating a proposition which we have entertained for more than forty years, during over thirty-five years of which we were engaged in administering the criminal laws of the State, and which we have never seen any reason to change or modify.  This view of the character of crime and its treatment will be found on examination to satisfy all the demands of justice, and to secure all the ends which legislators have sought to obtain through the infliction of punishment.  It excludes all idea of vindictiveness, or the rendering of evil for evil, and harmonizes all the dealings of governments and communities with offenders against the criminal laws with the highest standard of benevolence and human kindness and duty.  It eliminates from punishment the character of atonement or retribution suffered as an expiation, to appease the wrathful indignation of society or the State, and removes all the difficulties which have puzzled moralists and confused courts and juries, who have based the right to condemn and execute judgment for wrong done upon the mental or moral condition of the perpetrator at the moment when the act was done.

To many, and perhaps a large majority, of the educated, moral, and religious portion of our people, who have given no special attention to the subject, the proposition that punishment for crime is wrong, and ought to be discarded as barbarous and inhuman, suggests no other idea than that of opening the prison-doors and allowing all criminals to go free and commit fresh crimes with impunity, and without restraint or control,—the idea of anarchy and a relapse into the worst condition of savagery. Nothing could be more erroneous, or farther from the thought of those who repudiate *punishment*. Philanthropy, justice, and mercy alike require that those who are so morally diseased as to be capable of committing crime should be restrained and subjected to such treatment and discipline as are calculated to cure the disease, if curable, and, if incurable, that such restraint shall be perpetual. No one of sound mind doubts the right of the government or of the family and friends of one afflicted with insanity to restrain and control such insane person, and, if necessary for the protection of the community or the individual thus afflicted from doing or receiving harm, to subject him to confinement and bonds, however painful such treatment may be. But in no civilized country are insane persons held to be subject to punishment or to any moral accountability, even for the taking of a human life; and the treatment they are subjected to is not for atonement or retribution, and does not proceed from a spirit of resentment or vindictiveness. We say of such that they are the subjects of mental disease, or some physical disease which affects the mind and renders the subject of it incapable of acting rationally, or impels him to act irrationally; and hence we attribute to him no moral turpitude in the commission of acts otherwise criminal, and impose no punishment as a consequence of such acts. But if the mental faculties are not so clouded or obscured that the actor is not capable of distinguishing what is morally right from what is wrong, he is held amenable to the criminal law, and deserving of punishment according to the degree of moral turpitude manifested by the act committed. But if we assume that all crime ought to be treated as a moral disease, or as caused by an unsound condition of the mind proceeding from disease, it is evident that we can no more determine the moral responsibility of the perpetrator of a wrongful act in the one case than in the other. In a former chapter we have quoted the language of Sir William Blackstone on the end or cause of human punishment, wherein he states not what was then practically regarded as its aim or purpose, but what should not, and what should, be treated as the final cause or end of punishment for crime. We repeat this language because of the great truth it expresses, the full import of which does not seem to have been understood by its eminent author, but to have flowed from his mind and pen as an inspired utterance, and a prophecy of a more exalted social state for man upon the earth. He says, "This is not by way of *atonement* or *retribution* for the crime committed, for that must be left to the just determination of the Supreme Being, but as a precaution against future offences of the same kind." ⟋

Not by way of atonement, or satisfaction to the State or community for the wrong done, nor yet by way of expiation, to allay the resentment or appease the wrath of the community because of the offence, but as a necessary precaution against the commission of other public wrongs. But in this statement of a great and pregnant truth, the most important of all the just objects of what is denominated punishment is wholly omitted,—viz., *the cure of the offender.*

It is true that, in enumerating the means of attaining the ends of punishment, he says they are effected in three ways, one of which is the amendment of the offender, "for which purpose all corporal punishments, fines, and temporary exile are inflicted." These means of effecting the amendment of the offender are all directed to the lower instincts and baser qualities of the wretched violator of the criminal laws,—to his fears, his sense of shame, and his dread of physical suffering, and contain no hint of reformation by the enlightenment and cultivation of the moral faculties and higher sentiments of the man. Neither do they suggest any idea of that duty which, in every just government, the whole owe to each individual, of securing to him the greatest practicable amount of benefit.

Now, while we are repudiating *punishment* for crime, it seems best that this term should be clearly defined, in order to avoid any misapprehension in regard to our position. To punish, as defined by Webster, and as it is commonly understood, is "to afflict with pain, loss, or calamity for a crime or fault; primarily to inflict bodily pain, as to punish a thief with pillory or stripes," etc.; "to reward with pain or suffering inflicted on the offender." "Punished" is defined as "afflicted with pain or evil as the retribution of a crime or offence; chastised." It is thus seen that in the strict sense of the term, which is also the popular one, punishment embraces the idea of retribution for crime, by the infliction of bodily pain or suffering, and implies vindictiveness, resentment, retaliation, atonement to appease the anger of an injured community. If, therefore, we eliminate from it all idea of atonement or retribution, and leave these to the just determination of the Allwise Father of us all, it is no longer punishment, but the just and merciful administration of such treatment as the nature and circumstances of the case and the good of the offender may require.

The elements of vindictiveness and resentment in punishment for crime, according to the common acceptation of its meaning and purpose, have been recently illustrated in a neighboring State. A cruel and wanton murder was committed, and the supposed murderer was arrested and committed to prison to await his trial, upon which, if convicted, his sentence would be that he should be hung by the neck until he should be dead. For safety the supposed murderer was placed in a cage, constructed of strong bars of steel; and, in consequence of the excitement which the report of the murder had created in the community, the prison was barricaded and guarded for the purpose of protecting the alleged murderer by resisting any assault that might be made upon it. It is reported that the man confessed his guilt to the prison officials, and that so great was the feeling of resentment and the indignation of the people towards the perpetrator of the crime, that a thousand men, moved by a common impulse, gathered about the prison, destroyed the barricades, overcame the guards and entered the prison, broke down the steel-barred cage, took the prisoner out, and appeased their wrath by putting him to death. Here, if this account be true, were a thousand citizens of an American State, residing in or near Viroqua, Wisconsin, acting in concert in the commission of a murder, by voluntarily imbuing their hands in the blood of a fellow-citizen, each one of them, whether actively engaged in the commission of the deed or aiding and abetting it, thereby rendering himself a murderer and amenable to the penalty of death. How much the prevailing sentiment which demands vindictive punishment for crime may have had to do with fostering the vengeful spirit by which these men were actuated cannot be told, but that it tends to such results cannot be doubted. Had the perpetrators of this great crime against humanity and the laws of the State been imbued with the great principle of a common brotherhood among men, and been taught that all crime proceeds from some inherited or ✗ acquired disease which gives force and activity to the lower propensities, and obscures or perverts the action of the higher sentiments, the thought of putting to death a helpless man under the circumstances detailed would have been abhorrent to their own feelings as the crime of which their victim himself was supposed to be guilty, and would have appeared to them as cowardly and mean as it was criminal.

When we consider that crime is caused by inherited tendencies derived from ancestors; from evil example, teachings, and associations in childhood and youth; from ignorance, poverty, and idleness, and from strong appetites and passions, avarice, cupidity, and unholy ambitions, the seeds of which were implanted in the nature of the individual before his birth, or imbibed from his surroundings afterwards, and before he was capable of distinguishing between right and wrong, we perceive that he may be the creature, and perhaps the victim, of circumstances beyond his control, and we may well hesitate to pronounce any judgment against him based upon his moral accountability, of which he can have very little or no appreciation until his moral perceptions have been opened and his higher faculties developed and cultivated.

Phrenology locates the organs of the moral sentiments, such as benevolence, veneration, hope, ideality, firmness, conscientiousness, in the superior or higher portion of the brain; and the organs of the propensities, or animal appetites, passions, and proclivities, such as destructiveness, combativeness, acquisitiveness, self-esteem, love of approbation, etc., in the inferior or lower portion of the brain, and hence infers that the moral sentiments, acting through the intellectual or reasoning faculties, should control the action of the propensities; and that unless these, with the other organs of the brain, are so balanced that each shall perform its legitimate functions in perfect harmony with the healthful action of all the others, without excess, or the undue preponderance of any, the character of the individual will necessarily be faulty in proportion to the inharmony resulting therefrom. Thus, if acquisitiveness be large, and conscientiousness small, the individual may cheat, defraud, or steal; or if combativeness and destructiveness be large, and benevolence and conscientiousness small, he may be a murderer, and delight in cruelty. If, as the devotees of this science (or what is claimed as such) assume, the several faculties, sentiments, propensities, appetites, passions, and proclivities natural to men are all indicated by certain organs of the brain which are manifested externally upon the surface of the cranium that encloses the brain, so as to be clearly discovered by the skilled craniologist, whereby the true character of the individual may be read as in an open book, by comparing the relative power of each of such organs, and if these exist without any choice or volition of their possessor, who shall dare undertake to judge how far he is morally responsible, or amenable to human punishment, if the natural qualities of his mind and character shall lead him to the commission of crime? To be qualified for such judgment it would be necessary that we should be able to do so from the same stand-point which he occupied when the criminal act was committed, and this would evidently be an impossibility.

Now, whether the faculties of the mind and the qualities which constitute individual character are typified by certain prominences or depressions that may be traced upon the exterior surface of the head or not, we know that such faculties exist, and manifest themselves in the actions of men. We know, too, that in the character of the best and noblest of our race there is, and has ever been, an admixture of evil; and to us it appears equally true that in the characters of the worst and most desperate of men there is still " a little leaven" of good that may eventually "leaven the whole lump." If there is not sufficient strength of the moral perceptions to control our evil propensities, the latter will inevitably lead us into wrong-doing. The tree of life may be within our view, and its fruits may be fair, but so long as to us it is guarded by a flaming sword we shall not reach it, though that sword be only the shadow of the evil existing in our own natures.

Mr. Horsley says, in the preface to his " Jottings from Jails," " One frequently hears a story of John Bradford quoted with approval, in which it is said that, seeing a condemned criminal on his way to Tyburn Tree, he exclaimed, 'There, but for the grace of God, goes John Bradford,' and the thought has often occurred to the writer, when called upon to sentence men to imprisonment for high crimes, including murder, that had I been born with all the mental and moral characteristics and natural proclivities which the prisoner inherited from his ancestors, and been surrounded by the same influences to which he has been subject through his past life, I should certainly have been capable of committing similar crimes. This thought disarms the mind of the judge of all austerity or resentment in the infliction of the punishment which the law demands, and constrains him to look with pity upon his unfortunate brother, who was thus born to be the victim of his evil passions and propensities. We are perfectly well aware that when we represent the criminal as the victim of his moral, mental, and physical constitution, and therefore as a proper object for commiseration, we are antagonizing that public sentiment which has been almost universal, and which still inheres in our criminal laws, to which we have more than once adverted, and which demand exemplary or vindictive punishment for criminal wrong-doing. But we are also aware that, until a new and more humane popular sentiment was aroused in the latter part of last century by John Howard and those whom he was able to interest in behalf of the prisoners of his day, the general sentiment of the most enlightened nations approved of such cruel and inhuman treatment of criminals as now appears too shocking and barbarous ever to have been tolerated even by a half-civilized people. Our present systems of treatment, though vastly more humane and just than the old, are not satisfactory in their results, and some of them are so faulty in principle as to be entirely disapproved by the best and ablest of our philanthropic citizens who have devoted attention to the subject; and the lamentable fact that our penitentiary systems have failed to greatly diminish the number of convictions for crime is too clearly shown by reliable statistics to be denied. One of two conclusions, then, is certainly true,—either our modes of dealing with crime are based upon wrong principles, or the results are inevitable and must continue. The latter conclusion we cannot accept, nor do we believe a majority of our intelligent fellow-citizens are willing to adopt it.

What, then, is the principle upon which crime may be treated, with the reasonable hope of diminishing the number of criminals in a degree proportionate to the increasing intelligence and material prosperity of our people? This is a momentous question, but it is one which in our opinion, the history and experiences of the last quarter of a century has answered by indubitable and conclusive evidence, as it had been answered by the wisest moral and religious teachers centuries ago, in the language we have recited in preceding chapters. It is the great principle of humanity and common brotherhood, which forbids that we shall ever cease to seek to do good to the meanest of God's children in their most miserable conditions, and commands us to do them no evil. When this principle is accepted as true, it is still asked, How is it to be applied in practice, so as to secure the desired results in the treatment of criminals? Our mental constitution is such that, in order to understand this, we must have the most forcible and simple illustrations. The parables and similitudes by which Jesus illustrated the great truths which he taught made a more profound impression upon the minds of his hearers than did the direct and simple language of his Sermon on the Mount. In order to illustrate, and show the practical application of the principle of humanity and brotherhood in the treatment of crime, we have laid it down as an axiom that all crime should be treated as a disease. Now, it is denied that the mind can ever be diseased, and it may be impossible to detect the bodily disease which produces that mental disturbance or aberration of the mind which is called insanity; yet the similitude of lunacy to physical disease is so perfect, that it has almost universally been so denominated, and so we speak of " ministering to a mind diseased." That the same similitude as perfectly and truly illustrates the condition of the sinful violators of the criminal laws of the country, we have endeavored to show. For this view of crime we have the highest authority. The ancient prophets represented the rebellious and obdurate Jews as covered with putrefying sores from the crowns of their heads to the soles of their feet. When Jesus was rebuked for associating with publicans and sinners by some who claimed to be more holy, he explained to them that " the whole need not a physician, but they that are *sick*," and one of the most lovely and endearing appellations applied to him is that of " the good physician," the healer of sin-sick souls. How many men, in their prayers and supplications for grace and strength to resist the temptations of the world, have represented themselves (as I have heard my venerable father do hundreds of times before the morning meal) as covered with wounds and bruises and putrefying sores, invoking the ministration of the Great Physician, and the application of " the balm that was in Gilead,"—" A healing balm for every wound, a cordial for our fears," as expressed by the poet. We cannot conceive of any motive which should actuate the physician in the treatment of physical disease, or the nurses and friends of his patient, or which should control the action of those having the treatment and care of an insane person, which should not equally dictate and govern the treatment of the criminal. Any exhibition of cruelty or resentment, or infliction of unnecessary pain upon a sick or insane person, is shocking to the moral sense of every one who is possessed of ordinary benevolence and that sense of justice which is common among enlightened people, and would be considered as evidence of a low, ignorant, and vile character. The sentiment that would justify such conduct is demoralizing in its tendency and effects, and equally so, in our opinion, is that sentiment which justifies vindictive punishment for crime.  Indeed, as we have shown by one out of thousands of instances which might have been referred to, this sentiment is a fruitful cause of many of the most fearful crimes,—crimes which this sentiment justifies, while it secures immunity to the perpetrators of them.

Sixty years ago, George Combe, of Edinburgh, Scotland, published his great work on " The Constitution of Man, considered in Relation to External Objects," wherein he treated, among other things, of punishment under the natural laws.  This work, which advocates the truths of phrenological science, though criticised by some theologians as tending to conclusions not in harmony with their interpretation of the Scriptures, has been ably defended by others, who believed there was no conflict between phrenology and revelation, but that, rightly understood, they are in perfect harmony with each other.  However this may be, the great truths of physiological, mental, and moral science which it advocates are now too thoroughly established in the minds of the best thinkers of the present age, who are seeking after truth without regard to preconceived opinions or prejudices, to be successfully assailed.

After treating of the sentiments and propensities which make up the character and affect the actions of the individual, and pointing out such as tend to the commission of crime, and those that tend to its opposite, he says, " We perceive, therefore, as the first feature of the moral and intellectual law, that the sentiments, absolutely and in all circumstances, declare against offences, and demand imperatively that they shall be brought to an end.  There is a great difference, however, between the means which they suggest for accomplishing this object and those prompted by the propensities.  The latter blindly inflict animal resentment, without the slightest regard to the causes which led to the crime or the consequences of the punishment.  They seize the aggressor, worry, bite, or strangle him, and there they begin and terminate."

" The moral and intellectual faculties, on the other hand, embrace even the criminal himself within the range of their sympathies. Benevolence desires to render him virtuous, and therefore happy, as well as to rescue his victim. Veneration desires that he shall be treated as a man; and conscientiousness declares that it cannot with satisfaction acquiesce in any administration towards him that does not tend to remove the motives of his misconduct, and to prevent their recurrence. The first step, then, which the moral and intellectual faculties combine in demanding is a full exposition of the causes of the offence, and the consequences of the mode of treatment proposed." This writer, assuming that every crime proceeds from the abuse of some faculty or another, and that the causes of such abuse arise from three sources,—first, from particular organs being too large and spontaneously active; second, from excessive excitement from external causes; or, thirdly, from ignorance of what are uses and what are abuses of the faculties,—says, " The moral and intellectual powers next demand, What is the cause of particular organs being too large and active in individuals? Phrenology, for answer, points to the law of hereditary descent, by which the organs most energetic in the parents determine those which shall predominate in the child. Intellect, then, infers that, according to this view, certain individuals are unfortunate at birth in having received organs from their parents so ill-proportioned that abuse of some of them is almost an inevitable consequence, if they are left to the sole guidance of their own suggestions. Phrenology replies that the fact appears to be exactly so." He states, as evidence of the truth of this proposition, that " In the phrenological hall is exhibited a large assemblage of skulls and casts of the heads of criminals, collected from Europe, Africa, and America, and an undeniable feature of

I    *n*                 17

them all is a great preponderance of the organs of the animal propensities over those of the moral sentiments and intellect." "I have," he says, "examined the cerebral development and inquired into the external circumstances of a considerable number of criminals, and have no hesitation in saying, that if, in the case of every offender, the three sources of crime here enumerated were investigated, reported upon, and published, the conviction would become irresistible that the individual was the victim of his nature and external condition. . . . The public err through ignorance, and need only to know better to insure their going into the right path."

"Further, intellect perceives and the moral sentiments acknowledge that these causes subsist *independently of the will of the offender.* The criminal, for example, is not the cause of the unfortunate preponderance of the animal organs in his own brain, neither is he the cause of the external excitement which seduces his propensities into abuse, or of the intellectual ignorance in which he is involved. Nevertheless, the moral and intellectual faculties of the indifferent spectator of his condition do not, on this account, admit that he ought, either for his own sake or that of society, to be permitted to proceed in an unrestricted course of crime. They absolutely insist upon arresting his progress, and their first question is, how may this best be done? Intellect answers, by removing the causes which produce the offences.

"The first cause, the great preponderance of animal organs, cannot by any means yet known be summarily removed. Intellect therefore points out another alternative,— viz., to supply by moral and physical restraint the control which, in a brain better constituted, is afforded by large moral and intellectual organs; in short, to place the offender under such a degree of effective control as absolutely to prevent the abuses of his faculties. Benevolence acknowl-

edges this to be kind, veneration to be respectful, and conscientiousness to be just, at once to the offender himself,
and to society; and intellect perceives that whenever it is
adopted it will form an important step towards preventing a
repetition of crimes.

" The second cause,—viz., great external excitement, may
be removed by withdrawing the individual from its influence.
Thus, any restraint and control which serve to remedy the
first will directly tend to accomplish this second object at the
same time.

" The third cause, being moral and intellectual ignorance,
may be removed by conveying instruction to the higher
faculties of the mind. If these principles be sound, the
measures now recommended ought, when viewed in all
their consequences, to be not only the most just and benevolent, but at the same time *the most advantageous that
could be adopted.*"

Contrasting the animal system in the treatment of crime
with the moral, Mr. Combe says, " Under the animal
system no inquiry is made into the future proceedings of
the offender, and he is turned loose on society under the
unabated influence of all the causes which led to his in-
fringement of the law, and, as effects never cease while
their causes continue to operate, he repeats his offence, and
again becomes the object of a new animal infliction. Under
the moral system the causes would be removed, and the
evil effects would cease. Under the animal system, the
lower propensities of the offender and of society are maintained in habitual excitement, for *the punishment proceeds
from the propensities, and is addressed to the propensities.* . . .
Under the moral system again, the whole faculties exercised
and addressed in restraining and instructing the offender
are the human powers. The propensities are employed
merely as the servants of the moral sentiments in accomplishing their benignant purposes, and benevolence is as

actively engaged in behalf of the offender as of society at large."

After referring to the fact that the office of public executioner " is odious, execrable, and universally contemned," Mr. Combe adds, that " under the moral system the criminal would be committed to persons whose duties would be identical with those of the clergyman, the physician, and the teacher. These are the executioners under the moral laws; and just because their avocations are highly grateful to the sentiments, these are the most esteemed of mankind." Dr. Buchanan, in "The New Education," contrasts the animal and moral systems of treatment in an equally forcible manner. He says (p. 115), "The vindictive sentiment which comes in and clamorously asserts that justice requires the *punishment* of the criminal, and is basely defrauded when he is kindly educated into virtue, is the fierce inspiration of the malignant passions which are themselves the essence of crime, and which are roused into action by the aggressions of the criminals. He who cannot look upon criminals of every grade with the sentiment, ' Father, forgive them, they know not what they do,' has not yet learned the chief lesson of ethics. The criminal and his victim are both objects of compassion, and the compassion for the criminal is greater as his misfortune is greater, involving his soul, and extending its calamitous effects beyond the present life.

" True, it is right to defend ourselves against the criminal, because it is a necessity; but he is a poor thinker whose judgment becomes entangled in the meshes of passion, and cannot see that the criminal is the victim of an adverse fate (which might have overtaken himself), whose reclamation calls for our help as loudly as the spectacle of a drowning man. If we cannot control him we may be compelled to fight him for the protection of ourselves; but whenever we have physical power to control him, and do not proceed to his redemption, we become criminals ourselves. The State which *punishes* instead of reforming its criminals, is a criminal itself, or a victim to the contagion of crime, for all crimes are contagious. The knave tempts other men to tricks and treachery to circumvent him, and the homicide makes homicides of others who are tempted to kill him in advance. Thus the mob hangs the murderer, and governments have only of late risen a little above the animal contagion of crime, and begun to think seriously of reformation instead of torture."

We hope that we have now made it clear to the mind of the intelligent reader that the moral system of treatment, as explained and illustrated in this chapter, is not only based upon the true principles of equity and justice, but that its adoption is calculated to secure, in the highest degree, the greatest amount of benefit, both to the offender and to society; and that it has been shown to be equally clear that so long as punishment is inflicted upon the animal principle, both are injured by the infliction; and that there can be but little hope of diminishing crime and improving the condition of society, until the latter system shall be abandoned, and the former adopted. In the next chapter we shall treat of some of the evils of our present system of punishment for crime.

## CHAPTER IV.

### OF SOME OF THE EVILS OF OUR PRESENT SYSTEM OF PUNISHMENT FOR CRIME.

It has, we believe, become an almost universally accepted fact in the public sentiment, that all public exhibitions of corporal punishment for crime are demoralizing in their effects upon society, and injurious, instead of being beneficial, to the offender. Hence the whipping-post, the stocks, the pillory, the ducking-stool, and other devices for inflicting bodily pain in an open and public manner, have almost everywhere been abolished, and criminals condemned to death are executed within the prison walls or inclosure, and only a few persons who are designated for that purpose are admitted to witness the deliberate extinguishment of a human life under the sanction of a human law. It is within our recollection when the greatest publicity was given to executions of criminals, upon the idea of inspiring terror in the minds of the beholders as a deterrent from crime, and on these occasions thousands of men, women, and children congregated to witness the tragic horror. But when attention was directed to the fact, which was confirmed by observation, that the effect of such exhibitions was brutalizing, and tended to increase, rather than diminish, crime, public executions were abolished. The same principle which prompted this change, if rightly understood and logically followed out, and practically applied, would indubitably lead us to the approval and adoption of "the moral system of treatment," as explained in the last chapter, and effectually eradicate all thought of retributive punishment. The right which the State exercises to restrain and control the action of its citizens, in order to secure the peace, good order, and safety of society, is limited by the necessity upon which the right is based, and involves a corresponding duty. This duty, in case of a violation of the criminal law, is to inquire into the causes which led to the offence, the circumstances attending it, and what discipline or treatment is most likely to reform the criminal and make him a useful citizen. And until this duty has been performed, and the true character of the offender is known, no judgment can be formed as to how long the restraint should continue in order to make the discipline effectual, so that a restoration to liberty will be safe to society or just to the offender. It is obvious that with

our penitentiary system and our criminal laws and jurisprudence as they now exist, the performance of this duty is
impossible. The spirit of *punishment* which pervades the
criminal laws for what are known as felonies or penitentiary
offences, as well as for many minor offences, is vindictive in
its character and not reformatory, and does not seek, by
appropriate treatment, to remove the causes which have
made the individual a criminal.

All sentences to imprisonment under our statutes, except
in cases of some juvenile offenders, are required to be for a
specified period of time, according to the kind and grade of
the offence; and when that period has expired the prisoner
is set at liberty, however desperate his character may be.
Practically he is considered as having *atoned* for his crime
by suffering the punishment inflicted for it, and has a right
to the opportunity to commit fresh crimes, against which
society has no protection, however strong the probability
may be that he will do so. How large a proportion of
those thus punished repeat the offence afterwards is not
known, but many of them are returned to the same prison,
and many others are known to have been punished in other
prisons for crimes committed in other States or countries.
The shrewd thief or burglar is most likely to perpetrate his
offences where he is not known, and if detected and convicted but little if anything can be ascertained in regard to
his previous character before his sentence is pronounced.
On being arraigned for sentence, and asked if he has anything to say why judgment should not be pronounced
against him, he may appeal for mercy, assume an air of
innocence, claim that it is his first offence, that he was led
into it by others while under the influence of liquor, and is
ready to promise that this shall be the last he will ever
commit. He has been convicted of a burglary or theft, and,
so far as the judge knows, his statements may all be true.
The statute requires that he shall be punished by imprison-

ment in the penitentiary, at hard labor, for a term not exceeding five, ten, or fifteen years. The judge is now on trial. If he is a man possessing ordinary benevolence and conscientiousness, and moderate combativeness, he may be inclined to give some credence to the prisoner's story, which there has been none to contradict, and fearing lest he should make the punishment excessive he gives the prisoner some excellent advice, and sentences him to imprisonment for perhaps one or two years, and the sheriff or his deputy receives his warrant and takes him to the penitentiary, and delivers him into the custody of the warden. On his return, the officer informs his honor, the judge, that the prisoner whom he had dealt so leniently with, and given such fatherly counsel, was fully recognized by the officers of the prison, who at once saluted him with " Hello, Jake! got back again, have you ?" " Yes," replies Jake, " for a short time. The judge wa'n't so hard on me as that other one was that sent me here for five years." His name was Richard Jackson when last tried. On his former trial it was Richard Munson, and when his history is known he is found to have been a professional thief and burglar under various names. Such cases are not of very unfrequent occurrence. The judge has formed the best judgment he could from what appeared in evidence on the trial and the appearance and deportment of the prisoner in court and while in jail awaiting his trial. Many noted criminals are known to the police in all the large cities, but not all of them. When one has become notorious and is "wanted" to answer for some villanous crime, his photograph, if one has been secured, with some account of his character and history, are sent to such places as he may be likely to visit. In such cases the judge may obtain some general information to guide him in pronouncing judgment. But no matter how desperate the character of the prisoner may be, nor how utterly hopeless his reformation, he can only be com-

pelled to endure the punishment which the law has determined to be his due for the specific crime of which he has
been convicted. If the judge, upon inquiry, becomes satisfied that the prisoner has committed other crimes, and that
he will be likely to pursue the same desperate course of life
as soon as he regains his liberty, still he cannot transcend
the limit fixed by law as due to that particular offence, and
must leave him to the chances of his committing other
crimes, without any adequate protection to the community.

We have in the State of Michigan twenty-eight judicial
circuits, and thirty-one circuit judges, besides judges of
municipal courts of criminal jurisdiction. In these courts
all offences punishable by imprisonment in the State prison
are adjudicated. These judges are men of high character
and ability, who probably would not suffer by comparison
with judges exercising similar powers and jurisdiction in
any other State of the Union. But they are still men, with
differing temperaments and experiences, and varying in their
views and feelings in regard to crimes and punishments.
Some of them are by nature austere and rigorous, while
others are sympathetic, so that where one would deem five
or ten or even fifteen years' imprisonment none too much in
a given case, another would deem it more just and more
likely to be beneficial to impose only imprisonment for a
term of two or three years; and so the amount of punishment inflicted for similar offences, under like circumstances,
varies according to the varying views or tempers of the
trial judges before whom the adjudication is had, and it is
scarcely to be supposed that any two of them would pronounce the same judgment. If it be supposed, then, that
two years' imprisonment for an offence under given circumstances is all that justice demands, and the offender is required to serve a term of five or ten years, it is evident that
great injustice is done. If, on the other hand, the offence
justly requires the greater punishment, and a less is in-

flicted, justice is not satisfied, and evil may be expected to result in either case.    This is an infirmity which is inherent in our present system of criminal jurisprudence, in which punishment is meted out in *definite quantities* to be fixed by the trial judge within certain limitations, and this evil must continue so long as *definite sentences* for crime are required. To us this appears as irrational as would be the attempt to fix in advance the period during which an insane person shall remain under treatment in an asylum, or a person sick with some chronic disease remain under the care of a physician, and then be discharged without regard to the mental or physical condition of the patient.    To determine in either case the period required for punishment or cure would require a prescience not vouchsafed to judges or physicians in general.    It may be said that if it shall appear to the governor of the State at any time that the judgment of the court is unjust for any cause, he may interpose in the exercise of his executive authority and pardon the offender or commute the sentence.    This is true in theory, but our governors have no power to enlarge the period of imprisonment, however strongly justice may require it, and they are not elected with reference to any special fitness for the exercise of this power; and the history of the State shows that men have been pardoned by the governor for high crimes who were, if possible, more desperate and determined villains when thus set free than when they were sentenced to the State prison for life or a long term of years.    However conscientious they may be in discharging the duties of their high trust, they are liable to mistake the proper objects of clemency, and to be deceived and imposed upon by interested or misguided parties.

Again, all *punishment* for crime is inflicted upon the idea of man's *moral accountability to society*, and of *atonement* or *retribution* through suffering, or the visiting of evil upon him for the evil he has done to society.    The right to punish, if it exists at all, must be based upon this idea. Hence it is a maxim of the law that the criminality of the wrongful act consists in the evil or felonious intent with which it is done. If a wrongful act, however disastrous it may be to others, is done by a person who presumably has no moral perception of the wrong he is doing, or of its consequences, the law will not adjudge him guilty of a crime, nor punish him for the act. Hence, if the accused is adjudged so imbecile, or idiotic, or insane when the act was done, that he had no rational conception of its nature and consequences, or of his moral accountability for its perpetration, he is acquitted for that reason, as not deserving of punishment. But if acquitted by reason of insanity (unsoundness of mind), he is not set at liberty if his discharge is considered manifestly dangerous to the peace and safety of the community, but is placed under such treatment as the nature and circumstances of his case require. The duty of the State in such a case to seek the cure of the unfortunate individual by the use of appropriate treatment, and to restrain and control him until his liberation becomes safe to others, is fully recognized; and if, as we assume, all crime ought to be treated *as a disease*, or as caused by disease, there is no difficulty in applying that treatment which has been explained, and denominated by Mr. Combe "the moral system," to every case of crime.

For a great variety of minor offences the punishment provided by our criminal code is a fine not exceeding a certain amount, or imprisonment in a county jail or in a house of correction for a few days or months. These petty crimes and misdemeanors are triable in the courts of justices of the peace and police courts, and the daily grist (as it is sometimes called) ground out in our large cities is enormous. Drunkenness, assault and battery, or other disorderly conduct, and petty larceny, are the principal offences our police courts have to deal with, and in many instances the number of times the same individual has been adjudged guilty cannot be counted " on fingers and toes." Every morning (except Sundays) the unsavory procession is brought in, and the cases are disposed of in a very summary manner, and the punishment announced without the least hesitation and with little ceremony. Thomas is convicted of having been drunk and disorderly, and, being understood to be able to do so, is adjudged to pay a fine of one dollar and costs amounting to fifteen dollars and thirty cents. Maria Therese, as she calls herself, is notoriously a depraved creature, and is convicted for the fiftieth time of being disorderly, and everybody knows that she intends to continue in her vile course of life. She is not old, and still has some personal attractions, and therefore has friends. She, or her friends for her, can pay another fine of fifteen dollars and costs, and the fine is imposed and paid, and she goes on her way. One miserable wretch has no money or friends, but gets his living by pilfering small amounts, and he is sentenced to imprisonment for thirty days. And thus these wretched children of iniquity are all disposed of. Those who have paid their fines have purchased their freedom and the opportunity to commit fresh offences, with perhaps the additional incentive to try to indemnify themselves for what has been taken from them.

That this is not an overdrawn picture all who are acquainted with police affairs can testify. Here we have punishment, pure and simple, with no other element in it but meanness. Had some one obtained the money that Thomas was compelled to pay as a fine and costs by false tokens or pretences, he would have been guilty of a felony, but the money is taken from him without any pretence of rendering the least benefit to him on account of it, under the sanction of the law. The effects of the debauch which led to his arrest were visited upon him by the operation of a natural law, and the moral consequences of his acts are determined

by an appeal to his conscience, and are not cancelled by fine
or imprisonment.

Of the hundreds of thousands belonging to the classes
of offenders above referred to, all or nearly all require treatment at the hands of the State or community. They are
diseased and need cure; they are immoral and debased because of circumstances that naturally lead to such conditions,
under the operation of a law of human nature, whereby
their character and conduct could be predicted beforehand
with almost unerring certainty. Those who know their
parentage and surroundings in childhood and youth antici-
pated and foretold what their destiny would be, unless adequate means were provided to avert it. They have grown
up under conditions which made them the enemies of society,
—a sort of Ishmaelites whose hands are against every man,
and every man's hand is against them. On this subject the
Rev. R. W. Hill, in a paper read before the National Conference of Charities and Corrections in 1887, under the
quaint title of "The Children of Shinbone Alley," says,
"Heredity as surely dooms the progeny of the depraved as
water runs down hill. It requires an outside force to save
them, and a power, too, greater and more kindly than the
public interest which usually concerns itself with the denizens of the haunts of vice. It is a hard saying to utter,
that children are criminals by fate; and yet with such antecedents and with such cruel surroundings the birth of children is the prophecy of crime for the future. In years hence,
when these young dwellers in the 'Shinbone Alleys' of the
country shall have grown accustomed, as they will be, to
an atmosphere of crime, there is nothing to be expected
save a series of crimes of which they are to be the perpetrators. It is time for society to awake to the fact that such
places are hot-beds of vice, where each generation will prove
worse than the one that preceded it." (Report, p. 233.) They
are ignorant, and need instruction and moral enlightenment,

and thousands of them are poor and destitute, and need the aid and guidance of those who are wiser and more prosperous to raise them out of the filth and pollution which surround and infect them, into a purer atmosphere and a happier condition of life.   The sins of many generations have been visited upon them, and will fall with added force upon their posterity if no preventive is applied.   Figuratively speaking, they are moral lepers, and constitute a festering sore upon the body politic, affecting every fibre and muscle, and infusing a baleful influence through the whole social fabric. But they are the children of the State, and are what society has made them, or permitted them to be.

Some of the prison notes made by Mr. Horsley while chaplain of Clerkenwell prison, London, in August, 1885, are very suggestive.   One statement in particular is worth transcribing, as indicating how farcical is the repetition of convictions for small offences.   Under date of August 1, he says, " I go in the afternoon to a workhouse infirmary, to visit poor Annie P.   When about a year ago the magistrate reproved her for having been four hundred times convicted, she was very angry, for she was sure it was not much more than three hundred times that she had been taken up for drunkenness or offences arising out of it."   And the kind-hearted chaplain expressed his thanks that poor Annie will die sober and penitent after so many convictions.   Under date of August 2, speaking of an old Brahmin who had been arrested for causing a disturbance, Mr. H. says, " He reminds me of another old Indian who eventually died in prison, his chief knowledge of English being ' Ninety-shix time,' he having been repeatedly convicted of begging."

Hon. John J. Wheeler, a member of the Michigan Board of Corrections and Charities, in a paper on indeterminate sentences, referring to convictions in the criminal courts of cities, and the prisons in which persons are confined for small crimes and misdemeanors, says, " The occupants are mostly men and women sent to prison or jail for a few days or weeks, time after time. By the time they get sober, out they go, to be back again before the week is up. Those women who are most capable of reformation have their fines paid. Tramps and vagabonds of all kinds, too lazy to work, men and women, the victims of rum, are all treated alike, with no chance of reform. Criminals spend more than half their lives in prison and are not reformed. The whole system is wrong." In our American cities the records of police courts will probably show hundreds and perhaps thousands of cases where repetition of convictions, followed by fines or short periods of imprisonment in jails, extend from two or three to fifty and a hundred times, at large expense to the tax-payers, but without any benefit either to the public or the individual.

Another great evil under our present system, which bases the right of the State to punish upon the moral accountability of the wrong-doer, grows out of the exceeding difficulty, in many cases, of determining whether or not the accused was morally responsible for his acts at the time the alleged crime occurred. In prosecutions for homicide, and for assaults with intent to commit murder, and for arson, one of the most common defences set up is that of insanity. The practical difficulties involved in the determination of the issue in such cases are best understood by those who have had the largest experience in criminal jurisprudence. There are cases so marked and clear that no doubt can exist in regard to the alleged insanity, but there are infinite degrees and shades of mental weakness or unsoundness of mind which affect the actions and conduct of men, that no balance can weigh nor rule measure, and to which no satisfactory test of moral accountability can be applied.

Mr. Bishop, in his excellent work on crime, remarks on this subject as follows: " It should also be remembered that the phases and manifestations of insanity are in number little less than infinite. No reason indeed appears why they may not be even more numerous, certainly more difficult to be understood, than the qualities and phenomena of sound minds; and our assurance may well be humbled when we reflect that what is called the learned world, much more the mass of humanity, still gropes darkly on the borders of moral and intellectual science."

After noticing some of the various forms of insanity and the attempts which have been made to define it by varying tests, Mr. Bishop further remarks, "This subject of insanity is, in its practical legal aspects, attended with great difficulties. Men of sane minds know themselves but imperfectly, and they comprehend others less than themselves; nor is there language to convey, in exact form, even the little knowledge we possess of the sane mind. When, therefore, we undertake to investigate the phenomena of insanity, to discuss them, and to deduce from the principles of the law the legal rules to govern them, we are embarrassed with difficulties which should make us cautious, and restrain us from any extensive laying down of doctrines for unseen future cases." And he adds further, that "Judges, counsel, and juries cannot proceed too carefully in their investigation of cases of alleged insanity;" from which the reader will infer, as the fact undoubtedly is, that in a large proportion, if not in most of the cases where this defence is set up, the verdict is as likely to be false as true. In a recently published and very valuable work on insanity, by Dr. T. R. Buckham, the careful perusal of which we earnestly commend to our law-makers, the author, referring to the uncertainty of verdicts in insanity cases, says, "That a feeling of profound and general distrust prevails with reference to legal decisions in all cases in which insanity is an element of the trial, is an under-statement of the fact," and refers to the statement of Dr. Maudsley, who says, "It is notorious that the acquittal or conviction of a prisoner, when insanity is alleged, *is a matter of chance.* Were the issue to be decided by tossing up a shilling, instead of by the grave procedure of a trial in court, it could hardly be more uncertain. The less insane person sometimes escapes, while the more insane is sometimes hanged; one man laboring under one form of derangement is acquitted at one trial, while another having an exactly similar form of derangement is convicted at another trial." Other distinguished medico-forensic writers express the same views, and the question, " Is not the travesty of justice in this class of cases shocking?" propounded by Dr. Buckham, can admit of but one answer. The folly, not to say absurdity, of calling in physicians who have had no special training to fit them to be judges in such matters, to testify upon the trial as experts, is forcibly pointed out and illustrated, and a safe, rational, and practical mode of securing the most competent and reliable expert testimony in these cases is indicated, and it is made very plain that if the proposed plan were adopted there need be no more uncertainty in determining the question of sanity or insanity than there is in determining the guilt or innocence in ordinary cases. Under the system proposed the experts would be officers of the State, and composed of men of the largest experience in the treatment of insanity in all its various forms, and they would, in each case, practically determine the question of moral accountability for the court and jury.

Dr. Buckham discusses the different theories in regard to the nature and causes of insanity, and concludes that the mind itself is incapable of disease, and offers the following as the true definition of insanity : " *A diseased or disordered condition, or malformation, of the physical organs through which the mind receives impressions, or manifests its operations, by which the will and judgment are impaired, and the conduct rendered irrational.*" And as a corollary he concludes that, " Insanity being *the result of physical disease*, it is a matter of fact to be determined by medical experts, not

a matter of law to be decided by legal tests and maxims."
The facts and arguments adduced seem to be very convincing in favor of this theory, which is denominated the
" physical media theory," in contradistinction to the " metaphysical" or " psychical" and the " somatic" or " material-
istic" hypothesis.

In regard to the distinction between the " physical media
theory" and the " metaphysical theory" he says, " The
' physical media theory,' like the ' metaphysical theory,' regards the mind as a distinct, intangible, incorporal entity,
not dependent upon the body for its existence ; but, unlike
the ' metaphysical theory,' it recognizes the most intimate
relations between mind and body, and holds that in this life
the mind is *wholly dependent* for the manifestations of its
operations on certain organs of the body which we designate physical media."

Assuming as we do the correctness of these conclusions,
and the analogy of the " physical media theory" to our
theory of crime is perfect, and most forcibly suggests the
perfect analogy which ought to exist in the treatment of
both.   If " the mind in this life is *wholly dependent* for the
manifestations of its operations on certain organs of the
body, which we designate physical media," and if crime of
necessity involves an operation of the mind, as we know it
does, is it not as certain that the criminal act proceeds from
a diseased or *disordered condition* or *malformation* of the
physical organs through which the mind receives impressions, or manifests its operations, as that insanity results from
the same cause ?   In the latter case the will and judgment
are said to be impaired and the conduct rendered irrational,
and criminality is not therefore imputed, because of the extent to which the will and judgment are impaired ; but if the
diseased or disordered condition or malformation of the
physical organs impel to the commission of crime so
strongly as to force the consent of the will, and overpower

the judgment, and yet do not so far destroy the understanding as to prevent the actor from distinguishing what is right and what is wrong, he is adjudged a criminal. The *intent* to do wrong distinguishes the character or quality of the act from the unconscious, *involuntary* wrong of an insane man, and indicates a difference in the kind or degree of the malformation or disorder from which the wrong proceeded, and one which requires a different mode of treatment. But what ground have we to assume that one condition proceeds from disease and the other does not? And why should not the purpose of the treatment in both cases be the same,— that is to say, the cure of the disease, and the protection of society?

Questions of the greatest import to society have arisen from time to time in the history of criminal procedure, which have greatly puzzled jurists and moralists, but which, upon the theory that all crime proceeds from disease or mal- formation of some of the physical organs through which the mind manifests its operations, as we have assumed that it does, are relieved of all difficulty in their solution. A few years ago a boy in Massachusetts, named Jesse Pomeroy, put to death small children, and seemed to derive the greatest delight from torturing them, and it could not be perceived that he had any consciousness that it was wrong, although he knew what he was doing. Having no con- ciousness that it was wrong, and being incapable of under- standing that he was violating any law, he could not be punished as for a crime, and the question arose, and was largely discussed at the time, whether the State had any right to restrain or punish where there was no moral ac- countability. If the right of the State to interfere rested upon the principle of moral accountability, there could be no interference by the State, but if it rests upon the neces- sity of protection to the community against the most re- volting evils, the case is relieved of all difficulty. Pomeroy had developed homicidal mania, evidenced by the destruction of human lives. Benevolence and justice towards the boy demanded that he should be restrained and controlled, and the moral faculties which were deficient developed and cultivated as far as practicable, and the duty of the State, both to him and to society, required that this should be done.

The case of Freeman, who slew his own child under the delusion that if he exhibited his faith and devotion to God by seeking the sacrifice of his child, He would in some marvellous way interfere to stay his hand, or place a ram or some other subject of sacrifice in its place and save his child, as Isaac was saved when offered as a sacrifice by Abraham, his father, is fresh in the recollection of all. Supposing Freeman to have been entirely honest in his belief that he had been called upon by his Creator to furnish such a test of his faith and devotion, and of God's power to interpose and thus verify the truth of biblical history, and that he was impelled by no other motive, then he had not only not intended any wrong, but was in the performance of what he regarded as the highest and most sacred religious duty, that of yielding obedience to God's command. When this delusion was dispelled, and the terrible consequences of his rash act were before him, who could desire to add anything to his punishment? Yet if his mental condition was such that he would be likely to commit other homicides or great wrongs, the necessity for restraint and proper treatment would be apparent, and the right and duty of the State to see that it was applied would be clear.

There are other infirmities in our criminal laws and their administration worthy of attention, but which it would not, perhaps, be profitable to discuss in detail here. The modes of treatment which we shall hereafter point out will, in our judgment, obviate most of the objectionable features of our present system, and we hope may commend themselves to the favorable consideration of legislators and philanthropists. There is, however, one mode of punishment still practised in most States and civilized countries, to which we have before referred, and which to us appears so barbarous and inhuman, and injurious in its effects upon the community, as to demand our most emphatic protest against its continuance. We allude to the punishment of death, or capital punishment for crime. The right of an individual, whether in a state of nature or as a member of society, to take the life of another is recognized only in cases where it is absolutely necessary in defence of life, or to prevent some great wrong which is attempted to be committed by force. According to the theory of all enlightened writers upon government, and which has been accepted as true, in the transition from a state of nature to a social state and an authoritative government, men surrendered up a portion of their natural rights to the body politic, in order that the just rights of all might be protected by the government thus constituted. Upon this theory, the government could exercise no power except such as it acquired by such surrender. Individuals could not surrender or invest the government with any rights which they did not possess in a state of nature. Hence they could never surrender to, or vest in the body politic the right to take the life of an individual, except in self-defence. In a civilized state, with ample means of protecting itself and its citizens by imprisoning the offender for life, there can be no *necessity*, and consequently no *rightful authority* in the government to pronounce the penalty of death upon any of its citizens. When Moses ruled the Israelites, and made the laws for their government, they had no prisons for securing offenders, nor any other means of protection against the acts of the violent and desperate, and hence the destruction of life for great crimes may be considered as having been necessary upon the principle of self-defence, and therefore justifiable.

But the effect of this practice was to so cheapen human life in the estimation of that people, that they stoned to death those who were guilty of what we regard as very trivial or venial offences, even for gathering a few sticks upon the Sabbath day. Those, therefore, who seek to justify capital punishment, because it was denounced by the Mosaic law, for the shedding of man's blood, seem to forget the different circumstances of that people from our own, and also to forget that Jesus, whose authority no Christian will dare dispute, abolished the law of retribution, and taught a doctrine entirely inconsistent with it.

The abolition of public executions is in itself a concession that the example is pernicious, and does not deter from the commission of crime. The idea of punishment by way of example being abandoned, capital punishment assumes the character of gratuitous and wanton cruelty, without justification or excuse.

If there are any who still believe that life is more safe in those States where the murderer is put to death for his crime, a study of the effects of its abolition ought, it would seem, to be sufficient to correct the error.

In Rhode Island, Michigan, and Wisconsin, where capital punishment was abolished from twenty-five to fifty years ago, human life has been as secure as in any other States of the Union, and much more so than in some of them where the death penalty is in force; and during the forty years since imprisonment for life was substituted for hanging in case of murder in Michigan, but one case of murder by lynching under mob law has come to our knowledge. In Switzerland, that model and most peaceful republic of the Old World, capital punishment has existed as a legal enactment in but eight of the twenty-five Cantons since 1879; and in Belgium, Russia, Bavaria, Denmark, and Sweden, though not abolished by law, its enforcement has practically ceased. So in France, where in one year there were one hundred and twenty-six convictions for murder, and but four executions, and in Italy, where a similar proportion of executions to convictions is found, the same evidence of the decadence of this mistaken policy is found. In Austria also capital punishments have for many years been exceeding rare. In the Kingdom of the Netherlands the death penalty was abolished in 1870, and in 1881, when an effort was made by a minority of the Chamber to re-enact the penalty, the Minister of Justice stated that "the convictions for crime which merited death, according to the law in force up to that time, in the ten years immediately following the abolition of capital punishment, were fifty-seven in number, while the number of those condemned to death in the ten years immediately preceding was eighty-two." "In 1867," says Mr. Sparhawk (late consul at Zanzibar), "the death penalty was abolished in Portugal. It was not until the third year after that any appreciable change occurred, and since then, year by year, murders have decreased in number till to-day they are not more than half of what they were, and are far below that of other countries, making allowance for difference in population."

A new law has since been enacted, by which murderers are sentenced to twenty years in the penitentiary, and are not employed upon public works, but are given a religious and industrial education ; and at the expiration of the sentence they go free, with two-thirds of the proceeds of their labor to start life anew. "It is asserted," says Mr. S., "that the instance is rare where one of these ever appears in Court again charged with any crime."

If any other evidence than we have already advanced were necessary to prove that capital punishment does not deter men from committing capital crimes, but rather tends to incite to such crimes, it may be found in the following facts quoted in the article above referred to. "A Paris executioner, during his term of office, hung twenty murderers, who, as he said, had been constant attendants at his gibbeting matinées. Rev. Mr. Roberts, of England, conversed with one hundred and sixty-seven convicts under sentence of death, all of whom but three had witnessed executions."

Mr. Talbuck, secretary of the Howard Association, relates that "It has often been noticed that executions have been immediately followed by an unusual 'crop' of murderers. For example, in 1870, shortly after the execution of Tropmann at Paris for a peculiarly atrocious murder, several similar cases of wholesale slaughter occurred, including the sevenfold murder at Uxbridge. Similarly, in 1867, the execution of three Fenians at Manchester was followed within three weeks by the abominable Fenian explosion at Clerkenwell, which sacrificed many lives. When men were hung up by the dozen for forging one-pound Bank of England notes, the crime did not diminish—it increased; though many were cut off at Old Baily Sessions, many escaped all punishment through the humane repugnance of juries to send them in shoals to the scaffold."

The execution of three Anarchists in Chicago, a few months ago, aroused a feeling among those who sympathized with them in their opinions that called forth expressions of the most ferocious desire for vengeance against those who participated in the trial and in executing the law, and resulted in a deliberate plan for destroying the lives of those most prominently connected with the trial, and perhaps a wholesale destruction of other lives most shocking to contemplate. Had the sentences of the three that were hung been commuted to imprisonment for life, and had the law only authorized such imprisonment, such a malignant revengeful feeling would not in all probability have been engendered. "The supposition that capital punishment deters men from homicidal crime," says Mr. Griffin, "is apparently founded upon a misconception of human nature." While the righteous regard human life as the most sacred of all things, and are shocked at the thought of its lawless destruction, and grieved when any supposed necessity exists for its extinction, the man with murderous intent, or who is capable of entertaining such intent, sees in the punishment by the penalty of death only an example of rendering evil for evil under the sanction of a law which is supposed to accord with the sentiment of the people who constitute the State. If it is right for the State to act upon the principle of rendering evil for evil, why should not he act upon the same principle? If he is capable of contemplating the de struction of a human life by his own hand, without such a feeling of horror as to deter him from committing so enor- mous a crime, it is not to be supposed that the decapitation or strangling of a malefactor by the authority of the State will have any salutary effect upon him. On the contrary, as the facts of history clearly show, the only effect such an ex- ample has upon this class of men, is to familiarize in them the homicidal thought, and incite them to the commission of murderous deeds.

Sir Wm. Blackstone in his Commentaries on the laws of England (A.D. 1765), in treating of capital punishment and its effects as a means of diminishing crime, asks, " Was the vast territory of all the Russias worse regulated under the late Empress Elizabeth than under her more sanguinary predeces- sors? Is it now under Catherine II. less civilized, less social, less secure?" " And yet," he says, " we are assured that neither of these illustrious princesses have, throughout their whole administration, inflicted the penalty of death ; and the latter has, upon full persuasion of its being useless, nay, even pernicious, given orders for abolishing it entirely throughout her extensive dominions." . . . " But indeed were capital pun- ishments proved by experience to be a sure and effectual rem- edy (says the learned commentator), that would not prove the necessity (upon which the justice and propriety depend) of inflicting them upon all occasions when other remedies fail."

# CHAPTER V.

## OF THE PROPER TREATMENT AND DISCIPLINE OF PERSONS CONVICTED OF CRIME.

HAVING attempted to point out the injustice and ineffi-
ciency of definite sentences for crime under our present
system, the alternative suggested is that of a system of indefinite sentences, with or without some maximum limit of
time.   This is not a new idea in theory, nor a new thing in
practice, and we are prepared to say, from reliable information on this subject, that wherever this system has been
adopted and intelligently put in operation, the results have
been in a high degree satisfactory.

But in order to accomplish the beneficial results which it
is capable of yielding in diminishing crime by the reformation of such offenders as are capable of being reformed, and
restraining those who cannot be reclaimed, it is an indispensable prerequisite that suitable prisons or reformatories shall
be provided with all necessary appliances for the work designed to be accomplished.   The places, their surroundings
and appointments, and the teachers and managers must all
be adapted to the ends designed to be accomplished.   That
our county jails are adapted to the purposes designed, no
one acquainted with the subject will assume.   From what
we have said, and quoted from the opinions of those most
competent to judge, it is evident that they are not only unfit
places for criminals under sentence, but that most if not all
of them are nurseries of crime.   If properly constructed,
with suitable sanitary arrangements, and kept in a cleanly
condition, and with arrangements for separating the sexes,
and those of the same sex who ought not to be allowed to
associate together, they are the proper and most convenient

places for detaining persons suspected of crime, and awaiting trial or sentence. Such prisoners cannot be subjected
to the discipline necessary in the treatment of convicts, nor
required to perform manual labor, either for their own or
the public benefit. The local jails in England are not used
at all as places of punishment, but only of detention while
the prisoner is awaiting trial or sentence. What then shall
be done with such as are convicted of minor offences, and
need the discipline of a prison or reformatory? The answer
which seems to us the most appropriate to this inquiry is,
Let the State provide for the construction of *district prisons
or reformatories*, under the exclusive control of the State
and its agents and officers. For this purpose the State may
be divided into so many districts as shall be deemed necessary, and the institutions be located at the most convenient
and suitable points in each district. Erect substantial and
convenient, but inexpensive, buildings, with arrangements
for the proper classification of the inmates, for their employment in useful labor, and the cultivation of their mental and
moral faculties, as a means of promoting reformation; and
this should be the main purpose and aim of the State in the
management of these institutions, and pecuniary profits a
minor consideration. In a paper on the county jails read
by Hon. Levi Barbour at a convention of the Board of
Corrections and Charities of Michigan in 1884, in which
the evils of our present jail system are graphically described,
he earnestly recommends that they be made houses of detention only where persons charged with crime can be detained until trial, and that all prisoners detained therein be
entirely isolated from each other; and that district workhouses shall be provided under State control, to which all
prisoners convicted of petty offences shall be sent on conviction and kept at hard labor. He also recommends that
the terms of all jailers, superintendents of workhouses, and
wardens of prisons shall continue during good behavior

and efficiency; and that all such institutions shall be removed from the hands of politicians and party influence;
and in our opinion the importance of these proposed changes
cannot be too strongly urged upon the attention of the people,
and especially of our legislators.

Under a judicious classification of the prisoners, the cottage or family system in the district prisons or reformatories
should, we think, be a prominent feature of the institution,
as affording a means of inspiring self-respect and manliness
of character.

The kinds of labor carried on at these reformatories may
be various, but of course should be such as are best calculated to fit the operators for obtaining an honest living when
restored to their freedom. The grounds should be so extensive that market gardening, perhaps general farming to
some extent, with horticulture and floriculture, may be pursued by such of the prisoners as prove themselves worthy
to be trusted with sufficient freedom for that purpose, and
as are adapted to such pursuits. Various mechanical trades
should be taught and carried on, and all who are capable of
doing so should be required to perform a reasonable amount
of labor daily, as well for the physical and moral improvement of the prisoner as for contributing to the expenses of
their support and instruction. Since the practicability of
reforming the younger classes of offenders has come to be
admitted and has been demonstrated by experiments, and the
interest and duty of the State to provide the means of such
reformation has been recognized and acted upon by the legislatures of several of the States, reformatory institutions
have been established for the accomplishment of this most
humane and beneficent purpose. An inspection of these
institutions and a careful inquiry into their management
and methods of procedure will afford the best means of
gaining the necessary information in regard to the most
suitable buildings, their arrangement with reference to the

objects to be attained, and the details of their management, to enable the agents of the State to devise and construct, with such variations as may be required to adapt them to the ends to be secured, suitable and convenient structures for all the reformatory institutions that may be required. A fact in reference to the institution of separate prisons for juvenile offenders is worthy of especial note, as showing the vast progress which has been made towards the adoption of the "Moral System" in the treatment of this class of criminals. It is that when first established they were in every respect prisons, with high walls, and bars and bolts and prison cells, and guards to prevent escape. The youthful wrong-doers were assumed to be desperately wicked, and were punished accordingly. But when the idea dawned upon the minds of those who had charge of them, that the boys might be reformed and made good citizens by moral means, all was soon changed. The prison walls were torn down, bolts and bars and cells dispensed with, and the prison turned into a school for educating and training them for usefulness. One of the most conspicuous examples of the beneficent effects of this radical change occurred at Rauen Haus, near Hamburg, of which the Rev. Calvin E. Stowe some years ago gave the following account:

"Hamburg is the largest commercial city in Germany, and its population is extremely crowded. Though it is highly distinguished for its benevolent institutions, and for the hospitality and integrity of its citizens, yet the very circumstances in which it is placed produce among the lowest class of its population habits of degradation and beastliness of which we have few examples on this side of the Atlantic. The children, therefore, received into this institution are of the very worst and most hopeless character. Not only are their minds most thoroughly depraved, but their very senses and bodily organizations seem to partake of the viciousness and degradation of their hearts. Their appetites are so perverted that sometimes the most loathsome and disgusting substances are preferred to wholesome food. The superintendent, Mr. Wichern, states that, though plentifully supplied with provisions, yet, when first received, some of them will steal and eat rancid grease that has been laid aside for the purpose of greasing shoes, and even catch May-bugs and devour them; and it was with the utmost difficulty that those disgusting habits were broken up."

"The place was a prison," says Dr. Buchanan in "The New Education," "when he took it. He threw down the high walls, and took away the bars and bolts. He made the children love him, and he converted them into estimable characters." Horace Mann says of this institution, "The effect attested the almost omnipotent power of generosity and affection. Children from seven or eight to fifteen or sixteen years of age, in many of whom early and loathsome vices had nearly obliterated the stamp of humanity, were transformed, not only into useful members of society, but into characters that endeared themselves to all within the sphere of their acquaintance. The children were told at the beginnnig that labor was the price of living, and that they must earn their own bread. . . . Charity had supplied the home to which they were invited—their own industry must do the rest." At the great Hamburg fire, it is said that these boys acted like heroes, but refused all compensation, and after the fire gave up their provisions and beds to the sufferers. At the reformatory farm school of Mettray, in France, says Dr. Buchanan, founded by Judge Demitz for children who were condemned in Court for their crimes, a similar system was pursued, and the number of children thoroughly reformed was about eighty-five per cent. of all.

In England reformatories for youthful offenders have been a success. The reformatory farm school at Red Hill, in Surrey, takes charge of youths who are convicted of crime, or who are the children of felons. They are so successful that they impose no restraint or confinement, and their schools are as orderly and well-behaved as the schools patronized by the better classes.

In the American reformatories for juvenile offenders a similar method is adopted, and instead of being prisons they are schools in which no more restraint is imposed than in ordinary schools, and it is very seldom that an escape is attempted ; and they afford wonderful examples of what can be accomplished by the " Moral System" of treatment. The Ohio State Reform School was located on an open farm, surrounded by forest, offering every facility for escape. Mr. Howe, the manager of the school, related an incident at the Prison Reform Congress, in St. Louis, in 1874, which forcibly illustrates the efficacy of moral power in the management of youthful criminals. He said that on one occasion his heart sunk in momentary despair and alarm when, on a dark night, the boys, having just come from the chapel, started off with a sudden impulse for the woods, and left him alone to meditate on disappointments. It was not long, however, after their voices had been lost, before he heard them again emerging from the forest with the cry, " We've got him! we've got him !" A rough young convict, recently arrived, thought the dark night offered a fine opportunity for escape, and started off at full speed. His comrades pursued and captured him, and brought him back. Such was the general sentiment of the school that the boys would not favor or tolerate running away. In this institution none are received but youths convicted of crime.

It is stated that " Since the establishment of this reform school in 1858, about two thousand of these criminal youths have been received, and all but a very small percentage have been restored to virtue, having earned an honorable discharge by good deportment for a sufficient length of time to satisfy their teachers that they are really reformed."

This school occupied nearly twelve hundred acres of

elevated hilly land, with buildings capable of accommodating about five hundred boys,—a main building one hundred and sixty-one feet long, eight family buildings, four
large shop buildings, a chapel, barns, and other buildings. ⅄

"In this healthy and pleasant home," says Dr. Buchanan,
"they are received and managed with unwearied kindness
and love, and carried through a course of moral instruction
perhaps the most complete and efficient that has ever been
successfully applied on so large a scale. If there is in our
country any better system of *intellectual, moral, and practical
education* happily combined, I am not aware of it. So perfect is the system that, although they receive so many young
criminals from jails, they have no jail, no prison walls, no
bolted gates, but occupy an open farm in the forest, where
the boys are as free as in any country academy, and are
often sent to the village or the mill without any guards;
and there are fewer escapes than from other institutions
where boys are kept strictly as prisoners within high walls
and bolted doors."

In the year 1855 the Legislature of Michigan provided
for the establishment of a "House of Correction for Juvenile
Offenders, including both sexes," which was declared to be
for the instruction and reform of juvenile offenders, and
entirely disconnected with the State penitentiary. A board
of control of this institution was provided for, and it was to
be located at or near Lansing, providing that a suitable
piece of land, of not less than twenty acres, should be
donated for that purpose. The land was donated, and the
institution located near Lansing, and prison buildings were
erected as required by the act of the legislature. The
original act contemplated the confinement in this institution
of all who at the time of their conviction should be under
the age of fifteen years, and such others so convicted between the ages of fifteen and twenty years as the courts
pronouncing sentence should deem fit subjects therefor, for

the term of their imprisonment, to be designated in their sentence, not exceeding the limitation of imprisonment prescribed by law. The board of control was authorized to bind any such offenders to any suitable person residing within the State who would engage to instruct such offender in some proper art or trade, when such offender should be so far reformed as to justify his or her discharge.

In 1857 the legislature made some amendments to the former act, one of which made it the duty of the board of control to " prepare and carefully digest and mature a system of government for said house of correction for juvenile offenders, embracing all such rules, regulations, and general laws as may be necessary for preserving order, for enforcing discipline, for imparting instruction, for preserving health, and generally for the proper physical, intellectual, and moral training of the offenders ;" and for the purpose of enabling them to mature such system of government and discipline, the board was given power to authorize one of their number to visit similar institutions then in operation, and of the best repute ; to acquire an insight into the principles and practical working of the model system thus selected, for the information and benefit of said board. The subsequent action of the legislature, and of the board of control, attest the wisdom of these provisions. In 1879 the name of the institution was changed to that of " Reform School."

In 1861 it was made a school for boys only between the ages of seven and sixteen years who were convicted of any offence punishable by fine or imprisonment, or both, excepting such as were punishable for life. At the present time only boys over ten and under sixteen years of age are received, and those between these ages are sentenced, on conviction, to the reform school until they respectively reach the age of eighteen years, or until discharged by law. The board of control may place any of the boys of the school in the care of any resident of the State who is the head of a

*p*

family and of good moral character, on such conditions and with such stipulations as it may establish; but no boy can be placed in the care of any person engaged in the sale of intoxicating drinks, or who is in the habit of getting drunk. If any boy sentenced to the reform school is deemed by the board to be an improper subject for its care and management, or is found to be incorrigible, or who ought from any cause to be returned from said school, it may return such boy to the place from whence he came, to be dealt with as if he had not been sent to said school. The board may, when it deems it expedient, give any of the boys leave of absence in writing, with conditions therein expressed, for a limited period, or during good behavior; and in case of misconduct or other satisfactory reasons, they may be reclaimed and returned to the school without other trial or process of law. The board also has power to return any boy to his parents or guardian, on sufficient surety being given for the good behavior and care of such boy.

This institution was used as *a prison* for a few years only, when "all bars and bolts, cells and whips" were abandoned. "No unsightly fence shuts away the beautiful world without, as the love of home keeps our boys within its sheltering arms. The boys are generally contented," says the board of control, "and realize to a great degree the fact that the Reform School supplies for them a real need, and furnishes for most of them a better home than they had been accustomed to before their admittance here."

At the conference of county agents of the Board of Corrections and Charities, in December, 1885, Mr. Gower, the superintendent, made a statement in regard to this institution, in which he said, "The reform school is about twenty-eight years old, and was originally established as a 'House of Correction for Juvenile Offenders,'—a boy's prison with all the adornments of a full-fledged penal institution. The character of the institution has been much changed during the past ten years, and we believe greatly to the advantage of those committed to its care. Most of our boys are now in cottages, where there is an entire absence of anything to suggest that the institution is at all penal in its character, and where, as far as possible, it is intended that the boys shall have the surroundings, comforts, discipline, and instruction of a good home. In each of these cottages we have fifty boys under the care of a man and his wife. The wife is teacher of the family school, while the husband is employed during the day working with the boys upon the farm or in the shops. Experience in our own and other institutions has taught that boys in an institution can be more judiciously trained and educated when divided into families than is possible in the 'congregate plan' formerly in vogue throughout the country, and still retained in city institutions.

"We have at present four hundred and fifty boys in the school between the ages of ten and eighteen years; the average is about thirteen years and ten months; the average time of remaining in the school is about twenty-two months.

"Our boys have ten hours each day to sleep, four and a half hours for school, four and a half for work, and the other five hours for meals and recreation. On Sunday we have services in the chapel, conducted by some clergyman from the city, and a Sunday-school. When the weather will allow, many of the boys attend church in town, where they are always welcome.

"The industries of the school are largely those necessarily and directly connected with the work of the institution,—viz., the preparation of food, laundry work, making and mending clothes, bedding, and shoes, caring for the buildings and grounds, and work upon the farm. Besides this, many of the smaller boys are engaged in chair-caning. We hope soon to be able to introduce some mechanical industries which will be helpful in enabling us to put our boys upon a self-supporting basis when they leave us. As it now is, at least fifty boys each year go out from our tailor-shop, shoe-shop, bake-shop and engine-room, well prepared to earn a living by the trade they have learned while in the school, and as many more go to live with farmers, having acquired a taste for that work during their stay with us.

"During the past three or four years we have released many boys on 'leave of absence,' and with the happiest results. By this plan we are able to release conditionally many boys whom we would not feel warranted in granting a full discharge. In case a boy thus released does not do well, or is not properly cared for, he can be immediately returned to the institution. One hundred and twenty-six boys have been granted leave of absence during the past year, most of whom have gone with farmers and are doing well."

In his report to the Board of Control, in 1884, Mr. Gower says, "We are happy to say, not boastingly, but in simple justice to the institution, and for the encouragement of those who are interested in our work, that, for every instance brought to our notice where our boys have failed to do well after leaving us, we could name at least five who are honorable and worthy members of society.

"It is one of the most pleasing and encouraging experiences of our work that we are frequently receiving letters and calls from those who left the institution years ago, and are now filling positions of honor and trust in the communities where they reside."

The advantages growing out of the teaching of mechanical industries in our reform schools, both to those who are taught there and to the State, cannot be overlooked if the best results are to be obtained. If the boys are sent out without the knowledge of some useful trade or occupation by which they can gain an honest living, especially if they have no friends able and willing to aid them, they will be

likely to relapse into crime, however good their intentions
may be when discharged from the institution.  This necessity, as we have seen, has been felt and appreciated by those
in control of the Reform School at Lansing, and efforts are
being made to supply the deficiency.

The history of the Industrial School at Rochester, New
York, is instructive on this subject, and as showing the progress made in reformatory institutions within the last few
years.  That institution, like the one at Lansing, was established as a prison for boys convicted of crime, and for several
years bore the name of the " Western House of Refuge."
The labor of the boys was let by contract, and consisted
mainly in seating chairs and making shoes.

At the National Conference of Charities and Correction
in 1887, Mr. L. S. Fulton, superintendent of the school, after
stating the difficulties in the way of introducing a variety of
trades during some fifteen years of his experience as superintendent, says, " I could find no way out of the dilemma
until about two years ago, when I received a communication
from Mr. Litchworth, saying that he was coming to see me
on an important subject.  In a few days he came, and during
a long conversation that I then had with him he told me
about the technological system of the Massachusetts Institute of Technology, in Boston, and said he had a set of their
models.  After he got through I said, ' That is a very practical idea, I would like to have it adopted in this institution.'
We then agreed that we would see the president and secretary and treasurer of the board.  After a conference with
them, it was decided to call a meeting of the board.  A
meeting was held, a committee was appointed to consider
the subject, a favorable report was returned, which was
unanimously adopted by the board, and an appropriation
was asked and granted by the Legislature with which we
established in our institution this technologic idea of trade-
schools." . . . " I had been ambitious," continues Mr. Fulton,

" to accomplish the largest amount of work with the smallest expense, for it was then considered that he was a model superintendent who could do this. I was trying all I could to make these boys earn a large amount of money, so as to make the *per capita* expenditure as small as possible. But I have changed my views. I believe that the cost of maintenance should not be taken into the account. We should be economical in our expenditures, but should not seek to have large earnings. We should try to make what we can *of* the boy, not what we can make *out* of him.

" Our first shop was a carpenter and joiner's; the second, a wood-turner and pattern-maker's; the third, a blacksmith's; the fourth, a bricklayer and plasterer's; and the fifth a foundry. We have already a shoemaker's and tailor's-shop. We have it in contemplation to establish three other industries,—a machine-shop, a drawing-school for free-hand and mechanical and architectural drawing, and the erection of greenhouses to teach floriculture. The shops now in operation are models of their kind."

In these shops the boys are taught by competent instructors who feel a deep interest in the work. " The boys," says Mr. Fulton, " are greatly interested in their work, because they are not working for the State, but for themselves. They are more manly, self-reliant, and cheerful than under the old system. The teacher of carpentry and joinery not only gives instruction in the use of tools, but he tells them all about the lumber that they use; the different kinds and qualities; how pine differs from hemlock, oak, ash, or other timber; what they are used for, and why; how they season, shrink, and warp; such things as a master mechanic never thinks of telling his apprentices. Everything is done by rule, and in a scientific manner. The last half-hour he takes them to a class-room, and gives them an exercise in drawing. They make everything after a drawing, making their own measurements from a scale; plain butt-joints, mitre, dovetail, and blind dovetail-joints, doors, window-frames, newel-posts, brackets, etc.

"We recently erected a laundry, thirty by sixty feet. The entire work of carpentering, joinery, masonry, painting, etc., was done by the boys; and it is as good a building of its kind as there is in Rochester."

After describing the modes of instructing in different trades, Mr. Fulton adds, "Thus they become skilled workmen. Besides this work, they have three and a half hours each day in school, and three more hours for recreation, and they are as cheerful and happy as any like number outside.

"If any of you are interested in reform schools or similar work, let me advise you to go to work at once and convince your board of managers or directors of the practicability of teaching your boys trades; transform your institutions into schools of technology, where you will not only educate the head, but the hands also, and make of your boys skilled workmen at some trade or calling, sending them out armed and equipped to fight life's battles honorably and successfully, and to become self-reliant, self-respecting, and self-supporting citizens."

Boys are committed to this institution for an indefinite time, and may be held during their minority. But the board of managers have the power to discharge a boy, when they believe it is for the best interest of the boy, his parents, and the State to do so. Each boy is allowed to learn what he is best adapted for. Most of them learn to do very good work in six to eight months. They learn very much more rapidly under the system of instruction adopted in the school than they could from imitation.

The institutions of which some account has been given above, and institutions of like character in other States and countries, are designed for the reformation of youthful offenders, and not for adults. But the general principles upon which they are conducted may be applied to the conduct of district prisons or reformatories for the treatment or discipline of older offenders, who are convicted of crimes and misdemeanors not punishable by imprisonment in the penitentiary. That a majority of such offenders may, by judicious treatment, be transformed into good citizens we can entertain no doubt.

Dr. Buchanan, referring to the reports of the commissioners of the Ohio Reform School, says, " It is an encouraging fact, too, as stated in the report of 1870, that instead of finding reformation more difficult with the older boys, they have been more successful in establishing their moral principles, for, having more strength of character, they take a firmer hold of good principles. In this fact I think we have great encouragement to believe that many of the still older criminals who are confined in State penitentiaries will prove good subjects for moral reform when they receive the benefit of a similar institution.

" Indeed, I think this was fully proved by the experience of Burnham Wardwell, superintendent of the Virginia State Prison, a man whom nature designed for the management and reformation of criminals. I think we owe a much deeper debt of gratitude to moral heroes in an humble sphere than to many whom the world honors.

" Fellenburgh at Hofwyl, Mr. Wichem at Hamburg, Mr. Howe and his associates at Lancaster, and Mr. Burnham Wardwell in the Virginia prison, are the men we should love and honor. Mr. Wardwell is not an educated man, but he has the genius of reformatory love. He treated the prisoners as brothers, and instead of governing them by handcuffs and bayonets, he dismissed his guards and brought the six hundred and fifty prisoners unchained and unguarded into the chapel to hear the fervid appeals of a truly Christian minister. He so elevated their sense of honor that he could trust them anywhere, and often sent them out of prison with no escort but his little son.   He tells an amusing story of a party whom he allowed to leave the prison and make a donation visit to their chaplain.   One of his fiercest prisoners carried a long sharp knife for his donation, and when asked about it on the return of the party, he said he would have cut the throats of any who would have attempted to run off."

The institution for the discipline of adult offenders which has attracted the largest share of public attention is the reformatory at Elmira in the State of New York, under the superintendency of Mr. Z. R. Brockway, a man of large experience, broad and liberal views, and indomitable energy and perseverance in the work of reformation, to which his life is consecrated.

In an article by Charles Dudley Warner, entitled "A Study of Prison Management," published in the *North American Review* for April, 1885, he gives a somewhat detailed account of this institution, its management, and the result claimed to have been attained therefrom.   Mr. Warner says, "Here is an experiment in the personal treatment of convicts, unique, so far as I know, in the world." The reformatory is described as "a somewhat pretentious building, situated upon an eminence. . . . In point of arrangement, light, air, roominess, ventilation, etc., it conforms to modern notions.   It is as little gloomy and depressing as a place of penal confinement can be.   What distinguishes it, however, is that it is provided with school-rooms sufficient for the accommodation of all its inmates.   And it is, as we shall see, a great educational establishment, the entrance to which is through the door of crime.   The key-note of it is compulsory education.   The qualifications for admission to it are that the man convicted of a State-prison offence shall be between the ages of sixteen and thirty, and that he has not been in State prison before.   In his discretion any judge in the State may send a convict of this description to Elmira.

He is sentenced to the reformatory, subject to the rules of the institution, not for a definite time; but he cannot be detained there longer than the maximum for which he might have been sentenced under the law. For instance, if for burglary he might have been sentenced to the State prison for ten years, he may be held at Elmira for ten years; but he may, in the discretion of the board of managers, who are appointed by the governor, be discharged in one year.

" The institution is practically managed by the superintendent. The discharges are made only by the board, who consider the man's record in the prison, and the probabilities, from all the evidence concerning him, that he will behave if set at liberty. He must have a perfect record before the board consider his case; and, besides this, the board must have confidence in his will and ability to live up to it."

Mr. Warner states the course of a man's institutional life in the reformatory as follows: " Upon his reception he is subjected to a bath, clad in the plain suit that is worn by the intermediate grade, and locked up in a cell for a day or two, to give him time for reflection. He is then taken before the superintendent, who makes a thorough examination of him,—a complete diagnosis of his physical, mental, and moral condition. His antecedents are ascertained, the habits and occupation of his parents (and grandparents if possible), whether they were temperate or intemperate, lived cleanly and honestly, or otherwise; what the man's home-life was, if he had any, and at how early years he was turned loose upon the world; what had been his habits and associations up to the commission of the crime for which he was sentenced. An examination is then made of his physical condition, his inheritances, and not simply the actual state of his health, but his physical texture, whether fine or coarse-grained. His intellectual capacity is next ascertained, and then his acquirements. Is he bright or dull, can he

read and write, and how far has his education gone? Inquiry is then made into his moral condition. Has he any
sensibility, any shame, any susceptibility to praise or blame?
What sort of moral fibre has he? After a keen investigation of an hour or so, Mr. Brockway thoroughly knows his
man. Long practice and a very deep knowledge of human
nature enable him to diagnose the case pretty accurately.
The subject finds himself in the presence of a man who
probably wins his confidence, and who, he may soon discover, it is of no use to try to deceive. The result of this
searching examination is entered at length on the page of
a big ledger; the superintendent commonly outlines at the
bottom the proposed treatment; and the new-comer is instructed in the rules of the institution, and what is expected
of him, and what he must do in order 'to get out.'

"He goes at first into the second or intermediate grade,
and it depends upon himself whether up to the first or down
to the third. He is made to understand the minute rules
of behavior that he must attend to; he is assigned to the
class in school fitted to his capacity and acquirements, and
he is put into the workshop that is best adapted to his
health and training. He is informed of the maximum time
for which he can be detained, and that he can, by perfect
conduct in these lines of effort, win his release in one year.
To effect this he must gain a certain number of credit
marks, and these credit marks are constantly liable to be
cancelled by negligence or ill behavior. He is tested at
every step by the mark system. In the shop he is marked
according to his diligence, his sharp attention to his work,
his voluntariness at his labor. If he is listless, slights his
work, and does not give his mind and energy to it, he not
only misses credit marks, but will get discredit marks.
There is no escape for him; he must work with a will. In
behavior he must be perfect in obedience to the many and
minute rules laid down, of which he is furnished a printed

copy.  In school he is required to study according to his
capacity, and the marking is much the same as in a well-
regulated high school.  But while he must be perfect in
work and behavior, he will pass in school if he gains 75 in
the scale of 100.  As soon as he enters upon this course
of discipline and study an account is opened with him in
another big ledger."

The process of his release is stated to be this : " If he is
reported perfect in three things, labor, school, and conduct,
—for each of which three marks are required each month,
making nine in all for six months,—he is advanced to the
first grade,  If he remains perfect in the first grade for six
months more, gaining nine good marks each month, he
may then, at the discretion of the managers, be sent on his
parole.  But he is not released on parole until a place is
found for him in which he can get employment and earn
his living.  If his friends cannot find a place for him, or he
will not be received back into his former employment, if he
had any, the institution places him by means of correspondence.  On parole he must report his conduct and condition
every month to the superintendent, and this report must be
indorsed by some one of known character.  If the paroled
continues to behave himself for six months, he receives his
final discharge; if he backslides he is rearrested, brought
back, and must begin over again.

" The grades are three, and they mark considerable difference in privileges.  The first-grade men wear a light-blue
uniform with a military cap.  They occupy better cells than
the others.  They dine together in the large mess-room, at
small tables, accommodating from eight to twelve, and are
permitted to talk freely and to spend the noon hour in social
intercourse.  Up till recently a summary of the news of the
day, culled from the newspapers, was read to them once a
week at table, but there is a substitute for that now.  They
have somewhat better food than the other grades.  When

they march from cells to work-shops, to dining-room, etc., they march in columns of four, and they are officered by cap· tains and sergeants, chosen by the superintendent from theii own number. Monitors in the corridors, clerks, and officers for the next grade are chosen from them. Besides these privileges, a measure of confidence is reposed in them, but they are also under strict discipline, and are liable to be degraded for neglect of duty or failure to report delinquencies in their capacity as monitors and sub-officers.

" The second or intermediate grade wear citizens' dress, with Scotch caps. They march in columns of two, officered by members of the first grade. They take their meals in their cells, and have generally less privileges than the first grade. The third, or convict grade, wear suits of red clothes, eat in their cells, march in the degraded prison lock-step, are officered by officers of the institution, and in various ways are made to feel the dishonor of their position and greater rigors of prison life. It should be noted that the three grades mingle in the workshops and in the schools, for they take places in them on other standards than that of conduct.

" Eight hours a day labor is required, and the evenings are devoted to the schools. The various branches of an English education are thoroughly taught, mostly by able men outside of the institution, while some classes are conducted by inmates. Their education also embraces political economy, and such a knowledge of the law and the government of society as is necessary to make them intelligent citizens. The end kept in view in history, elementary law and morals, political economy, etc., is the fitting of the student to play his part well as a citizen, and to be an orderly member of society. These tend to broaden his view of life and his interest in it as an orderly process, and to discipline his perverted faculties. This is often very difficult. These are not normal minds or dispositions. By inheritance or bad practice their natures are warped. Most of them have neither the knowledge nor the will to do right.

"It is a mistake to suppose that criminals are naturally bright. The moral failure has affected the intellect in most cases. If they are bright, it is usually in a narrow line, the development of a ferret-like cunning and smartness. They lack intellectual breadth as they do moral stability. . . . They are, in short, in an abnormal condition, and any real growth or reformation must be radical, built up from the foundation. The skill of the superintendent is shown in awakening the interest, in arousing hope and ambition, and in creating a moral steadiness of will."

At the time of Mr. Warner's visit to the reformatory it contained a little over six hundred prisoners, and all working and studying at first under the strong incentive of gaining their liberty, but gradually becoming deeply interested in the subjects of their study and labor, and stimulated by the hope of attaining the means of living honestly, and of being respected as good and intelligent citizens. "Sunday morning," says Mr. Warner, "the casuistry or morality class meets in the chapel. This numbers about two hundred, and is selected from all grades, according to intellectual brightness and attainments. It is for the discussion of questions of morals and the conduct of life. The men all take notes, for they must pass a written examination upon what they hear. The conductor reads or lectures, and free but orderly discussion takes place. The first Sunday the writer was present they were concluding the reading of Socrates. Each man had a printed syllabus of the morning's reading, and questions propounded. The next Sunday would be a review preparatory to examination. Each man took notes as the reading went on. Questions were asked and opinions given, the interlocutor raising his hand, and rising when recognized by the lecturer. Such absorbed attention I have seldom seen in a class-room. . . . Never was compulsory education so completely applied. But it must be confessed in this case that the class had got thoroughly interested in the subject. The expression of their faces was that of aroused intelligence. Nothing seemed lost on the majority of them; the finest points made by Socrates, his searching moral distinctions, his humor, you could see were taken instantly by the expression of their faces. The discussions and essays in this class show a most remarkable grasp, subtilty, penetration, and power of drawing fine moral distinctions, and the vigor and fitness of the language in which they are couched are not the least notable part of the display.

"The previous Sunday there had been a lively discussion of the question, 'Is honesty the best policy?' The study of the morality of Socrates led the class naturally, and by their request, to a study of the morality of Jesus and the New Testament, though not at all as a religious inquiry; and thus a result was reached in moral investigation that a clergyman, beginning at the other end, probably never could have brought this mixed and abnormal class to attempt willingly.

"The reformatory is a busy place; it has the aspect, as I said, of a great industrial and educational establishment. What first impresses one accustomed to visit prisons is the aroused physical life. The old convict heaviness and hopeless inertness of flesh are gone,—gone with the depressing hang-dog look. The men work, move about, run up and down stairs with alertness and vigor and apparent enjoyment of motion. We see here the well-known criminal type of head, but the expression of face is altogether changed; stupidity and hopelessness have given place to intelligence and ambition. The change is astonishing. New life has been awakened all through the mass; and the mental and physical activity, first aroused by the desire to get out, has now, in a large number of prisoners, passed into a desire to know something and to be somebody."

The contrast these men presented to the inmates of the penitentiaries is shown by the account which Mr. Warner gives of visits which he had then recently made to two New England prisons,—viz., one of the old type at Wethersfield, Connecticut, which he describes as "an old and ram-shackle establishment, patched up from time to time, and altogether a gloomy and depressing place. It is, however," says Mr. Warner, "well managed; it is made to pay about its running expenses; many of the modern alleviations of prison life are applied there,—a library, occasional entertainments, a diminution of the sentence for good conduct, and so on,—whatever such a place is capable of in the way of comfort consistent with the system. But the inmates are the most discouraging feature of the exhibition. They are in appearance depressed, degraded, down-looking, sluggish; mentally, and morally tending to more degradation. There is no hope or suggestion of improvement within. The discipline is good, and the men earn time by good conduct, but there are no evidences that the alleviations (which take from the former terrors of prison life) are working the least moral change. It is a most depressing and dispiriting sight."

He also visited the State prison at Cranston, Rhode Island, which he described as "a new, handsome granite building with the modern improvements. Perfectly lighted and ventilated, with roomy cells, a common mess-room, and admirable hospital, a more than usually varied dietary, with a library, and all the privileges that humanity can suggest as consistent with discipline and security, it is as little gloomy and depressing as a State prison can well be. Having occasion to look into this matter officially, I confess that I expected to find at Cranston a very different state of affairs from that existing at Wethersfield. The improved physical condition ought to show some moral and physical uplift in the men. I was totally disappointed. Here were

the same hang-dog, depressed, hopeless, heavy lot of convicts. The two prisons might change inmates and no visitor
would know the difference."

This contrast is certainly very marked, and the cause of
it very apparent to those who have made a study of crime
and its treatment. The two systems are wholly unlike in
their aims and methods, and the results are as different as
darkness from light. Under the system of definite sentences
the prisoner is paying the allotted penalty of his crime;
under the reformatory system the prisoner is working out
his own salvation with all the moral aids that can be applied
to effect his cure and restore him to the condition of honorable manhood. Under the former system the prisoner is
*punished and turned loose to commit other crimes;* while under
the latter he may be honorably discharged, with the strong
probability that he will not only abstain from the commission
of crime thereafter, but that he will exert a good moral
influence that will tend to the prevention of crime. That
" depraved, degraded, down-looking, physically sluggish appearance, mentally and morally tending to more and more
degradation," described by Mr. Warner, characterizes the
inmates of all our penitentiaries, whereas in all our reformatories stupidity and hopelessness give place to intelligence
and ambition.

Of those sent to the Elmira reformatory, a certain percentage are incorrigible. Mr. Warner says, " It is believed,
however, that this percentage could be greatly reduced by
universal indeterminate sentences, giving a longer time to
work on obdurate natures."

He further says, " The reformatory has been in operation eight years. The *morale* of it has been gradually
changing for the better. At first the heroes (as in other
prisons) were the biggest, sharpest, most successful rogues.
The standard has changed. These men are no longer
looked up to. There is a considerable *esprit du corps* of

good conduct and progress, and goodness and intellect are respected. There is a strong moral influence among the inmates themselves in favor of good order and good conduct."

The reports show that eighty per cent. of those who go out from this institution are reformed. The men are closely watched for six months after they go out, and a general run of many of them is kept afterwards. "In many cases," says Mr. Warner, "where a man would probably prefer an honest life, he is so morally debilitated by inheritance and indulgence that it takes a long time to build up in him enough moral stamina to carry him along safely through life; and the time of detention is too short. This result—eighty per cent. put in a better way—is astonishing when we remember that of those ordinarily discharged from State prison, sixty per cent. have to be caught and imprisoned again."

A fact in regard to those who are sentenced to this reformatory is noticed by Mr. Warner, which tends to show the diseased and perverted condition of those who are disposed to pursue a criminal course of life. He says, "I was at first surprised to learn that men do not like to be sent to this institution; many of them, perhaps most of them, would prefer to go to the regular State prison. Their whole nature revolts against the idea of discipline, of study, of reform. They like crime and an irregular life, and they hate any influences to turn them away from it. They hate the notion of behaving, as some boys out of prison hate moral restraint and religious instruction. They resent the pressure as long as they can; and some of them, of course, never do surrender, and go out unregenerate."

The evidences of this abnormal and diseased condition are stamped upon their countenances, and may be read as easily by the adept in the science of human nature as the physician reads the evidence of physical disease in its recognized symptoms.

" As to economy," says Mr. Warner, " I notice by the report that the Elmira reformatory does not pay. Its inmates earn by labor from sixty thousand to seventy-five thousand dollars a year, but the State has to appropriate annually about thirty thousand dollars to carry it on. It is money well spent; for it would cost the State in cash a good deal more than thirty thousand dollars a year to catch, try, and send to prison those who would repeat felonies on being discharged, if these men followed the state-prison rules. And this does not take into account the depredations they would commit, the injury to individuals, their bad moral influence, and the cost of police to catch them. With such results, the Elmira reformatory is worthy of the most thoughtful attention of tax-payers, as well as sociologists."

Had the thousands of juvenile offenders, who have been saved from a life of crime through the education and discipline of reform schools, been sentenced to jail or the penitentiary for definite periods, as adults now are under our present system of punishment, the amount of crime they would have committed, and the expense attending their repeated arrests, trials, and convictions, would have been enormous; and the injury to individuals, and the demoralizing influence of their conduct upon society could not be computed. If, therefore, we consider the reformatory system in its economical aspect, it seems very certain that it must result in a very large financial gain to the State; but if we also consider the good that is done to the class of offenders treated, by transforming them into useful, law-abiding citizens, and the moral influence of their future lives upon society, instead of the evil which they would otherwise have effected, the advantage derived from it is incalculable.

To realize the benefits that such institutions are intended to yield, and are capable of producing when wisely conducted, it is indispensable that men be found who are qualified by nature and habit for their management and superintendence. No one doubts the fitness and adaptability of Wichern, Stowe, Gower, Fulton, Brockway, and Wardwell to conduct the several institutions of which they have had charge, for they have proven their fitness by their success. But these positions require a combination of very rare and exceptional qualities, physical, mental, and moral; a commanding presence, a sound judgment, and a moral force capable of subduing the fiercest nature, and with a heart full of human sympathy and kindness towards all, and especially towards those under his care. To all these must be added business tact, experience, and skill, with a general knowledge of all branches of education and of all the trades and manual occupations carried on in the institution. It is not strange, therefore, that the inquiry should suggest itself, whether others can be found to fill their places successfully when these men become incapacitated.

Mr. Warner, in view of the manifold duties performed by the superintendent of the Elmira reformatory, and the complicated details of its management, after remarking that the experiment was unique, so far as he knew, in the world, says, " I suppose it is an open question whether anybody except Mr. Brockway could carry it on." The importance of this experiment in reforming criminals cannot be overestimated. It appears to us to present one of the great questions of the age, if not the greatest, and it would be a startling proposition if it were admitted that success or failure depended upon any one man. We have no apprehensions upon that score. Every beginning of a good and useful thing is the assurance of its completion. Watt discovered the fact that steam was a force, but others applied it to the uses of men. Arkwright invented the spinning-jenny, but others improved and applied it. So every valuable invention and discovery has laid the foundation for new inventions and discoveries, and men are constantly becoming qualified to take up and carry forward the work which their predecessors had left uncompleted. Mr. Brockway is a man of broad views and keen perceptions, with extraordinary capabilities for organizing and managing such an institution, and with the experience he had gained as the superintendent of the Detroit House of Correction, and his observation of the working of reform schools for juvenile offenders, he was able to organize a full-fledged reformatory for adults, and make it a success. Such men are worthy of all honor, and his labors and example will tend to enable other men to qualify themselves to take up and carry on the work and improve upon it, until the institution will be in a large measure changed to a school instead of a prison, where students of the first grade, if no others, will be allowed the same freedom that is allowed in the reform schools of Ohio and Michigan.

Prominent among those whose names and deeds are worthy of being held in everlasting remembrance was Barwick Baker, of Hardwick Court, Gloucestershire, England, recently deceased. He was a country squire, possessed of large landed estates with an ample income, who devoted his life unsparingly to works of benevolence for ameliorating the condition of mankind. He was active in the preliminary legislation necessary to the establishment of reformatory schools throughout England and Scotland, and one of the first to establish a reformatory school for boys, which he did on his own estate, and which is still in successful operation, having accomplished a vast amount of good at no slight sacrifice to its original projector.

General Brinkerhoff, at the annual Conference of Charities in 1887, said, " In the death of Barwick Baker the world has lost a man who, in some lines of philanthropic work, and in results accomplished, has had no superior and but few equals during the generation in which he lived. From the time he became a magistrate, in 1833, at the early age of twenty-six years, to the time of his death, December 10, 1886, he was identified with every progressive movement in dealing with the dependent or criminal classes, and to his personal and persistent efforts England is largely indebted for her present advanced position upon these subjects."

*The Gloucestershire Chronicle*, published on the day succeeding his death, giving some account of the character and extent of his work, says: "Half a century ago he was appointed a visiting justice of the county jail, and in this apparently not very important though useful office, held by hundreds of other country gentlemen until the prisons were tranferred to the State, is found the 'moving why' of his career of public usefulness. . . . Speaking in a meeting at Gloucester five and thirty years ago, Mr. Baker said that the seeing of children in prison time after time had occasioned him great pain, and he had thought much as to whether it could not be remedied. One day the Hon. Miss Murray, maid of honor to the Queen, called his attention to the possibility of reclaiming vicious children, and said if he would bring to her any child that had sufficient strength of character to distinguish itself in vice, she had no fear that she should not be able to make that child distinguish itself in virtue. She urged him to visit a school then established in London. He did so and became warmly interested in it. Having interested a young friend of his by the name of Burgough, he established a reformatory in a small brick building on his own lands, near his home at Hardwick Court.

"George Henry Burgough was in every respect a worthy coadjutor of a man like Baker. He was only twenty-four years old, and he had in his own right an income of ten thousand pounds a year, and yet for two years he resided in Mr. Baker's little reformatory, and acted as instructor for the young criminals until, broken down by his labors, he went to Florence, in Italy, and died.

"The school at Hardwick was commenced in 1852, the first inmates being three young London thieves brought into the country for treatment. For some time the work was carried on almost secretly, Mr. Baker and Mr. Burgough having misgivings as to their success. Mr. Burgough died; but Mr. Baker persevered, and after a while the results were such as to attract attention, and in 1854 even the *London Times* made note of it, and similar institutions were established; and now all England is covered by reformatories for young criminals, and other nations have followed their example.

" Mr. Baker's work, however, was not confined to juvenile reformatories alone; but, *pari passu*, he carried along to success various other reformatory measures. Perhaps the most important of these was the police supervision of criminals on ticket of leave, which has so largely reduced the volume of crime in England, and which is now beginning to receive acceptance in America."

In all these reformatories the "moral system" of treatment prevails, and the abnormal activity of the lower faculties is overcome, not by punishment, but by the development and cultivation of the moral perceptions; and the demand for competent teachers is everywhere supplied.

In contemplating the wonderful power of the moral and mental forces of the human mind as displayed in the influence they are capable of exerting upon the lives and conduct, and in developing the latent capabilities of others, we find ourselves utterly incapable of assigning any limits to its possibilities. Intellect, operating through the organs of the brain, gathering the rich fruits of knowledge from every field of human research, and inspired by the influx of that divine spirit of love to God and love to humanity which give the light and the wisdom to guide and direct it to the service of mankind, appears almost omnipotent to accomplish any and every conceivable benefit to the human race.

By patience and perseverance, and the skill which is acquired by diligent and oft-repeated experiment, man teaches
the deaf and dumb to converse intelligently with him and
with each other, not only by certain motions or signs, and
by writing, but by oral speech.    He teaches the blind also
to read and write and perform many useful services for
themselves and others.    He teaches the lower animals to
understand and obey him, and to display a marvellous degree of intelligence; and, stranger still, he develops and cul-
tivates mental and moral faculties in idiotic children who seem
scarcely to possess the smallest spark of intellect or reasoning power.    Cruiser, the most vicious and one of the most
powerful horses in England, who had resisted all efforts for
his subjugation by kindness or force until he was regarded
as untamable, was wholly subdued by Mr. Rarey, without
punishment or the use of any cruelty or hardship.    Like
many vicious men, he didn't want to be good, and seemed
determined that he never would be brought under the influence of any other power but that of force.    But when Mr.
Rarey had, by an ingenious device, overcome his physical
power and rendered him incapable of resistance, and then
applied gentle, kindly treatment, though at first against the
strong will that had never been curbed, the latent nobility
of the animal, which had been so long hidden, was aroused,
and he became docile and submissive, and ever after exhibited a strong affection for his conqueror and friend.

The "moral system" of treatment of criminals, while it
excludes all idea of punishment, does not exclude the idea
that force, even to the infliction of some degree of pain, may
be used when necessary, in order to bring the subject of it
under the influence of moral teaching and kindly discipline.
Force may be necessary in his capture and to prevent escape,
and while under treatment to compel obedience to institutional rules and regulations that are intended for the prisoner's benefit and are necessary for the orderly conduct of the

institution. Such force has in it no element of *punishment* or *retribution*, but is applied upon the same principle that the surgeon inflicts pain by the amputation of a limb or the cauterizing of a wound. Mr. Brockway, it is said, in some cases does a little judicious "strapping" or "spanking" with good effect, but it is always done by his own hand, and in such manner and under such circumstances as to engender no feeling of resentment.

When my father used the rod upon my back and shoulders in my boyhood, and I was persuaded that he did so from a sense of parental duty for my benefit, I felt no resentment; but when, at about the age of twelve years, a castigation was administered, apparently more from passion than duty, I felt intensely indignant, and, after receiving the last blow without flinching, demanded the cause of the infliction, and, feeling that there was no sufficient reason for it, I then, in a tone and manner that convinced him that I was deeply in earnest, declared that it was the last flogging but one that I would ever submit to at his hands; and no attempt was ever made afterwards to repeat the experiment. It was in those days the general custom to administer corporal punishment for disobedience or neglect of filial duty, the proverb "He that spareth the rod hateth his son" being constantly kept in remembrance and often repeated. Solomon had said it, and he was wiser than they, and they felt bound to manifest their faith by their works, as did Freeman in seeking to destroy his child; but we have no evidence or belief that any mere punishment ever administered was attended with benefit. It has extorted thousands of promises from children to do better, only to be broken when a new temptation came.

Neither does the "moral system" of treatment afford any sanction or encouragement to the sickly sentimentality which makes heroes of great or small criminals, "and which, under the guise of humanity and philanthropy, confounds all moral distinctions."

"The mawkish sympathy of good and soft-headed women," says Mr. Warner, "with the most degraded and persistent criminals of the male sex is one of the signs of an unhealthy public sentiment. A self-respecting murderer is often compelled to write upon his cards 'No flowers.' This foolish display of weak sentimentalism has been so earnestly condemned, and satirized by the public press to such a degree, that we may earnestly hope that hereafter instances of its existence will be few and far between."

Mr. Hough makes the following very sensible and truthful remarks on the subject of sentimentality towards criminals: "Those who are in control of penal institutions meet with no more pernicious influence than that exerted by certain well-meaning but mistaken philanthropists who are impelled by kindly hearts to slop over with sentiment. No criminal is so hard to reach as the one who fancies himself injured, or has a grievance against society. Aside from treatment that compels him to feel this resentment, there is no one thing that will so quickly bring this feeling as to have some tender-hearted, benevolent person tell him that they think his penalty is far more severe than his offence warrants, especially now that he has promised to pray regularly and abandon his wicked ways."

Crime, including all conscious wrong and injustice done by man towards his fellow-man, is a sad subject to contemplate, and the treatment of criminals is one of the most serious that can occupy the minds of good men and women; and to make it effectual for reformation requires the utmost coolness and deliberation and soundness of judgment, uninfluenced by emotions of sympathy or prejudice. Stern justice, administered in a grave but kind and friendly spirit, rebuking crime but encouraging repentance, and affording hope only through discipline and sincere endeavor, is the greatest mercy, and no encouragement based upon any other condition can benefit the criminal.

If men are able, by the exercise of their mental and moral powers, to exert such a wonderful influence in transforming the characters and conditions of animals and of their own species, it would seem, by parity of reason, that they should also possess the power of reforming men and women addicted to crime, and making good citizens of those who have been enemies to society and themselves. But when it has been demonstrated by successful experiments, as it certainly has been, that a very large portion of our criminals can be reclaimed by processes that are simple, rational, and practical, as well as economical, it would seem to require no argument to convince any of the fact, or that it is the policy of the State to adopt the measures necessary to secure so benign a purpose. To accomplish this requires legislation. Changes of a somewhat radical character in our criminal laws are required. The definite sentence must be abolished and the indeterminate or indefinite substituted in its place, and reformatories provided for to take the place of our penitentiaries, which should be retained only for the confinement of such as may prove to be incorrigible; and these should never be allowed the opportunity of committing further crimes. Under the "moral system" the criminal is treated for the cure of his disease, and the incurable criminal should receive the same care as the incurably insane, and the public be protected alike from the injury that either might do if turned loose upon it; the only difference in the treatment being such as the different character of the disease renders proper. Thus the criminal may be required to labor, which the insane person may not be capable of doing.

Why has not such legislation been had? The Legislature of a State represents the average of public opinion, and follows rather than seeks to lead it, and public opinion has not been educated up to an understanding and appreciation of the vast importance of the great principle involved in the proposed "new departure." The churches have been for ages professedly seeking the conversion and reformation of sinners, and appropriating millions annually for missionary work, and millions of voices have sung in numberless ears the old hymn containing the encouraging assurance that

> " While the lamp holds out to burn,
> The vilest sinner may return ;"

but they have not asked the Legislature to make the sentences of criminals indeterminate, and turn our prisons into schools for the reformation of offenders. Within the last few years conferences of charities and corrections and prison congresses have been held in Europe and America, and hundreds of enlightened philanthropists, including many eminent clergymen, have attended them and advocated reformatory measures, and their proceedings have been published. But a knowledge of what these men have said, and what they are seeking to accomplish, has not been so diffused as to attract the attention of the general public, and they have not had the appreciation which their great importance demanded. Many also, who are satisfied that the system is right in principle, find difficulty in determining what the necessary details shall be, and to what extent changes ought to be made. These obstacles will, we have no doubt, be overcome at no very distant period, and when the system shall be established and perfected so as to become the settled policy of the State, those then living will see, as the English people in their own country have seen, a rapid and most encouraging diminution of the volume of crime and of the number of our prisons in proportion to our population. In an article by Mr. Eugene Hough, published in the first volume of " The Open Court," page 703, some very pertinent remarks are made on the treatment of crime, which are worthy of attention. Mr. Hough says, " Abolish prisons, keepers, and all degrading rules. Institute moral hospitals with trained instructors, with rules that will and may be enforced without destroying self-respect. . . . Abolish the definite sentence; let the patient return into society when he is cured, and not before. Abolish the death-penalty; give all an opportunity of regaining their normal social and moral standing.

"The idea of punishment is as old as history. Old ideas are tenacious of life, but they have to die some time, and the time has now arrived to kill and cremate this heathen idea of punishment. Within the present century many acts were thought deserving of punishment that to-day are thought best to be treated in a scientific manner. The time was when insanity was punished with beating, stoning, and death. Lunatics are not thought to be deserving of punishment to-day; they are subjected to treatment. What makes the difference is that we of to-day recognize the fact that lunatics are not possessed by devils, but are diseased. No one outside of the detective force, who has given two minutes' scientific thought to the subject of crime, but has arrived at the truth that it is a disease—a disease of the morals. Like consumption, it may be inherited or contracted, acute or chronic. Like mental disease, it takes many phases. It may be moral imbecility or moral lunacy, and each divided into numberless forms of the disease, each having a distinct aspect of its own. Acknowledged as a disease, how absurd to think of curing it by punishment! Why not punish a small-pox patient into good health? . . . Little need be said of indeterminate sentences. The protection of society plainly demands that a criminal shall not be let loose until he has recovered the use of his moral powers. No wise judge can foretell how long a time it will take to develop the man's moral faculties sufficient to warrant his being set at liberty. . . . When the wrong-doer has been subjected to the thorough treatment of this reform system, and competent scientists (for it will

---

be a science) have pronounced him a man of sound morals and good enough to be trusted with his freedom, what folly to follow him with social and legal ostracism!"

Mr. Wheeler, in the paper referred to in the last chapter, expresses his views on the treatment of criminals as follows: "Let the criminal understand that his interests are not so important as the public safety; that not his punishment but the public good is aimed at in his confinement; that the length of time that he will remain in prison is altogether uncertain, and depends entirely upon himself; that as soon as he becomes a safe member of society, able and willing to care for himself, and live on his own honest labor, whether in one month or twenty years, he will be released, and no sooner; with the certainty that he will be protected and guarded and guided in efforts to do right, and arrested and imprisoned if he again does wrong, and criminals will fear crime and its consequences where they now laugh at it. . . . No one can say he is confined too long where all depends upon himself. If they cannot feel this and reform, they should be prevented from living on the proceeds of their own crimes.

"The true reformation of a criminal is largely dependent on a discipline that will make him self-controlling and self-reliant. Hard work, kind treatment, and strict discipline, with the idea constantly kept before him that he will be liberated just as soon as he becomes able and willing to live an honest life, will do more to reform than any system now in vogue. . . . Those in charge of the prison can ascertain the prisoner's previous history, his hereditary tendencies, the full history of the crime for which sentenced, his character and conduct in prison, his record in other prisons, if any, and this, with their knowledge of the characteristics and methods of the criminal classes, will enable a decision to be reached as to proper date of discharge."

Having considered the nature and effects of crime and its causes so far as we can discover them, and indicated the principles which, in our opinion, ought to be recognized and adopted in its treatment, there would seem to be no reason for hesitancy on the part of the Legislature in providing for the changes necessary to carry into effect the reformatory system which we have outlined. The success of this system wherever it has been adopted has been so marked as to afford no ground for doubt that its results have been, and must continue to be, in every way beneficial. Among the many reform and industrial schools in Europe and America, model institutions may be found from which all the necessary details of construction, management, instruction, and discipline may be obtained, and there need be no fear that a sufficient number of trained and experienced men cannot be found to properly conduct all reformatory institutions. The great and beneficent purposes and aims of these reformatories, when their institution shall become the settled policy of the State, will inspire an enthusiasm in the grand work that will be everywhere felt, and will engage the attention and command the devotion of the ablest and best men in the country to this service. It will be like the revelation of a new religion to man, embracing all the truths of all historical religions, made clear, simple, and practical, with their errors, superstitions, and mysticisms eliminated, so that the wayfaring man, though a fool, need not err therein, and so that, though a man may not comprehend the law and the prophets, he can understand and obey the two simple commandments of Jesus, upon which "hang all the law and the prophets." It will be a religion of humanity, in which all can agree, whatever speculative opinions they may entertain, and under whose benign influence all can labor together for the common good of all. It points out a practical and rational way of overcoming evil with good, such as the world has never before attempted, or had any proper conception of until within the last few years, and its contemplation, when understood in all its grand proportions and simple harmonies, will fire every righteous soul with zeal for the accomplishment of its benign purposes. It is reverent and devotional, while it is simple and rational. It conflicts with no truths of science or philosophy, but is all-embracing in its lofty aims and purposes of redeeming men and women from sin and folly and leading them into the ways of wisdom, which are the ways of pleasantness, and whose paths are peace. There is no intellect so great, and no character so elevated, that the possessor would not be honored, as well as benefited and ennobled, by engaging in its service.

# ARTICLE IV.

## PREVENTION OF CRIME.

---

## CHAPTER I.

### EDUCATION AS A MEANS OF PREVENTING CRIME.

It is a trite saying that " an ounce of prevention is better than a pound of cure," and there are few that contain more truth and good, practical common sense than this. If our people were all educated as they should be during the period of childhood and youth, by teaching them those things which they ought to know, and surrounding them with protecting influences against those which they ought not to know, there would be little necessity for prisons and reform schools; for character built on a right basis needs no reforming.

Not only the general government, but the several State governments, as we have had occasion to repeat, have recognized their interest in the education of the people for good citizenship, and the public duty of each to provide for the education of its youth. In most of the States education in the primary and high schools is free to all, the schools being supported by a property tax, levied upon the same basis as that for the support of the State and municipal governments, in proportion to the value of taxable property within the district; and we are satisfied, after much reflection upon the subject, that it is the right and the duty of the State to make education compulsory; and if the parents or guardians of children are unable to educate their children or wards, the State should perform that duty for them.

Dr. J. D. Scouller, superintendent of the State Reform School at Pontiac, Illinois, in a paper read before the Eleventh National Conference of Charities and Corrections, discusses the question, "Can we save the Boys?" in which he divides them into three classes, and concludes that all classes of them except the first need to be educated and surrounded with saving influences, as well for promoting the welfare and safety of the community as for the best interests of the boys through every period of their lives.

Dr. Scouller reminds us that "the plan was once tried of having men 'ready made' without the boys." "The man," says Dr. Scouller, "was such a failure that the experiment was never repeated." The first class of boys treated of by the doctor are mostly too good to live, and ninety per cent. of them accordingly die young. The second class are good-hearted, full of life and activity, but full also of impulses that might lead them astray if not guided and controlled by good counsels and proper discipline. The third class, he says, are "the boys who will make our criminals, who will be our law-breakers; the boys who love the world, the flesh, and the devil, . . . the boys who prowl our streets at midnight, whose hands are too soft for manual labor, who are too young and delicate to work, belong to this class. The streets at midnight, and no work, will damn the best boy that ever a mother nursed."

Of the boys who are not blessed with parental care he says, "Many of the Arabs belonging to the community have no such care. They are left to fight the battle of life alone, the world for their step-mother, sorrow their only school-master. It takes far more innate virtue for a boy under such circumstances to grow into an honest, God-fearing man than it does for a boy who is kindly watched and cared for; and, for this very reason, the more loudly comes the Macedonian cry, 'Help us! Help us!' 'What can I do for you?' a lady once asked a weeping orphan. 'Oh,

ma'am, you can aye speak a kind word to me, for I have no
mother like the rest.' If there be no help or kind words
for such boys from good men and women, then 'may God
hear the voice of the lads' and rouse us to our duty. The
saving of such boys is a work, not a myth; a fact, not a
theory; a privilege as well as a duty.

" Sir Humphry Davy was once asked for a list of his
greatest discoveries. He answered, ' My greatest discovery
was Michael Faraday.' He found him, a poor boy, washing bottles in his labaratory. He lifted him up till he became
one of the world's greatest men. The Christian worker
who discovers a good mind and soul, though amid poverty
and rags, is among the greatest of modern discoverers.

" Dr. Guthrie, of Edinburgh, one of the fathers of ragged schools, was once at a meeting where a speaker described Dr. Guthrie's ragged school-children as 'the scum
of the country.' When the doctor's turn came for speaking,
he seized a sheet of writing-paper lying on the table, and,
holding it up, said, ' This was once the scum of the country,
—once foul, dirty, wretched rags. In it, now white as the
snows of heaven, behold an emblem of the work our ragged schools have achieved.' "

In regard to those whom Dr. Scouller designates as the
third class, he says, " I have had some little experience
with this class, and I am convinced, after no little thought,
that the State should demand the guardianship of the
children of all parents who, either from their criminal proclivities or actual transgressions, are unfit to manage their
children other than raise them as law-breakers or vagabonds.
The State should take them when they are young enough to
be susceptible to moral lessons, if there be any moral soil to
plant on. A man found sowing thistle-seeds upon another
man's land, or scattering fire-brands in a city, should at once
be punished. Yet this nation, founded on democracy, whose
very existence depends upon the virtue of its members,

suffers a criminal class to grow whose whole aim and object is to undermine the confidence of the community and to weaken the strength of the commonwealth."

In our public primary schools we are professedly attempting to educate the children of both sexes in the common branches of learning, excepting only those whose condition requires some special treatment or discipline on account of exceptional characteristics or circumstances. In our high· schools, colleges, and universities every branch of knowledge which goes to make up a complete education is supposed to be imparted. Immense sums of money are raised and expended annually by the people of the State for education, and in many of our cities the taxes levied for school purposes are a heavy burthen upon the tax-payers. The object of all this expenditure is to make intelligent, good, and useful citizens of the youth who are soon to take the place of those now upon the stage of active, busy life,—an object so desirable, so philanthropic and beneficent, as to challenge the hearty approval of a vast majority of our citizens, while few are found to question its wisdom or its policy. If this object were accomplished in a degree proportioned to the financial outlay for its attainment, we should need fewer prisons or reformatories for the treatment of criminals. But after devising a system of schools, and providing for their proper organization and the erection of the necessary buildings for the accommodation of teachers and pupils, comes the most important consideration, What and how shall the children be taught?

To the first part of this question no wiser or truer answer has ever been made than that given by Agesilaus, King of Sparta. When asked what boys ought to learn, he replied, "Those things which they are to practise when they come to be men." If a similar question be asked in regard to girls, a similar answer would be appropriate : " Those things which they are to practise when they come to be women."

In other words, education of the young should be practical, and the aim of all their teaching should be to make them good and useful and intelligent, and to shield and guard them against any influence which would have an opposite tendency.

An enlightened sense of moral obligation and duty, and a thorough training in such industrial arts and occupations as they are respectively best adapted to pursue, are the equipments and armor with which every young person, male or female, should be provided on starting out in life. The intellect and the moral faculties should be developed and cultivated in every school, and industrial pursuits taught in the higher institutions of learning, in conjunction with the arts and sciences and literature. Dr. Buchanan, in his "New Education," to which we have before referred, states what he conceives to be the indispensable elements of a proper education, of which he designates five, as follows:

*First.* "The first and most necessary is physiological development; the formation of the manly, healthy constitution, competent to live a hundred years,—competent to win success in life by unflagging energy,—competent to enjoy life and health, and thus become a source of happiness to others, instead of a pauper or an invalid,—competent to transmit life and health and joy to thousands of future ages,—competent to meet all the difficulties of life triumphantly, instead of struggling in misery and railing at society and Divine Providence. . . . A male or female school which does not develop its pupils, which does not send them home in better health and development than when they were received, ought to be abolished as a mistake or a nuisance."

The exceeding great importance of such physical development can hardly be overestimated, and the neglect of such training and instruction as are necessary to secure and maintain a sound and vigorous physical condition is an egregious fault, if not a crime.

*Second.* "The second element of a liberal education is training for the business and duties of life,—in other words, *Industrial Education,* without some share of which it were better for a man that he never had been born, for without industrial capacity (unless a hereditary capitalist) he must be either a beggar, a thief, or a swindler.

"In neglecting physiological education we have degenerated the human race, impaired its efficiency, and saddled on its back a costly medical profession—ten times as many physicians as should be needed, who struggle to prolong lives that are hardly worth preserving—that perpetuate physical and moral degeneracy. In neglecting industrial education, we have produced a race of soft-handed, soft-muscled men, who struggle to escape man's first duty, *useful production,* and to live at others' expense by the innumerable methods of financial stratagem. The reign of fraud will never cease until each man is taught that life presents this sharp alternative,—useful production or the *life of the vampire.* He who has attained manhood without being trained to useful production may justly utter maledictions against parents and schools for having blasted his life and deprived him of the only solid foundation of honor and prosperity."

*Third.* "The third element in a liberal education, next in importance to the physical and industrial, is the *medical.* . . . The first duty of a man is to sustain himself that he be not a burden to others. This corresponds to industrial education. It is to sustain himself in full vigor of mind, soul, and body, that he may perform every duty, and be a help instead of a burden to all around him. Without this second duty performed, physiological development and industrial culture are both failures; and *without either of these three indispensable qualifications, the man himself may be a total failure.* . . . I mean an education by which disease shall be stamped out in its incipience. . . . Its first approaches are easily repelled. The great majority of diseases can be repelled without the use of drugs."

To know how to avoid or to repel disease is an acquisition the value of which we can all appreciate, for all suffer more or less from its effects, and there are no evils in the world, excepting moral evils, that produce so much misery as proceeds from ignorance of man's physical constitution and its requirements, and the thousand dangers to which it is constantly exposed.

*Fourth.* " With physical, industrial, and medical education man is *just prepared to live.* But that his life shall be *worth living,* shall be a blessing to himself and the world, we need the fourth element of a liberal education, which is to make him a good and happy man,—the *moral,* or *ethical,* or *religious* education. Either of these words, rightly understood, conveys the full idea, for each mean the same; although contracted and perverted by vulgar usage, each word has but half its proper meaning. I mean the education which shall exalt man to the plane of a happy, a holy, and a glorious 'life, in harmony with the Divine nature,—a life so high that it shall be in communion with the angels,—a life so beneficent that it shall diffuse happiness around to all, and leave a blessed fragrance in all the atmosphere that it filled."

*Fifth.* As the fifth and last and least important element of education, as it has been heretofore considered, Dr. Buchanan places the literary or the *intellectual.* " Colleges," he says, " are supposed to be devoted to intelligence, but I affirm that they should be devoted *first to virtue,* and that it is as practicable to take the plastic elements of youth and thereof make *a good man* as it is to make an *intelligent* or a wise one. Intellectual without moral education simply increases the dangerous and corrupting elements of society. It gives the sceptre of knowledge into the hands of the social Lucifers. . . . A perfect liberal education should extinguish the elements of hereditary disease and fortify against their possible development. . . . A perfect liberal education would prepare every individual for his life pursuit as thoroughly at least, as the lawyer is prepared for practice. . . . Our illiberal system of education, confining its training for life to the literary professions, degrades labor, drives ambitious men into non-manual vocations, and leaves the industrial classes, or a large portion of them, ignorant and degraded, unable to better their condition, crushing each other in blind competition for employment, helpless to employ themselves, dependent on capital and corporations, struggling for a meagre subsistence, living half the length of days enjoyed by the prosperous, and their short lives beclouded by disease and the grief of premature deaths in their families ; while the whole struggle of life lowers their moral nature, tempts to crime, and invites to suicide,—in which they find uniting with them many of the superficially prosperous, but ill-trained, to whom life yields no substantial joy.  Of such material is society composed, which continually threatens, by social convulsions, to fall into anarchy, —a disorder that is kept only at bay by the policeman's club and the soldier's bayonet. . . .

" Liberal education makes the school-room a delightful place, to which the children resort with eagerness, in which their songs maintain a spirit of harmony, obedience, and love, and the voice of threatening is never heard ; in which they grow into habits of politeness, friendliness, hospitality, obedience, diligence, zeal, energy, manliness, self-respect, truthfulness, and cheerfulness, which enable them to set examples that improve their seniors, and to begin life with a stock of religious virtue sufficient to defy temptation. . . .

" As for the elements of present and eternal life, illiberal education has left its subjects as it found them, or perhaps has left them to dislike authority, to avoid books of useful instruction, to consider idle sport the supremest pleasure and labor the greatest degradation; to be moved chiefly by rivalry and jealousy, to scoff at profound moral truths, to assail or ignore whatever does not accord with their prejudices, or with a low animal view of life; to trifle with all solemn thoughts, to ignore the welfare of others, to look to money, power, and ostentation as the goal of life, and to pursue that aim without regard to the laws of health, without regard to any high principle (perhaps even without regard to law), and to ignore our eternal destiny until the cold hand of hovering death shuts out all scenes of earthly ambition and raises a debased soul to the consciousness that it is plunging into the darkness of eternity.

"In short, illiberal education is responsible for the vast increase of debasement, of crime, suicide, insanity, pauperism, and mortality which statistics alarmingly prove to have occurred in the present century, during which, while religion and morals have declined, intemperance has much more than doubled in that English-speaking race which is destined to be the leading power of the world. . . . The entire degradation and perversion of education *has been caused by the exclusion of ethical influence and principles*, and will cease when the ethical element shall be introduced. Uninspired by love, primary education has been simply a tyranical enforcement of tasks, generating, like all tyranny, sullen discontent, secret hate, furtive evasion, or restless disobedience, and steadily maintaining a low moral status. With proper ethical sentiments, the teacher, who has all the world's wealth of intellectual delight and information at command, would be the most fascinating companion to whom his pupils could approach, and the school would be their favorite resort, exclusion from which would be keenly felt as a punishment. Uninspired by love, the higher education has been a selection of themes and tasks without regard to the welfare of the pupil, and without any thought of qualifying him to reach a higher stage in civilization, or to get rid of the errors inherited from ancestry or instilled by teachers."

What Dr. Buchanan says of the education given at the Reform School of Ohio may be taken as indicating what should be regarded as the proper education of every youth. He says, " It is *intellectual, practical, and moral.* They give half their time to instruction, the other half to work, and throughout the whole they are under moral influences. Industry—the daily performance of duty in work—is the very foundation of moral culture, without which the moral nature has little stamina, and may degenerate into mere sentimentality. It is the resolute doing of duty every hour in the day which makes the substantial moral character that will stand the conflicts of life; and as labor is the chief duty of life, it follows that no moral education is entirely substantial that does not include labor. This is the secret of the wonderful success of the reform school. Another open secret is, that in a school of three hundred youths, disciplined to duty and friendship by love, labor, and song, there is a public sentiment, an irresistible moral power, which at once corrects and assimilates the new arrivals, as dead flesh is assimilated into the human body."

The moral leverage of this public sentiment which belongs to an institution with a large and well-trained band of pupils, under the control of their teachers, isolated from surrounding society, may not be expected to pervade families and schools in general with the same potency that it does such a body of pupils in a reform school. But if parents or guardians and teachers are, each in their several relations and offices, fitted for the positions they occupy towards those under their charge, a moral sentiment will animate each member of the household or the school that will inspire to labor and to duty, and secure cheerful obedience on the part of the children and pupils to all proper and just rules for their guidance and the government of their conduct.

While the child is with its parents or guardian, and attends the schools of the township or city where they reside, its industrial education depends upon such parents or guardian, and is often sadly neglected for various reasons. Among farmers, gardeners, mechanics, and others who are their own employers, the boys can, when of a proper age, be instructed in the trade or calling to which the head of the family is devoted; and if this is done intelligently, and with such explanations of the uses and importance of labor, and its true dignity, as it justly deserves in the economy of life, and with an appreciation on the part of the instructors of the capabilities and adaptation of the learner for the employment in which he is engaged, it may be made a pleasure and not a burdensome task, and may be prosecuted with much of the zeal and enjoyment that boys find in a game of ball or other kind of play.

Appreciating the benefits, both physical and mental, and the satisfaction that we have derived from the habitual performance of a considerable amount of manual labor every year for more than seventy consecutive years, we cannot but conclude that those who despise useful labor and prefer a life of idleness, or who squander their time in amusing themselves and others without giving any valuable equivalent for what they consume of the products of others' labor, must have failed to receive such an education as their interests and the interests and duty of others justly demanded, and that their moral standard is far below what it should have been. The moral law requires that we shall not only abstain from things hurtful to ourselves or others, but that we shall do what we can in our several circumstances to make the world better and its people wiser and happier.

That there is a lamentable deficiency in the qualifications of our school-teachers is generally admitted. Of the thousands employed to teach, scarcely one in a hundred is really qualified for the position. They may be competent to instruct in those branches of learning commonly taught in our schools from books, after the usual manner of teaching, but they do not know how to reach the heart and soul of the pupil, engage his attention, secure his affections, and command his reverence, and must therefore fail to enlighten his understanding and implant in his susceptible mind those ideas and principles which go to make up a strong, vigorous, morally healthy, and admirable character. However learned a teacher may be, if he has not this power, and does not take pleasure in exercising it for the benefit of his school, he will do more harm than good in attempting to teach. The old way of governing a school through appeals to the *fears* of the pupils, and compelling obedience by the use of the rod and the ferrule, is almost universally repudiated, and milder means of government have been adopted, and higher qualities in the character of the teacher are demanded in order to insure success.

A brief sketch of our first experience in teaching a common school in the State of New York will perhaps best illustrate our ideas as to the proper mode of governing and teaching a school.

At the age of nineteen, having formed the design of making teaching a profession, and having labored hard under adverse circumstances to acquire the necessary learning for that purpose, and yet feeling great diffidence and some doubt as to possessing the requisite qualifications, I deemed it most prudent to commence my professional career in a backwoods district, where the pupils would be unsophisticated and backward in their studies, and where the position of the school-master would command such respect as to secure ready obedience to school rules and make its government easy. Upon making inquiry I heard of a district that seemed to offer the conditions that corresponded with my wishes, and where it was said a teacher was wanted for three or four months of the ensuing winter season. I accordingly went to make my application, and finding one of the trustees in the woods chopping near a small clearing, inquired of him whether they desired to employ a teacher. He seemed to be a frank, honest, straightforward sort of man, and replied to my inquiry, " Yes, we want a teacher,—one that can govern our school. We have a turbulent set of young fellows to manage,—some of them larger and older than you look to be,—and for the last two winters they've broken up the school and turned the teachers out of doors, so we've had no school to amount to anything for two years, and you look rather young to undertake the job." This was unpleasant news for me. I did not covet the chances of being turned out of doors, nor of having a fight in order to maintain my position, but the alternative of withdrawing my application and acknowledging that I had not the courage to meet the emergency, whatever it might be, was much more repulsive. I did not hesitate, therefore, to say that I thought I could manage the school, and informed him that I was willing to undertake it, with the assurance of the trustees that I should have their support in such measures as I might deem necessary for preserving order and decorum in the school. We therefore entered into a contract by which I was to teach the school during three months, and was to be paid ten dollars per month and board around among the patrons of the school.

During the few days between my engagement and the commencement of my work I reflected very seriously upon the subject of school government, and applied myself earnestly to devising some plan by which I should get control of the school and bring it into subjection, without attempting the use of physical force; for it seemed altogether probable that such an attempt would be resisted by the united force of the whole set of " turbulent fellows" referred to by the trustee, and that in such a contest I should be put out as my predecessors had been, and the school broken up for another year.

From my experience as a pupil under different teachers in common schools, and what I had learned of the character and disposition of the boys of my own age, and the opinions entertained by them in regard to the methods of government adopted by their teachers, I had arrived at the conclusion that *moral power* ought to supersede physical force, and that corporal punishments should very rarely be administered. I had observed that the teacher who assumed an air of authority, and came into the school armed with a rod and ferrule, failed to command a willing obedience, but, on the contrary, provoked a disposition in his pupils to secretly disobey his injunctions and take pleasure in annoying and vexing him when they could do so without detection. I had observed also, that those teachers who were most patient and friendly with those under their charge, and invited obedience by suggestion and appeals to the reason and understanding of the pupils rather than commanded it, were more successful, both in government and in communicating instruction. I therefore determined to adopt this course in the management of the school I had engaged to teach, though I formed no definite plan as to how I should accomplish it.

In observing and reflecting upon the methods of instruction generally adopted, it had appeared to me that but little, if anything, was done by the teacher to enlarge and cultivate either the mental or moral faculties of the pupils, and that *memory* was the faculty mostly brought into exercise.

Remembering the many puzzling questions that had arisen in my early experience, and the strange notions that I had imbibed from some of my reading lessons, and which, from want of encouragement on the part of the teacher, I had been too timid to ask a solution of, I discerned the necessity of making every lesson an occasion for exercising and enlarging the intellectual and, as far as practicable, the moral faculties of the learners. The system which I adopted for this purpose will be explained as I proceed with my narrative.

On the day appointed, I was present and commenced my labors as teacher. The school-house was built of rough logs, with a large open fireplace in one end, and furnished with board seats and long writing-tables next the walls. There were thirty-five or forty present of both sexes, five or six of whom were young men from fifteen to twenty years of age, and a corresponding number of young women of similar ages. The first day was spent in classifying the pupils and going through the usual school exercises, without any attempt to lay down or require a compliance with rules. It was very perceptible that most of the time of the pupils was occupied in trying to size up the new teacher and satisfy themselves as to his temper and disposition, and the teacher was as sedulously occupied in observing the conduct and studying the characters exhibited by them. During the day the whole school seemed possessed by the spirit of disorder. Whenever they thought they could do so without attracting my notice, they indulged themselves in grimaces and contortions of the facial muscles, in rising suddenly from their seats and as quickly returning to them, and in other disorderly conduct for their own gratification and the amusement of the school. The prospect of success at the close of the school on that day did not appear very flattering, but without administering any rebuke I resolved that on the following day I would make a determined effort to bring them to order. To this end I requested the pupils present to give notice to their parents and others interested, that I desired as full an attendance as possible of those who were to be pupils in the school on the following day, and stated that I should have something very important to say to them, in which all would be interested.

The following night was one of sleeplessness and deep anxiety. The situation was critical, and my future prospects in life seemed to depend very largely upon the issue. If I could succeed in bringing the school into willing subjection, I had no doubt of my ability to benefit my pupils and give satisfaction to all who were interested; but if I failed, the consequences might be disastrous both to me and to the school. Before reaching the school-house on the following morning I had laid out a plan of procedure which I hoped and believed might be successful. As the pupils came in, and before opening the school, I extended a cordial and friendly greeting to those whose acquaintance I had made the previous day, and saluted the others in the same friendly spirit, and thought I perceived a more respectful manner on the part of the older pupils than they had exhibited on the previous day. The feeling indicated by their furtive glances at the teacher and at each other, and the defiant air which I had observed the previous day on coming among them, seemed to have given place to one of serious inquiry and expectancy as to what was about to take place, of which they had as yet had no intimation; and I am satisfied now that no wiser course could have been pursued than that which was adopted, of leaving them for a time in entire ignorance and suspense as to what were my intentions in regard to their government. If I had undertaken to govern them, or to lay down rules for the government of the school on the first day, the attempt would probably have inspired a feeling of opposition which it would have been difficult to overcome. The course pursued was unexpected and puzzling to them, and excited inquiry and reflection upon the subject, and led them into a different frame of mind from that which they at first exhibited. The same principle is acted upon, I observe, by Mr. Brockway at the Elmira Reformatory. Each prisoner when received is locked up in a cell for one or two days to give time for reflection before he is placed under discipline, or the rules of the institution are made known to him.

At the usual time of commencing the school exercises I called the pupils to order, and they gave me their earnest and undivided attention while I addressed them in substance as follows:

"When you were dismissed last evening I informed those of you who were then present that I should have something very important to say to you this morning, in which all of you would be interested. You are all aware that I have been employed by the trustees to be your teacher during the present winter. Now, lest you should be under some misapprehension as to our relations as teacher and pupils, I wish to explain to you my ideas of what that relation means, and what is required in order that you may reap the benefits which you have a just right to expect from my labors in that capacity, and as I proceed I wish you to carefully weigh and consider what I have to say, and to reason upon it so as to form a judgment for yourselves as to whether I am right or not, and if I express any idea that any of you think is wrong, I desire you, in a proper manner, to tell me so. First, then, I wish to say that I have not been engaged to tyrannize over you, nor to rule the school in any rash or unreasonable way, but I understand that in my office of teacher I have undertaken to instruct you to the best of my ability in the various branches of learning usually taught in common schools, such as reading, spelling, writing, arithmetic, geography, and grammar. I shall assume that you all desire to become intelligent and respectable, as well as useful men and women, and you all understand that in order to become so it is necessary that you acquire a knowledge of all these different branches of study, and your parents and guardians evince the interest they feel for your welfare and happiness in life by sending you here to gain this knowledge. That I possess the requisite qualifications to give the instruction you need appears by a certificate which I was required to obtain from the school inspectors of your township, and I hope to make it more manifest to your understanding as the school progresses. In some of your studies I shall adopt a method which I have no doubt will be new to you, the object of which will be to cultivate not only your intellectual but your moral faculties at the same time. This will require great labor on the part of your teacher and close attention and study on your part, but the satisfaction we shall both derive from it will more than compensate for the labor and study devoted to it. I am here to be your friend, and the friend of each of you, and next to your fathers and mothers I hope you will learn to esteem me as one of your best friends, and treat me accordingly. It will be understood that this is a *democratic school, in which all the pupils are equal,* and no one can claim any special or exclusive rights or privileges. There will be no high and no low among you, but all will stand upon the same level, each one being at liberty to excel the others in good conduct and in acquiring knowledge by being more studious and diligent. Knowledge is acquired only by effort, and you will find some rough places and difficult problems as you progress with your studies, and I hope you will desire to gain all you can during the time I shall be with you ; and in order that you may do so, it will be a pleasure for me to help any of you along who may desire it, out of the regular school hours.

" I now call your attention to another subject of some importance, which, however, is only an incident to the main purpose of the school. I refer to the government of the school. It is obvious to all of you that in order to prosecute your studies successfully some rules of order must be observed so as to avoid confusion and constant interruption, and the question arises, What rules are necessary to secure this object, and who shall make these rules? I have said that this was to be a democratic school, and that I do not come here to tyrannize over you, and now I propose that you shall be your own legislators and governors, and establish for yourselves the rules by which you are to be governed. These should be few and simple and reasonable, and I will proceed to suggest such as I, from my experience and observation, deem necessary, and you will each vote for or against them according to your own individual judgment, and if any of you deem any proposed rule unnecessary or otherwise objectionable, you will be at liberty to state your objections freely, and it is my desire that you should do so."

A few simple rules were then proposed and adopted by a unanimous vote of the pupils who were old enough to understand them, and a more orderly, well-behaved school than this it would have been hard to find. It was truly a self-governed and well-governed school, and the progress made in the studies pursued was very satisfactory.

The pupils were informed that they were expected not only to exercise and cultivate the memory, by committing the rules of arithmetic, grammar, and their lessons in geography and history, but also to enlarge and improve their understanding by searching out and endeavoring to comprehend the reason of every rule or proposition contained in the books they were studying, and that they ought to know the signification of every word and the meaning of every sentence read by them; that every word, every letter and figure, and every mark printed in the books they used had some meaning which they ought to understand, and that every reading lesson contained some relation of facts, or instruction in arts, science, or morals, which it would be beneficial for them to comprehend.

The reading-book of the most advanced class was "The English Reader." The class, being called up for exercise in reading, were questioned in the following manner: "What book have you?" *Answer*, "'The English Reader.'" "Why is it called the English Reader?" None of the class could answer. I explained that it was called a *reader* because it was a book containing lessons for their instruction and ex-

ercise in reading; and it was called the *English* reader because its contents were in the English language. I then
called their attention to the observations on the principles of
good reading contained in the " Introduction," explaining
their importance and the necessity of studying them atten-
tively, and proceeded to ask them questions in regard to the
several divisions of the book into parts, chapters, and sections, and what was indicated by each, to which no intelligent answer could be elicited. After explaining that the
book is divided into two principal parts, one composed of
pieces in prose and the other of pieces in poetry; that the
chapters were the divisions of these several parts according
to the general character of the pieces embraced in each;
that the sections divided the chapters into pieces, and that
the pieces were divided into verses or paragraphs, which
were numbered consecutively by Arabic figures, the chapters
and sections being numbered by Roman numerals, and the
meaning of all these terms being made plain to their comprehension, we proceeded with our first reading lesson.

The pupil standing at the head of the class reads the
heading of Chapter I., " Select Sentences and Paragraphs,"
and the question is asked, " What do these words mean ?"
No intelligent answer can be obtained, though there are
pupils in the class who have read the book through several
times. I explain what these words indicate, and point out
the necessity of constant reference to the dictionary. This
pupil proceeds to read the first paragraph of section I:
" Diligence, industry, and proper improvement of time are
material duties of the young." The class is then asked to
define the words *diligence, industry, improvement*, and *duties*,
and by the aid of " Johnson's Dictionary" their several definitions are ascertained. They are then asked why these
should be regarded as material duties of the young, and
especially what advantages they themselves may expect to
derive from the faithful performance of them. The second

pupil in the class then reads the next paragraph : " The acquisition of knowledge is one of the most honorable occupations of youth." The words *knowledge, honorable,* and
*occupations* are then defined, and the sentiment contained in
this paragraph is commented upon, and the uses of knowledge indicated so as to impress them upon their minds.
Thus as each paragraph of the lesson is read it is followed
by definitions of the principal words, and practical observations upon the sentiment it contains or the moral it inculcates.
Examples were given, and the way to acquire knowledge
pointed out, and the pupil was then required, as far as possible, to find out everything for himself. In every branch of
learning the teaching was equally thorough ; and it was very
soon apparent that the scholars were deeply interested in the
studies they were pursuing, and trying to make the best use
of their time. After continuing in the course indicated for
a time, they came to their lessons prepared to answer such
questions as were naturally suggested by the subject of them,
with such intelligence and appreciation as showed that their
understanding and moral perceptions had been opened and
were being developed. During portions of several succeeding years I was engaged in teaching in public and private
schools, pursuing the same method, and with similar satisfactory results. I have visited many public schools since
that, and observed the systems of teaching adopted in them,
and have seldom found any attempt made to reach the understanding, or cultivate the moral faculties of the learners,
and I have found but few teachers in our primary schools
who were capable of doing so.

In the higher institutions of learning intellectual education has been the chief and almost the exclusive aim, and
the value and power of moral education have been ignored
or not properly estimated. Referring to the comparative
value of intellectual and moral education, Dr. Buchanan
says, " You will agree with me that it is not a debatable

question whether a man's moral or intellectual life is of the greatest value, for happiness is as high above intelligence as the heavens above the earth ; nor is it at all debatable whether it were better for our country to be filled with shrewd and intelligent scoundrels or with good but ignorant men. Ignorance is a trivial matter in comparison to crime, and intellectual shrewdness is no compensation for the loss of virtue and happiness. I claim therefore that moral education, in its highest sense, is incomparably more important than intellectual education, and as our educational systems have heretofore been not moral but intellectual, they are but left-handed affairs, and have yet to acquire their strong right arm. . . . If we could educate men forever on the intellectual plan, and if there could be no moral element in the education, they would be no better, no happier, in the end ; there would be as much of fraud and strife, murder and misery, as much of poverty, despair, and suicide as when we began. Two of the most intellectual, brilliant, and educated men I have ever known terminated their lives by their own hands, because all their intelligence brought them no happiness : their lives were hollow mockeries ; and just such a despairing mockery is that splendid civilization in which literature, art, science, machinery, and architecture make an outward display, while the whiskey-shop, the street mob, the workhouse, the penitentiary, the police court, the foundling hospital, and the insane asylum tell the inside story. Amid the brilliant civilization of Paris there are to-day many thousands of criminals. . . . The laborers of Europe, living on one to three dollars a week, are kept in squalid ignorance, and their bread is taken by taxes to feed four million men who live only for the purpose of homicide by bullet and bayonet. The great nations of Europe devote their wealth to standing armies and the debts of war ; and while they profess to represent the highest civilization of Christendom, which professes allegiance to the law of love, they live as brigands do, with their swords pointed at each others' throats, every one of them believing that if they could not defend themselves, their so-called Christian neighbors would invade, conquer, rob, and enslave them. Each nation thus declares that it considers its neighbors an organized banditti, and this universal opinion must have some foundation. Gloomy as it seems, this is the universal condition which is now and ever shall be, unless moral education can change the scene."

" All educational reform," says Dr. Buchanan, " must fail unless we have good teachers; but with a superior corps of well-paid teachers, who consecrate themselves for life to their business, and have all the necessary appliances, I claim that we can accomplish the moral regeneration of mankind by means which have been already tried and worked successfully. I do not mean by the ordinary appliances, for they are notorious failures. We have in use four methods of moral education: 1, homilies by text-book and lecture; 2, good advice; 3, scolding; 4, punishment. These methods are in use everywhere, and are everywhere failures. The bad boy hears the virtues talked about in homilies until he is tired of it. He gets good advice when he is doing right, and a double dose of good advice when he is doing wrong. But it is very rare to find anybody who would thank you for good advice, or who is willing to act upon it. The man who really knows how to appreciate good advice and to act on it is already so good that he seldom needs it. If he desires it he does not need it, and if he needs it very badly he does not desire it, but heartily resents it. The bad boy rejects advice with contempt, and receives a liberal supply of scolding, which makes him sullen, and so wicked that for the next offence he is whipped and left among the debasing influences of hatred and fear.

" Moral education is the reverse of this. It takes in criminals and turns them out good citizens by the familiar means that common sense recommends, of placing them in a moral atmosphere and keeping them in it until their whole nature is changed, just as men are made criminals by placing them in a criminal atmosphere and keeping them there until they are saturated with baseness. The same amount of moral power which can take criminal youths and elevate them to respectability can take the youths of virtuous families and elevate them to pre-eminence in virtue. It is no exaggeration to say that the schools which have reformed criminals have demonstrated an amount of power sufficient for the world's regeneration if rightly applied."

In a preceding chapter, in discussing the proper treatment of crime, we have shown how this moral power has been applied in reformatory institutions, and with what wonderful success. If, then, it is capable of changing the character of criminal youth and elevating them into a condition of virtuous respectability, it cannot be doubted that such youth might have been saved from crime by a similar power judiciously exercised while they were yet innocent and free from the contamination of crime. While moral education is of the highest importance, every sort of knowledge that can contribute to the welfare of the learner, or shield him from evil, should be communicated as soon as he is able to comprehend and apply it. In treating of ignorance as a cause of crime, we adverted to the helpless condition of a human being when born into this world, and to the fact that his origin and his surroundings during the period of infancy and early youth are matters of which he could by no possibility have any prevision or control. He may be the child of noble and virtuous or of debased and criminal parents. He may be born the inheritor of wealth and luxury or of squalid poverty, of health or disease. The laws prohibit no class or condition from propagating their species. The drunkard, the thief, the scrofulous and the epileptic, the weak-minded and the pauper, the lame, the halt, and the blind, may multiply and replenish the earth in marital relations, and their right to leave a progeny behind them, to suffer and be a burden and a curse to themselves and the community, is unchallenged. The mean and undesirable of our domestic animals are weeded out and are not allowed to multiply, and, by the skilful application of scientific principles, the various races of these useful creatures are vastly improved from age to age and their value increased. But any suggestion that the human race might be improved by incapacitating the vicious and criminal from multiplying their kind is met with superstitious horror, or with ridicule. Dr. Scouller advocates physical disqualification of criminals as the most sure and effective mode of preventing crime by stopping production, and thus eliminating the criminal element from society. Other distinguished men have advocated the same remedy, and there can be no doubt of the efficacy of this remedy if the proper subjects of it could always be distinguished and the application be made at the proper time. But the difficulties in the way of its proper administration will probably prevent its becoming popular or practical. The perpetual restraint of those who prove to be incorrigible may, however, accomplish the same end by milder means. The children now in being, whatever class they may belong to, are to be educated and taken care of and not only saved, as far as practicable, from becoming criminal, but made actively useful. The child's education and the formation of its character begins before birth. Whatever of good or ill, of pain or pleasure, has created any emotion in the breast of the mother, and whatever appetites or passions or ambitions have been indulged by her during the formative period prior to its separation from the silent tabernacle in which its inceptive life began, have had an influence in determining what manner of person it shall be. If the mother has been educated as she should have been, and instructed in the duties and responsibilities of motherhood in all its stages, and is surrounded, as she should be; with favorable conditions, her offspring may be what a mother most desires, well-born, with a sound physical frame and well-formed brain ; but if she has been left in ignorance of the duties and responsibilities pertaining to the great trust she assumes, or if adverse circumstances have prevented her from performing her maternal duties, the child of her love will need regeneration and a new birth, and may be a curse instead of a blessing to her and to the world.

In treating of ignorance as a cause of crime, we have referred to the ruinous consequences to the young resulting from abuse of the most delicate organs of the human body, and indicated the necessity of early instruction in regard to their uses and abuses. The extent of the evil adverted to is known and appreciated by but few outside of the medical profession and those who read the warnings contained in medical books, but by them its prevalence and ruinous effects are well understood. All necessary information and instruction upon this subject may and should be given by parents or teachers before any vicious habits can be formed, and may be communicated privately, and with such delicacy as not to offend against any rule of modesty and decency ; and parents should be made to understand that it cannot be omitted without great peril of irremediable injury to physical and mental health. Millions have impaired their physical health and thousands have been rendered insane through ignorance of that which every youth must be taught in order to be safe from these disastrous results. Dumb animals, left to the guidance of instinct, are free from this vice, as well as from many other vicious practices that debase and brutalize humanity and tend to degenerate the race, physically, mentally, and morally.

The value of industrial education in all our reformatory institutions, without which no intellectual or moral training would be effectual in producing reformation, is so well understood and everywhere admitted that no argument is required in its favor.

Mr. Charlton, superintendent of the reform school for boys in Indiana, justly and truly says that "Labor is the most blessed duty ever enjoined upon man, and should be performed with alacrity and with joy. At its magical touch springs into existence not only all the wealth peculiar to civilization, but all that adds to the comforts and luxuries of life. Labor not only conduces to happiness, but it is essential to the welfare of our race. No one, however well grounded in Christian faith, or however highly cultivated and refined, can live a truly moral life and be idle. The workshops of the devil open the moment those of legitimate and useful toil are closed. Dissipation hides its face in the presence of honest toil." Report of Conference of Charities, etc., 1885.

The restless activity of youth will not endure idleness, and if not directed into proper channels this activity will assuredly work itself out through improper ones. If ignorance is a cause of crime, the converse of this proposition is true, and knowledge is a preventive of crime. While the ignorant are not necessarily vicious, nor the educated necessarily virtuous, yet if it were not true that education tends to make men better, the State would have comparatively little interest in educating its people, and its duty to support schools for that purpose would not be apparent. But if common observation did not satisfactorily indicate that the tendency of such education as our schools have afforded, defective as it unquestionably is, has been to diminish crime, the statistics of illiteracy in its relation to crime incontestably prove this to be true. By the report of the United States Commissioner of Education for 1872, it appears that the aggregate number of prisoners in 1870 was 110,538; that the aggregate of those who could read and write was 82,812, and the aggregate number of those who could neither read nor write was 21,650, and of those who could barely read but not write, 5931 ; total illiterates, 27,581, or twenty-five per cent. of the entire number of prisoners.  These returns are culled from seventeen States, fourteen of these being Western or Middle States.

The census returns for 1870 show that in New York and Pennsylvania the illiterate in the entire population amounted to only four per cent., while the illiterate prisoners amounted to thirty-three per cent. of all the prisoners, and the very deficient included sixty per cent. of them.  Thus it appears that four per cent. of the population furnished thirty-three per cent. of the prisoners, or twelve times as many as an equal number who were not illiterate.

In the central West three and a half per cent. of the population was returned as illiterate, and forty-six per cent. of the criminals illiterate, or thirteen times their proportion of criminals in proportion to their numbers.

In the far West and the Pacific section the returns give three per cent. illiterate, who furnished thirty-one per cent. of the criminals, or tenfold their proportion.  In three of the Southern States twenty-two per cent. illiterate furnished sixty per cent. of the criminals.

These facts are gleaned from a paper by the late Bishop Harris, of Michigan, read before the Conference of Charities, etc., in 1885, on the subject of " Compulsory Education as a Means of preventing Crime."  In this article he commends, among other educational agencies, the kindergarten, and remarks that " It is clear, when we study the kindergarten, and come to understand its methods of utilizing play, that healthy amusement among young people could be made educative of the social sense more largely than it is, and thus be another preventive of crime."

He also advocates the industrial education of youth.  " Industrial education," says Bishop Harris, " in the form of the school, since the practical abolition of apprenticeship, is also important. The manual training school and the school shop, modelled on the Russian or on the Swedish plan, ought to be established to a limited extent in all our cities, and made free like our common schools. They give admirable instruction in wood-working and in metal-working," and he concludes by saying, " Compulsory education, in the forms of the common school, the kindergarten, the industrial art school, may furnish us the most valuable preventive agencies against crime."

In the article referred to, Bishop Harris refers to the increasing growth of cities in our country, due to the invention of labor-saving machinery, as one of the causes of crime, and remarks that " Increasing urban growth for the most part furnishes us our social problems." One of our greatest statesmen of a former age, deprecating the increase and growth of large cities in our country, characterized them as " sores upon the body politic." The deplorable condition of many of the youth in our large commercial towns has been adverted to, more particularly of those who are compelled to subsist on garbage or by thieving; and certainly no one who is susceptible to compassion for the unfortunate can contemplate their condition without feeling an earnest desire that some practicable means may be provided for their redemption. With the example before us of what reform schools are accomplishing, can there be any doubt that this may be accomplished by compulsory education and proper discipline? The way is simple, rational, and effective, and only requires wise legislation and active exertion to accomplish it. If " there is more joy in heaven over one sinner that repenteth, than over ninety and nine just persons that need no repentance," what rejoicing would there be, both among the angels in heaven and the righteous on the earth, when the thousands of city Arabs and hoodlums, as they are commonly denominated, are brought to repentance and good lives through the instrumentalities provided by the wise and good, whose names are already written in the book of life.

In order to secure teachers who are qualified for the work, training schools should be established in which everything that pertains to the government of schools and the proper mode of giving instruction should be thoroughly taught, and none should be permitted to become instructors in our public schools or reformatories but men and women of such character and acquirements that they shall deserve, and be capable of commanding, the confidence and love of their pupils.   In patience, gentleness, tact, judgment, candor, intelligence, and moral character every teacher should be a model worthy of the imitation of youth.   The silent influence of the teacher's character is more potent in moral education than the most admirable oral instruction, but when these are conjoined their power is irresistible.   Wendell Phillips once said that " Men succeed less by their talents than by their character.   There were scores of men a hundred years ago who had more intellect than Washington. He outvies and overrides them all by the influence of his character."   And who shall say at this day that the nobility of Washington's character, commanding as it did the respect and admiration of his country's enemies as well as of its friends, did not turn the scale of fortune in our favor in the doubtful struggle for liberty, and secure our national independence ?   If a teacher is discovered by his pupils to be deficient in any of the essential qualifications required, his usefulness will be impaired or destroyed, and his influence injurious instead of beneficial.

For the purpose of furnishing a supply of competent teachers for the public schools of Michigan, a State Normal School has been established at Ypsilanti, the exclusive purpose of which, as expressed in the act creating it, is " the instruction of persons, both male and female, in the art of teaching, and in all the various branches that pertain to a good common-school education. Also to give instruction in the mechanic arts, and in the arts of husbandry and agricultural chemistry; in the fundamental laws of the United States, and in what regards the rights and duties of citizens."

Training schools for teachers have also been established in connection with the higher schools in cities, and it is an encouraging fact that much progress has been made in this direction, and that great progress has been made in placing in our schools a much better qualified class of teachers than those who formerly occupied those positions. The example of Dr. Wichern in qualifying teachers for reformatories in Germany, as related in the " American Cyclopædia," is very suggestive on this subject. The necessity of a supply of teachers led Dr. Wichern to establish at the *Rauhes Haus* (some account of which we have given in a former chapter) what he denominated the " Institute of Brothers," intended for the gratuitous training of those who would become teachers, " elder brothers," and " haus fathers" of the children, or to fill situations elsewhere requiring the same patience, knowledge, and tact. They were at first attached to the families as assistants, and after an apprenticeship they undertook, in rotation, the direction, each brother, before the course of four years expired, having been twice in charge of each of the families, of which there were fourteen of vagrant children, occupying as many houses.

The establishment of reformatories in other parts of Germany and Europe, on a similar plan to that of the *Rauhes Haus*, caused a demand for these trained teachers, and they were also wanted for superintendents of hospitals, prisons, charitable institutions, etc.

The success of the *Rauhes Haus* as a reformatory was greater than that of any other institution of the kind then existing, the relapse into vice of the pupils after leaving it not exceeding four or five per cent. In 1852, Dr. Wichern was

appointed by the Prussian government director of prisons
for the kingdom, and the wardens and overseers of the prisons and bridewells were all selected from the graduates of
the " Institute of Brothers," who had been specially trained
for this work.

When we consider the incalculable importance of so
educating our children as to fortify them against the seduc-
tions of vice and temptations to crime, and arm them for the
conflicts and burdens they will have to encounter, as well as
to fit them for the higher enjoyments of righteous and pure
lives, the necessity of a thorough training of those who are
to be their instructors is too apparent for argument.

We would especially emphasize the importance of industrial education. An editorial in the *Globe-Democrat* says,
" The great discovery of our age is industrial education.
Its advantages prove large in all ways. It gives every
child a chance to find out what it is fitted to do best. It
enables every child to grow up able to earn a living. It relieves the professions of those utterly unfit by nature for
professional life. It destroys the unworthy prejudice against
manual labor. It brings all grades of society nearer together. It develops a hand-cunning or handicraft that relieves the brain from over-use and exhaustion. It enables
brain-workers to secure easy reaction from brain toil. It
encourages industry and saves many from falling into crime.
Industry underlies moral behavior. Education of the brain
can never be a perfect affair without hand skill."

In the education and treatment of children and youths,
both parents and teachers ought fully to understand all the
tendencies to vice and crime which they may have inherited
or acquired, and sedulously endeavor to protect them against
their development. As soon as a child is old enough to understand the nature and possible effects of ancestral taint, he
should be warned of his danger, and encouraged and advised
to refrain from any conduct or course of life which might

develop or strengthen the inherited infirmity. Towards such the utmost caution and prudence are required. Their moral perceptions should be cultivated and the principles of right and justice made clear to their understanding at an early period of their lives, and the contrasts of good and evil, and their effects respectively in bringing happiness or misery to men and women, should be sharply presented to their consciousness. They should never be permitted to entertain the thought that they are victims of an adverse fate, and that their inherited appetites or passions cannot be resisted and overcome; but however charitably we may look upon their faults, they ought to be taught that they are to be regarded as fully responsible for the wrongs they do as a natural and necessary consequence thereof. If such an inheritance may in some sense be regarded as a fatality, it does not follow that it cannot be eradicated or controlled by suitable training and culture. On the contrary, the results of such training and culture in the reform schools, both of this country and of Europe, conclusively prove that from ninety to ninety-five per cent. of the criminal youths may be cured by the methods adopted for that purpose; and as knowledge advances it is reasonable to conclude that these methods may be improved so as to become still more effective. The power of human kindness and love, directed by wisdom and stimulated by a broad, all-embracing philanthropy, has never been so intelligently appreciated and practically applied in any former period of the world's history as within the last half of the present century.

There are still stupendous evils to be eradicated and threatened evils to be averted, but the spirit of our people, which has been awakened to a comprehension of their magnitude and importance, we may well hope will move forward in the work of reformation, regardless of hoary traditions and superstitions, until life shall be made a blessing to all and a curse to none.

# CHAPTER II.

## THE PREVENTION OF INTEMPERANCE.

WE have treated of intemperance as one of the principal proximate causes of crime; and assuming our premises to be true, it is obvious that if intemperance can be prevented, it will tend, in a great degree, to lessen the volume of crime. The simplest rules of sanitary science teach us that the most effectual way of preventing disease is by removing its causes. But while a vast majority of all enlightened peoples deplore the evils growing out of the intemperate use of intoxicating liquors, the question, How shall it be prevented? remains a problem yet to be solved. If all who regard it as an evil were agreed upon some practical mode of effecting the desired end, its solution would be easy enough. But herein lies the difficulty. Some propose one means and some another, and the diversity of opinion among the friends of temperance prevents the application of any effectual remedy. One of the greatest obstacles, however, to the adoption of any mode of prevention is the fact that there is a wealthy and powerful class of men engaged in distilling and brewing, who, from motives of pecuniary interest, are opposed to all restrictions upon the manufacture or traffic, and a very active, energetic, and politically influential class in every town and city who are engaged in the liquor trade, all of whom, from the same motive, are opposed to any measures for its suppression. These men, though constituting but a lean minority of voters at the elections, by their activity and zeal, and the political influence they are capable of exerting under our corrupt system of caucusing and bargaining, very often control the nominations to office and influence legislation.

They well understand the political machinery in their several localities, and the vulnerable points in the characters of leading politicians of all political parties, and how to bring " the proper influences," as they are derisively called, to bear to prevent adverse legislation. They do not so much object to paying a tax to the government for a license, and to be protected in their business, as to any measure looking to its suppression.

Some of the friends of temperance advocate the immediate and entire prohibition of the liquor traffic by legislation. Others, believing this to be impracticable in the present state of public opinion, favor taxing and regulating the manufacture and sale of intoxicating liquors, under a system of " high license" and strict accountability for all damages arising from intoxication caused by the licensees, and prohibiting the sale of intoxicants to minors and persons addicted to drunkenness, and forbidding such sale on certain days and times.

Temperance associations have existed for many years, and have made noble and praiseworthy efforts to reform inebriates and stay the tide of intemperance by warning, admonition, and diffusing information upon the nature and extent of this great evil. Statutes have been enacted in some of the States forbidding the traffic under heavy penalties, but these have been evaded or openly disregarded to a great extent, especially in communities where the public sentiment has been strong against prohibition.

Even in Maine, where these statutes have existed for a longer period than in any other State, and where the most strenuous efforts have been made to enforce them, it has been boldly asserted by some that there has been fully as much liquor drunk as if the prohibitory statute had not existed, and that statistics have shown no diminution of crime resulting from the prohibitory law, while others claim that the law has been generally obeyed. In some States local option laws have been enacted, under which the electors of the respective counties are authorized to determine, by a majority of their votes, whether any intoxicating liquors shall be manufactured or sold within their limits. These laws are based upon the assumption that if a majority of the electors are shown by their votes to be in favor of prohibiting the traffic within their territory, they will see that they are enforced and the traffic therein prevented. But unless the principle of prohibition is generally adopted throughout the State, the difficulties are still greater than they would be if the traffic were everywhere forbidden by a general law. A few isolated counties in which prohibition has been adopted, surrounded by counties in which the traffic is licensed under the general law, are open on all sides to invasion by habitual law-breakers, while their own inhabitants, living near their respective boundaries, can easily pass over where liquor is freely sold "according to law," and gratify their appetites without restraint. Until the great enormity of the evil and the overwhelming necessity for effective measures for the suppression of intemperance is more generally understood and appreciated, prohibitory laws, whether general or particular will be of little avail.

Temperance societies have accomplished much good by enlightening the community in regard to the effects of strong drink upon the minds and bodies of individuals, and in deteriorating the race physically, morally, and intellectually, and in establishing a strong public sentiment in some States and localities in favor of legal prohibition and the enforcement of prohibitory laws. The ministers of religion have preached against intemperance from their pulpits, while a large proportion of them have indulged in the habitual use of intoxicants, and thousands of their church members not only use the fatal poison habitually, without ministerial rebuke or admonition, but many of them are manufacturers of or dealers in intoxicating drinks; and intoxicating wines are dispensed by gospel ministers to the members of their churches in administering the communion service, as an emblem of the blood that washes away the sins of the penitent,—an emblem of blood surely, and an efficient cause of sin and crime and the destruction of all that renders life of any value.

Thus, notwithstanding all the efforts which have been made to suppress intemperance, statistics seem to show a constant and steady increase of intemperance in all civilized countries of the globe, and the prospects for the future are indeed gloomy.

A few years ago the *London Times* said, " In our time we have suffered more from the intemperance of our people than from war, pestilence, and famine combined." In March, 1881, the same paper said, "Something must be done to redeem the nation from the slough of drunkenness in which it is now wallowing. The drink bill of the country has enormously increased since 1860, with multiplied horrors of every kind coming from drunkenness. In that year the drink bill was £86,897,683 [or $434,488,415]. In 1879 the cost of the liquor consumed in the kingdom was £147,288,760 [or $736,443,800]." The *Times* further said, " Suppose an unexpected visitation of prosperity, how high would the total stand in the last year of the century? If there be any probability one way or the other, it is that the year 1900 will be as much above 1880 as that is above 1860, and that the drink bill will then be £246,000,000 [or $1,230,000,000]. For the whole population of these isles the average expenditure in drink is more than £3 [or $15] for every man, woman, and child, and more than £15 [or $75] for each family. It is vastly more than the public revenue, vastly more than the most inflated and extraordinary expenditure we have had for twenty years. It is more than ten times as much as is spent for the poor, watched by economists with such jealous eyes. As for the revenue of the Church of England, which many call monstrous, and which certainly is exceptional in comparison with other churches and religious communities, if it were brought to the hammer to-morrow—glebes, rent-charges, parsonages, churches, episcopal and capitular incomes, everything down to church furniture and parish stock of vestments—it would scarcely fetch the amount of last year's drink bill. The workingman grudges a few pence for the education of his children, and spends often as many shillings in drink. He will not lay up as much as a shilling a week to provide for probable sickness and inevitable old age, but he spends perhaps ten times that amount in beer and spirits. But he is not the greatest sinner; far from it. His betters—lay, spiritual, professional, or trading—are generally far worse than he is. The gentleman in the pulpit, who delivers weekly diatribes against drunkenness and improvidence, . . . often spends ten times as much, though he really wants it less. It is a very ordinary thing for the wine and beer bills to amount to £50 [$250] out of a total expenditure of £500 [$2500]."

"The testimony of the church," says Dr. Buchanan, "as given by a committee of the Lower House of Convocation in 1869, is that ' a careful estimate of the mortality occasioned by intemperance in the United Kingdom, including the lives of innocent persons cut short by the drunkenness of others, places the mighty sacrifice at fifty thousand persons every year,—a number twice as great as that which perished on both sides upon the fatal field of Waterloo.' This statement is very moderate. Dr. Norman Kerr, unwilling to believe in such fatality, more recently investigated the question, and decided that the mortality directly produced by alcohol is greatly above a hundred thousand annually." The horrible intemperance of Great Britain during the last ten years has been fully displayed by the calculation of William Hoyle, who shows that the expenditure for drink is more than twice the entire rental of the kingdom. In Ireland, with far lower rents, the average amount expended on liquors in ten years was £13,823,162, and the total rental £11,518,392.

In continental Europe the steady increase of intemperance is shown by statistics to be equally alarming. In a former part of this work its desolating progress among our own people is shown. All other causes of moral degeneracy increase the flow of alcohol, and they reciprocally act together as cause and effect. " Brutality," says Dr. Buchanan, " demands alcohol, and alcohol feeds brutality, and hence they increase together. . . . This is illustrated by the statistics of the State of Maine under a prohibitory liquor law which is commonly called the ' Maine Law.'

" From 1851 to 1880 the population increased fourteen per. cent., or one-seventh,—from 587,680 to 648,945. During this period, in spite of temperance laws (enacted in 1852), churches, and New England education, the number of crimes has tripled,—the State-prison convicts, eighty-seven in 1851, were two hundred and sixty-seven in 1880. The high crimes of murder, murderous assault, arson, rape, robbery, and piracy increased from fourteen to sixty-seven. Divorce, insanity, and suicide have also largely increased during this period. . . . Thus enforced temperance has failed as signally as the church and the school to arrest the downward tendency."

As reciprocal causes of moral and physical degeneracy Dr. Buchanan enumerates the four following as the most prominent :

1. That " the whole civilized world has been gradually leaving the country and crowding into the large cities, in which the race degenerates so rapidly that, if it were not for the health and vigor of the country, the population of the civilized nations would actually decline, the deaths exceeding the births. With all their polish and intellectuality, great cities are known to be great ulcers, and their intellectuality has no more power to save them than sunshine has to prevent putrefaction.

2. "The conscription of the entire population for military service, the army, being a rebellion against the Divine law, a school of pessimism that debases the moral nature and, like a malignant tumor, absorbs the life-blood of the nation, driving the poor by exhausting taxation into pauperism and prostitution." This applies more especially to the countries of Europe, but its consequences reach us through the flood of emigration which is flowing in upon our shores from the most ignorant and impoverished populations of the Old World.

3. "The third cause is the industrial ignorance of laborers, which disqualifies them from profitable employments, and perpetuates their poverty by the enormous competition of hungry, unskilled laborers.

4. "The fourth cause is the selfish competition and gambling commerce, in which capital, in a few skilful hands, grows with magical rapidity by dividends, monopolies, and speculation, while labor, unenlightened, must struggle despairingly (as it is in excess) for a bare subsistence."

"The deep underlying cause of all," says Dr. Buchanan, "is found in the organization of society and all its institutions upon a basis of pure and intense selfishness, instead of the principles taught by Jesus. Life is altogether a desperate competitive struggle,—a struggle to grasp, monopolize, and indirectly enslave.

"For none of those great evils does our common education offer or suggest any remedy. It develops no high principles; it undermines more than it assists religion; it harmonizes with selfish ostentation and ambition; it increases the separation and alienation of classes; it aggravates discontent with the existing social orders; it stimulates wild, pessimistic speculations; furnishes intellect to journalism and politics, and incendiary leadership to discontented masses.

"The true full-orbed education of the moral and indus-

trial faculties annihilates intemperance and vice, assures the
prosperity of all, places the humblest laborer in the path
that leads to comfort, intelligence, and happiness; destroys
the social alienation of classes and the consequent jealousies;
forbids all future turbulence, and elevates women above the
sphere of prostitution; restores integrity to governmental
affairs, empties prisons and almshouses, unites industrial
pursuits in co-operative and profitable systems of stability,
. . . establishes the ideal republic, and prepares for the
advent of the Kingdom of Heaven by removing every
obstacle."

If there is any system of education possible by which all
or most of those great benefits can be gained, there is certainly no conceivable blessing that can be of greater value
to mankind. And what ground have we to hope for the
elevation and improvement of the race, when all existing
systems designed for that end have failed, if it is not in the
adoption of a wiser and better system of education for the
young? Will moral and industrial education of the youth
stay the tide of intemperance and vice and disperse the
murky clouds of pollution that hang like a pall of moral
death over the civilized world? Education in all reformatory institutions is directed to making the recipients of it
good and useful, self-respecting and self-sustaining, and their
wonderful success in eradicating vicious tendencies and im-
planting in their stead the elements of honesty, industry,
and virtue is shown by the histories of those we have referred to when considering the proper treatment of crime.
In all these institutions, as we have seen, every pupil is instructed in some useful industrial pursuit by which he can
earn an honest living and lay the foundation of future success. He goes out into the world a skilled laborer, artisan,
tradesman, or mechanic, whose services are in demand, and
carries with him a certificate from his teachers that he may
be safely trusted and employed. Without this industrial

education, all the intellectual training he might receive, and all the moral precepts he might be taught, would not make him good, nor fortify him against the temptations to evil which he would have to encounter. Industrial education is at once the sword and shield which are put into the hands of every pupil on leaving a reformatory, with which to carve out character and acquire competency and ward off the assaults of misfortune and vice, and no practical philanthropist or manager of a reformatory at this day would dream of accomplishing the reformation of criminals, whether youth or adults, without a thorough training in some industrial pursuit. Industry, wisely and intelligently applied to the benefit of ourselves and others, is a practical exercise of a high moral principle, which of itself affords happiness and strengthens virtue. To those who believe there are ministering angels in heaven, the thought that they derived no happiness from the execution of their missions of good to man would be repulsive. To be happy we must be *actively engaged in doing good.*

The repugnance which many of the prisoners sent to the Elmira reformatory felt to becoming good when received at the institution was attended by an equal aversion to industrial labor, and the same treatment which overcame this aversion overcame also their repugnance to becoming good men and useful citizens.

An industrial and moral education equally practical and thorough for every child in the State, either at home or in our public schools, would, in the course of a few generations, bring about such a vast improvement in the social condition and character of our people that intemperance would be effectually prohibited, and poverty, crime, and oppression would not prevail. Partisanship for selfish ends, with all the corrupting appliances, falsehoods, deceits, and corruptions which are now almost universally resorted to for the purpose of gaining or continuing political power and

influence, would give place to a noble and generous strife in
advancing the public good and securing the welfare and
happiness of all.

The Legislature of the State of Michigan has recently
incorporated into the statute relating to public instruction
and primary schools a provision that, in addition to the
other branches in which instruction is required to be given
in the public schools of the State, instruction shall be given
in physiology and hygiene, with a special reference to the
nature of alcohol and narcotics, and their effects upon the
human system. The text-books used for this purpose are
required to give at least one-fourth of their space to the
consideration of the nature and effects of alcoholic drinks
and narcotics. These are wise and exceedingly important
provisions, and if such instruction is thoroughly and intelligently given, its effects cannot but be salutary in a high
degree. Hygiene—the art or science of preserving health
—is a branch of knowledge that ought to be universally
understood, but of which the great mass are generally but
little informed, and even among the more intelligent its rules
are habitually disregarded. The deleterious effects of alcohol, tobacco, opium, and other poisonous substances upon
the human system, and the dangerous consequences resulting from their use even in the smallest quantities, if clearly
pointed out and impressed upon the youthful mind before
any appetite for them has been acquired or habit of using
them formed, will, with proper moral and industrial training,
operate as a protection and saving influence to the man
through his entire life, and enable him to overcome even a
strong inherited tendency to intemperance.

Every means of prevention adopted by churches and
temperance associations for reforming those who have already become the slaves of strong drink should be continued. They have accomplished much good in the past
and may do more in the future, but the hope and trust of

the true philanthropist and reformer must be based upon the educating of the young by instructing them in the principles and practice of temperance, morality, and industry. If our youth of both sexes shall be so educated, the sentiment in favor of prohibition will become practically unanimous when they become men and women, and laws forbidding the manufacture or sale of alcoholic liquors for any other than medical and scientific purposes will be strictly enforced, without any formidable opposition. The causes of intemperance and vice will be understood and removed, and the disease prevented by removing them or contracting their influence.

Such an education will put an end to ignorance and idleness, and expel avarice, cupidity, and selfish ambition, with the long dark list of crimes that follow in their train and cast their lurid shadows over the hearts of men and women throughout the civilized world. It will diffuse its healing influence over all nations, and bring peace and security instead of wars and tumults. It will broaden the sense of a common brotherhood, so that geographical lines shall no longer divide friends from foes, and standing armies to protect the one by destroying the other no longer be supported by imposing excessive burdens upon industrious, peace-loving citizens.

## CHAPTER III.

### HOW SHALL THE INTERESTS OF CAPITAL AND LABOR BE HAR-MONIZED AND THE CONFLICT BETWEEN THEM PREVENTED?

" Ye friends of truth, ye statesmen who survey
The rich man's joys increase, the poor's decay;
'Tis yours to judge how wide the limits stand
Between a splendid and a happy land."

WE have said that there is no necessary conflict between capital and labor. The true interests of the capitalist and the laborer are identical, and what benefits the one should benefit the other. The man of wealth may increase his store of gold by disregarding the just rights of laboring men and women, but he can do so only by dwarfing his own soul and debasing his manhood, and losing thereby what is of infinitely more value than material wealth, his own self-respect and the right to claim the sincere respect of others.

If all men had attained the requisite knowledge to perceive and the wisdom to be governed by that which is at once the greatest, most simple, most rational, and most sublime truth ever revealed or taught to man,—a truth which is upon so many lips, but really comprehended by so few,—and of applying it to all the exigencies of social, political, and domestic life, there would be no difficulty in giving a satisfactory answer to this question. We have referred to this great truth as contained in the teachings of Confucius and of Jesus. It is the common interest and brotherhood of man,—the law of love, of peace, and of good-will among men, embracing those of all nations, tongues, and races upon the earth. It required a long period of time and of progression from a state of barbarism and semi-barbarism

26

before there were any capable of accepting it.  It was not contained in the decalogue, which was supposed to have been written by the finger of the God of Israel on tablets of stone, and delivered to Moses amid clouds and thunders on Mount Sinai.  The God whom that ancient people worshipped was the God of battles, who taught them to destroy other nations and peoples, and take possession of their lands and of their goods as an inheritance.  "The Lord," says Moses, "is a man of war; the Lord is his name."  The author of Exodus represents him as saying, "I will do terrible things;" that he would drive out before them the Amorites, and the Canaanites, and the Hittites, and the Perizzites, and the Hivites, and the Jebuzites, and would cut them off.  Almost every European nation is at this moment prepared to make war upon its neighbor in the name of and under the guidance of the "God of battles."  His law for the government of his own peculiar people demanded "life for life, foot for foot, burning for burning, wound for wound, stripe for stripe," and there are millions of people who claim to be enlightened and Christianized at the present day who yet do not seem to know that this law was abrogated by Jesus and superseded by another which is its opposite.

The Israelites were a stiff-necked people, and, like too many of the present day, though very religious, were very full of evil.  They were capable of slaying "every man his brother, and every man his companion, and every man his neighbor" at the command of Moses, in order to appease the fierce anger of their God "of battles" and of his servant Moses, because of their having worshipped the golden calf which Aaron, his priest, had made for them while his brother Moses was upon the mountain holding converse with the Lord.

Love towards those deemed their enemies would have been opposed to the plans and purposes which were formed for their development and growth into a great and powerful nation, and the attempt to promulgate such a law would have been treated with derision, or as the teaching of some strange god or false prophet. The most enlightened peoples were then ignorant, superstitious, barbarous, and cruel, and utterly incapable of understanding the gospel of peace and good will. More than thirty-three centuries have passed since that period, with ever-increasing means of mental, moral, and religious enlightenment and culture; and truths of the most momentous importance to the welfare of mankind have been evolved.

The wise and good who have been able to perceive what is true, and to distinguish it from error, have had a double task to perform,—that of removing ancient and deep-rooted errors, and overturning systems of fraud and oppression against the most strenuous and determined opposition of those who were interested in maintaining existing institutions, and that of building up new systems, based upon the principles of justice and equality, in their stead.

If all who come into the possession of wealth, either by inheritance or successful business enterprise or other legitimate means, were to consider and treat it as a *trust*, to be administered in such manner as to produce the greatest amount of happiness and comfort of which it is capable to others as well as to themselves, and for which they are to render an account as stewards to a paramount proprietor and Lord of all, there would be no conflict between capital and labor, for the laborer, in whatever field of human enterprise employed, would be recognized as worthy of his hire, and would receive his just share of that which his industry and skill have aided in producing, and the disgrace and criminality of poverty and destitution, which are justly chargeable to our present selfish and corrupt social system, would cease to exist.

But the idea of absolute individual ownership of property, and the right to accumulate without limitation, and to dispose of it at the sole pleasure of its possessor, as if he were its creator, and the distinction which society accords to him on account of his riches, are so gratifying to human vanity and pride, and cast such a glamour over his state, that few have been able to realize this great truth, that *the real value of all worldly possessions consists in the good they may enable their possessor to do to others*, and that they can afford true happiness in no other way. The whole atmosphere of society seems to be infected by this glamour. It permeates all classes and all professions. It is conspicuous in the pulpit, the choir, the chancel, at the altar, and in the pews of our popular churches, and among all modern religious denominations. The elaborately ornate and expensive church edifices, the pomp and show introduced into the forms of worship, and the extravagances of dress and equipage indulged by members of churches, as well as others who can command the means of doing so, while there are thousands of their brother men and sister women suffering from hunger and cold, and disease caused by overtaxing the physical powers in ceaseless but unavailing toil, indicate too clearly the increasing tendency towards a division of our people into orders or classes of rich and poor, and render it more and more difficult for any to deal justly, and to live according to the precepts of divine wisdom.

An aristocracy of wealth is equally opposed to the principles of a just equality of rights as an aristocracy of privilege and hereditary authority. Both alike lead to the oppression and enslavement of the masses who inherit neither wealth nor privilege.

The aggressions of capital upon the rights of the people who labor for a subsistence have never been more audacious and utterly regardless of moral principle than at the present time. One of the latest and most iniquitous of all the heartless and soulless schemes for the accumulation of wealth at the expense of the people, and for the impoverishment of the wage-workers of the country, is that of *trusts*, by which not only the prices of labor, but of the products of capital and labor, are fixed by a central power which is wholly irresponsible to the people and defiant to the government. Through a combination of the owners of the coal-mines of the country, under the form of a trust, with railroad corporations and transportation companies which distribute their products to every city, village, and hamlet where it has become an indispensable article of consumption, the prices of coal are fixed for every retail dealer, all competition is precluded, and no such dealer dares to sell a pound of it at any other price, on pain of being denied the privilege of buying or selling it at all.

This central power determines what mines shall be worked and what shall not be worked, and does not hesitate to close any of them when the profits of the combination will be increased thereby, and to throw thousands of miners out of employment for an indefinite period of time. As an example of this arbitrary exercise of power, it was recently announced from Pittsburg, Pennsylvania, that on the 19th of November, 1888, at a meeting of the coal operators, " it was unanimously decided to shut down all the mines along the Monongahela River for an indefinite period. This will throw out of employment seven thousand miners, besides all the river men engaged in taking coal down the river." The suffering which these men and their families must endure in consequence of this action, during the most inclement season of the year, and the sickness and death that cannot fail to result from it, cannot be compensated for by all the blood-stained treasures that the coal operators can ever gain through such unhallowed means.

Neither our national nor any State government would dare attempt by legislation to fix the price to be paid for any article that enters into the daily consumption of its citizens, nor to grant such power to any corporation or municipality; and yet, as we have pointed out in a former part of this work, there is scarcely an article used or consumed in this country the price of which is not arbitrarily fixed by combinations of manufacturers, producers, or dealers.

If the millions of unjust gains accumulated by coal-mining, standard oil, and other combinations of similar character were fairly divided among those who are justly entitled to share with the capitalists in their distribution, it would enable every industrious citizen to live comfortably upon the proceeds of his labor, and to secure a competency to sustain him in sickness and old age, and would furnish a suitable provision for those who are unable to labor. No agrarian law for an equal division of property would be justifiable or salutary, but the principles of sound ethics and of a pure religion will be forever opposed to that vain pride and degrading selfishness which seek their gratification in the hoarding or display of wealth, and prompt men to seek its acquirement by means which may be justly characterized as robbery. The combinations to which we have referred exercise the powers and privileges and have all the odious characteristics of monopolies, than which no more monstrous tyranny has ever existed among civilized peoples.

The means adopted by the famous Captain Kidd and his associates—some of whom are said to have been persons of high rank and social and political position—to make or increase their fortunes, and which the law denounced as piracy, were scarcely more reprehensible in a moral point of view than those by which these combinations accomplish their purposes. Piracy and robbery are often attended by the destruction of human lives where resistance is offered by their victims, but who shall compute the daily sacrifice of health and life, and the suffering worse than death, that are caused by the fraud and injustice of the worshippers of Mammon?

So long as the strong arm of the government does not interfere for its prevention, and a debased public sentiment pays homage to riches more than to moral worth, there can be no abatement of the evil expected, and the tendency will be to its increase. The same restless spirit of enterprise and mental activity which has been stimulated by the rapid increase and diffusion of knowledge during the present century, and which has produced so many wonderful inventions and discoveries adapted to benefit and bless mankind, has also stimulated the unscrupulous, the avaricious, and the seekers of power and place to devise and carry into effect a thousand new schemes and devices for deceiving, defrauding, and oppressing the people.

These monopolies are beginning to attract public attention and to create alarm among thinking observers of events, and it may be hoped they will, at no distant day, be met by such legislation and such moral force of awakened public sentiment as will check, if not destroy, their power for evil and afford some protection to the just rights of the toiling millions. Congress, during its late session, instituted an inquiry into the nature and effects of trust combinations, and we may hope that their true character will be clearly and fully exposed, and that salutary legislation upon the subject by the national and State legislatures will be had, and that all such conspiracies, and all stock gambling and gambling in grains, and other like schemes for making money by fraud and villany will be prohibited by law, on pain of forfeiture of the money invested or property acquired, and the discipline of a State or national reformatory.

By the common law of England such acts of individuals or associations as were calculated to enhance the prices of merchandise or provisions for private gain, to the injury of the king's subjects in general, were held to be offences against public trade. Among these were *forestalling*, which was described as the buying or contracting for any merchandise or victual coming in the way to market, or dissuading persons from bringing their merchandise or provisions there, or persuading them to raise the price when there. *Regrating* was another offence, which consisted in the buying of corn or other dead victual in any market and selling it again in the same market, or within four miles of the place, and thereby enhancing the price of the provisions. *Engrossing* was an offence of similar character, and was described to be the getting into one's possession, or buying up large quantities of corn or other dead victual with intent to sell them again. " This," says Blackstone, " must of course be injurious to the public, by putting it in the power of one or two rich men to raise the price of provisions at their own discretion. And so the total engrossing of any other commodity, with intent to sell it at an unreasonable price, is an offence indictable and finable at common law." The general penalty for these three offences by the common law was discretionary fine and imprisonment.

Among the Romans these offences and other malpractices to raise the price of provisions were punishable by a pecuniary mulct. Bl. Com., Book IV., chap. 12.

Blackstone says that " Monopolies are much the same offence in other branches of trade that engrossing is in provisions," and were declared by statute, in the reign of King James the First, to be contrary to law (excepting certain patents for a limited period), and were punished with the forfeiture of treble damages and double costs to those whom they attempted to disturb.

To monopolize, as defined by Webster, is, 1. *To purchase or obtain possession of the whole of any commodity or goods in the market, with the view of selling them at advanced prices, and of having the power to command the prices. 2. To engross or obtain by any means the exclusive right of trading to any place, and the sole power of vending any commodity or goods in a particular place or country.* The power is expressly granted to Congress by the Constitution of the United States "to promote the progress of science and useful arts, by securing, for limited terms, to authors and inventors, the exclusive right to their respective writings and discoveries. (Art. I. sec., 8.) And this is all the power that Congress possesses to grant any monopoly whatever. But it has the power to "regulate commerce with foreign nations and among the several States," and may prohibit the forming of combinations for establishing monopolies by arbitrarily fixing the price of articles of commerce throughout the country, and rendering any attempt at competition ruinous. The greater includes the lesser, and so trust combinations, such as that of the coal-mine proprietors and operators, involve all the public evils of *forestalling, regrating,* and *engrossing,* as known to the common law, with that of *monopolizing* in its most odious and aggressive form.

The difficulty in legislating wisely upon these subjects under our complex system of government, so as to clearly define those acts which ought to be deemed criminal, and distinguish them from such as are allowable and beneficial, is very apparent to those who have had experience in legislation and the administration of the laws. We have adverted to this difficulty in discussing the proper definition of crime, and included many acts as criminal in their nature which, on account of this difficulty, are not made punishable as such. Every enlightened government should encourage trade, commerce, and manufactures, as a source of national and individual prosperity, and should place no restrictions upon private enterprise excepting such as are necessary for the prevention of fraud, injustice, and oppression; but a government which will not, or cannot, protect the masses of its people against the rapacity and cunning of those who possess the means of enslaving or impoverishing them is not worthy to be called just, much less to be boastingly proclaimed "a government of the people, by the people, and for the people."

Some, if not all, of the threatened evils growing out of the rapid development of the stupendous schemes we have been considering for concentrating immense wealth in the hands of the few by combinations to control the business of the country, and not only to fix the prices of all commodities consumed, but, directly or indirectly, the prices of labor also and the amount of production, have now assumed such a definite character that it appears to us practicable and the duty of the government to interpose, and by suitable legislation endeavor to avert them by declaring all combinations for such purposes criminal and providing for their suppression.

These combinations, unless promptly met and disarmed, will become a constant menace to the government itself, and an intimidation against the exercise of its just powers for their control and the prevention of their abuses. This danger is greatly increased by the general trend of politics under our system of government. It is now well understood, and a subject of regret and alarm to many, that the States are generally represented in the Senate of the United States by millionaires, or men of large wealth, many of whom have made their fortunes by successful speculation; and, whether justly or unjustly, the impression largely prevails in the public mind that their positions were secured by the lavish use of money. Some of them adopt expensive and extravagant modes of living at the national capital, such as men of moderate means cannot afford. It is a fact universally understood, and altogether too lightly regarded, that a seat in the national House of Representatives, especially from a district considered as at all doubtful, can only be secured by the expenditure of a large amount of money, while during the late canvass for Presidential electors it is represented, and is probably true, that the amount expended for carrying the election in a single State has exceeded a million of dollars. To the octogenarian whose memory extends back to the administration of James Madison it may well seem as if the ancient republican simplicity had departed, and with it the rugged virtue and integrity as well as the practical equality of our people.

Our danger does not arise from our great national prosperity, nor the increased production of material wealth, but from allowing it to be grasped by a few, instead of benefiting the many.

Mr. Powderly, Grand Master Workman of the order of Knights of Labor, at a recent meeting of the delegates of that organization, in calling attention to the work before them said, " The most important questions that can come before this body for consideration are those of finance, land, and transportation. These great questions are up before the people for discussion and solution, and must be settled by the people. . . . Those who control our public highways are reaching out with the hand of steel to grasp and control the government."

Of all the monopolies to be dreaded in the future, there is perhaps none more likely to be disastrous to the masses than that of land. We have referred to this monopoly as it exists in England and Ireland, and every student of current history knows full well the sad condition of the farm laborer under their tenant system, and how that by toiling early and late he can only obtain a stinted and meagre subsistence for himself and his family, and that when, from sickness or other cause, he is incapacitated for labor they must suffer want and may become paupers.

England has no written constitution, and the British Parliament is omnipotent in its powers of legislation. Hence it may interpose between the landlord and his tenants when the demands of the former become so exorbitant as to disturb the peace of the country, whatever con-

tract relations may exist between them, and appeals may be
made to the imperial legislature for relief or protection.
But under our written constitution no State has the power
to pass any law impairing the obligation of contracts, and
hence when contract relations have been entered into no
relief can be given by changing their terms or conditions.
Under the provision of the constitution referred to, it was
long ago decided by the Supreme Court of the United
States, after much discussion and deliberation, that an act
of a State Legislature creating a corporation for private
purposes constituted a contract between the State and the
corporation which it created, and could not therefore be
repealed without its consent. The soundness of this decision has been questioned by able jurists, and we deem it
unfortunate that such a determination was arrived at by
that tribunal whose construction of the constitution is binding upon all other courts, and we do not believe that the
framers of that instrument intended to include corporate
charters under the term *contracts.* If the court had taken
that view of it, this country would have been saved from
one of the great dangers that threaten the stability of our
government. This danger so impressed itself upon the
mind of President Lincoln as to cause him the deepest
anxiety. Just before the close of our civil war he penned
the following prophetic utterances: "Yes, we may congratulate ourselves that this cruel war is nearly to a close.
It has cost a vast amount of treasure and blood. The best
blood of the flower of American youth has been freely
offered upon our country's altar that the nation might live.
It has been indeed a trying hour for the republic; but I see
in the near future a crisis approaching that unnerves me,
and causes me to tremble for the safety of our country. As
a result of the war, corporations have been enthroned and
an era of corruption in high places will follow, and the
money power of the country will endeavor to prolong its

reign by working upon the prejudices of the people until all wealth is aggregated in a few hands and the republic is destroyed. I feel at this moment more anxiety for the safety of my country than ever before, even in the midst of the war. God grant that my impressions may be groundless."

If there was ground for such fears and apprehensions nearly a quarter of a century ago, how much greater reason have we now to apprehend danger from these causes, when corporations have multiplied and combined their power and influence, and wealth has been aggregating in the hands of a few with such unexampled rapidity, until it overshadows and controls all the important industrial interests of the country, and has become the most potent factor in every election of legislative, executive, and ministerial offices. Can this power be controlled by legislation or counteracted by other controlling influences, and the impending danger which so impressed and agitated the mind of the patriot Lincoln be averted? Surely no more momentous question was ever propounded to an enlightened people, living under a government emanating from themselves and theoretically based upon and controlled by their freely-expressed will. Are we now about to discover that, under the guise of freedom, and the encouragement of trade, commerce, and manufactures, we have created and fostered in the money power a tyranny as potent and as destructive of liberty and equality as that of the most absolute ruler in the world? There are some who believe this can be averted only through revolution and bloodshed, or some other great national calamity. The Rev. Dr. Talmage, in a recent Sunday discourse, alluding to the injustice and oppression practised towards some of the helpless victims of poverty, under the promptings of avarice, says, "There are evils in our world which must be thundered down, and which will require at least seven volleys to prostrate them. We are all doing nice work in churches and reformatory institutions

against the evils of the world, and much of it amounts to a
teaspoon dipping out the Atlantic, or a clam-shell digging
away at a mountain, or a tack-hammer smiting the Gibral-
tar. What are needed are thunderbolts, and at least seven
of them. There is the long line of fraudulent commercial
establishments, every stone in the foundation, and every
brick in the wall, and every nail in the rafter made out of
dishonesty; skeletons of poorly-paid sewing-girls' arms in
every beam of that establishment; human nerves worked
into every figure of that embroidery; blood in the deepest
dye of that proffered upholstery; billions of dollars of accumulated fraud intrenched in massive storehouses and stock
companies manipulated by unscrupulous men, until the
monopoly is defiant of all earth and all heaven. How shall
the evil be overcome? By treatises on the maxim, honesty
is the best policy? or by soft repetition of· the golden rule
that we must do to others as we would have them do to us?
No, it will not be done that way. What are needed, and
what will come, are the seven thunders. . . . Thunderbolts
will do it; nothing else will."

These utterances of Dr. Talmage, like many of his pulpit
declamations, may be tinctured with sensationalism, and his
denunciations may be too sweeping, but they nevertheless
truthfully describe the character of a portion of the commercial men of our great cities who have coined wealth out
of the tired nerves and overtasked muscles and brains of the
poor sewing-women, who have been compelled either to labor
for them for a bare subsistence, or else starve or resort to a
life of shame,—and of men who have enriched themselves
by gambling in stocks or grains, or by other dishonest
means.

The indiscriminate denunciation of the wealthy, or of
corporations and manufacturing associations which necessarily require the aggregation of a large amount of capital,
would be as unreasonable as to denounce the poor because

of their poverty. The requirements of the trade, commerce, and manufactures of the country, in which all our citizens are interested, and upon the successful prosecution of which depends the prosperity of each individual citizen, as well as that of the country in general, demand that these associations shall exist, and that they shall control a vast amount of capital. It is not the possession nor the use of money which, in itself, constitutes an evil to be deprecated or a danger to be avoided, for these afford the means, not only of physical well-being, but of intellectual, moral, and spiritual progression.

In legislating for the protection of the people against unjustifiable uses of capital, and of the power which wealth confers, the distinction must be carefully made between such as ought to be restrained or forbidden and such as are beneficial and not dangerous in their character. There should be no restrictions upon manufactures, trade, or commerce that are not clearly necessary for the purposes above indicated.

The trust combinations to which we have referred, and which are attracting the attention of the national Congress, and of the State Legislatures, as well as that of the public at large, have recently become the subject of discussion by able jurists, as well as of judicial animadversion. Professor Dwight, of Columbia College, in an article on " The Legality of Trusts," published in the *Political Science Quarterly*, of December, 1888, discusses the subject of trusts at considerable length and (taking the sugar trust as an example) arrives at the conclusion that they are not only legal, but that neither the State Legislatures nor the United States Congress can legislate upon the subject so as to suppress them. This conclusion is based upon the assumption that such trusts are not injurious to trade or commerce ; that, as a rule, they are not dangerous to the public; that " they cannot overcome the law of demand and supply, nor the resistless power of unlimited competition," and that they

are only a new step in the onward progress of the country
which it would be unwise and, as he clearly intimates, un-
constitutional for the Legislature to undertake to restrain.
It is needless for us to repeat our very emphatic dissent
from these conclusions.  Such combinations are confessedly
organized for the purpose of counteracting " the law of demand and supply" by an arbitrary limit of production and
destroying all competition.  Protected by a high tariff from
foreign competition, and controlling the entire production
of sugar, oil, coal, and other commodities of absolute
necessity consumed in the country, they can, as they have
done and are doing, arbitrarily fix the prices which the
consumer shall pay, unaffected by any natural law of demand and supply, or any possible competition.  If our government were powerless to afford any protection against
such overshadowing self-constituted powers, operating
through and controlling every branch of productive industry, trade, and commerce, and abstracting from a helpless and dependent people as much as they choose for what
they please to give, then it were time the people should
organize a new government, capable of protecting the equal
rights of all.  But this cannot be admitted, and we believe
that very few among the able jurists and statesmen of the
country will be found to agree with Professor Dwight in
his conclusions upon this subject.

The Supreme Court of New York is reported to have
held, in a recent case, that this same sugar trust was an unlawful organization under the rules of the common law, and
that the corporations which combined in its formation have
forfeited their charters by doing so.  But whether they are
punishable by the common law as conspiracies against the
public welfare and the rights of the people or not, their
character is the same, and the power and duty of the government to restrain and control or suppress them ought not
to be a matter of doubt.

We now proceed to consider some of the means by which labor has sought to secure its just share of the joint products of labor and capital. To those who have observed the operations of labor organizations and their effect from an unprejudiced stand-point, as they have existed and now exist in this country, it must, we think, be obvious that comparatively little good, and much evil, has resulted from them. The organization of great trusts on the one hand for the purpose of limiting production and controlling prices, and of laboring men on the other hand for the purposes of controlling the prices of labor and determining who shall be and who shall not be employed, only serve to enlarge and intensify the conflict by placing each in a hostile attitude towards the other, to the detriment of both. The most disastrous conflicts the world has ever witnessed have occurred where both parties were in the wrong, each giving a pretext for the wrong-doing of the other. The methods of strikes and boycotts adopted by labor associations incite to and encourage anarchism and lead to lawlessness and crime. They appeal to the evil passions of men, and afford opportunity for the most wicked and depraved to gratify their desire for plunder or revenge with comparative impunity. The great labor associations, and some of the smaller ones, establish a tyranny as odious as that which they seek to resist. In order to effect their purposes, the individuals, on becoming members of the order or association, surrender their freedom of action and subject themselves to the dictation of a Grand Master or chief, or an executive committee, who direct when, where, and upon what terms they shall labor or desist from labor. By the rules which govern most, if not all, of the trade associations the members are forbidden to work in the same employment with non-union men, or those not belonging to their society, whom they designate as " scabs." The spirit thus fostered by these associations is entirely opposed to the fundamental principle upon which our social and political systems are supposed to be based,—that all men are created equal,—and to that most ennobling and humanizing principle of common brotherhood, common interest, and universal sympathy and good will, upon the practical application of which rest all our hopes of harmonizing human interests and improving our social condition.

Of all the plans devised or suggested by philanthropists or political economists for harmonizing the interests of capital and labor, those which embrace the essential principles of *co-operation*, or profit-sharing, appear to us to be the most feasible, practical, and just, because mutually beneficial in their financial, social, and moral aspects. While the institution of great corporations and trusts, in the usual and customary management of affairs, separates the employer and employé so widely as to offer but little ground of sympathy between them, co-operation and profit-sharing bring the capitalist and the laborer into constant association, and inspire mutual respect and kindly feeling by each towards the other.

This plan does equal justice to all. The man of wealth who lends his money to those engaged in manufactures or other business enterprises may receive a fair return for its use. The manufacturer or other employer is entitled to a fair reward for the capital he puts into the business, and for his skill and enterprise, and the risks incident to the business. The laborer also is entitled to a fair remuneration for his toil and faithfulness; and when, after satisfying these claims, a surplus of profits remains, simple justice requires that this should be shared by and distributed to the capitalist and the laborer, the employer and the employed, whose combined labors and resources have produced it. If this system could be everywhere adopted and carried into practical effect it would solve the great problem of the equitable distribution of wealth, and all would have reason to be satisfied and content. There are, of course, various employments out of which no profit is produced, and to which this system could not be directly applied, but its influence would be reflected upon and benefit all classes of wage-workers and employés. Co-operation means mutual helpfulness, and its principles are adopted and practically applied in a great variety of ways.

One mode of co-operation consists in the adoption of a sliding scale of wages in those branches of business in which it is practicable, as in rolling-mills, mining, and various other industries. It is stated that Mr. Potter, president of the North Chicago Rolling-Mill, is a strong advocate of this system, and that he has succeeded in convincing the employés of more than one of the many establishments with which he is connected that it is for their interest to accept it. Under this system a minimum is in some cases established below which wages shall not fall, and a maximum above which they shall not rise. Mr. Potter, however, advocates the widest scope, so as to cover not only the lowest but the highest prices paid for products. A basis having been reached by mutual agreement, his plan is to have wages fall below or rise above that basis just as the prices of products rise or fall. This plan is illustrated as follows: Taking steel rails at thirty dollars a ton as the basis, and wages at three dollars per day, if the price falls to twenty-eight dollars, wages to fall to two dollars and eighty cents per day, and if the price of rails rises to forty dollars per ton, wages to be four dollars a day, and so in the same proportion as the price of the product rises or falls. Whichever of these plans may be adopted, if the basis be an equitable one, the system embraces the main principle of profit-sharing, and is simple and practical in its operation. In some branches of business the profit-sharing system would probably be preferable. This system has been adopted in several large manufacturing institutions with very satisfactory results. A writer in the *Peoria* (Illinois) *Journal* says, "We never heard of any striking among the workmen employed in the Pillsbury flouring mills at Minneapolis, and the reason is given in the plan pursued by the proprietors of the mills. Each year they set apart or name a certain percentage of their business as legitimate profits, and all over that percentage they divide among their employés, *pro rata.* Last year this excess amounted to thirty-five thousand dollars, and that handsome sum was given to the employés. Every employé has his salary or wages and, besides that, an interest in the business. It is for his personal advantage to do what he can to save waste and needless expense, to increase the profits, and prevent the destruction of property."

A writer on this subject in another journal says, "One of the best remedies for settling the supposed conflict between capital and labor seems to be the co-operative plan of dividing the profits over a stated amount with the workmen and employés, making the latter as closely interested in the success of the business, whatever it may be, as the employers and capitalists. The plan is recommended by economists who have studied the theory of the subject, and seems to be the most practical and successful in actual operation of any of the proposed remedies. A St. Louis manufacturing company has made an offer like this to its employés, which proposes to make each one of them personally and directly interested in the success of the company's business, it being a proposition to divide the profits of the business with the employés, after allowing seven per cent. interest on actual capital invested. The remainder of the profits will be divided equally upon the total amount of wages paid and capital employed. Each employé will receive his proportion of those profits, according to the wages paid him. All employés who have served the company six months or over within the year, and who have not been discharged for good cause, will share in the distribution.

In addition, the company offers the employés the privilege of conducting a co-operative store. Each employé contributes five dollars in instalments of one dollar a week, which is to be invested in groceries and provisions. These goods are to be sold at the usual profits, which are to be invested in other goods, as required, and the surplus divided among the members. The employés elect their own managers and operate the store, while the company offers to allow the regular buyer of the establishment to do the buying, and will also furnish the store-room. The store will be open at the noon hour and on Saturdays from 5.30 to 6.30 P.M." As this writer remarks, "it depends upon the nature of the business whether this plan can be adopted or not. In some it would be quite impracticable. In all manufacturing business, however, it seems it would be most practicable. It is but a modification of the co-operative plan, and has many advantages to recommend it."

Grand Chief Arthur, of the Brotherhood of Railroad Engineers, is reported as saying, "The great trouble is that there is too wide a chasm between employer and employé, and the sooner that chasm is closed up the better it will be for mankind." Whatever co-operative system may be adopted it will tend to close up this chasm by uniting the interests of capitalist and laborer, and will be a step towards that "federation of the world towards which, throughout all the past ages, thought and love, and hope and beauty, and good will in all the nations of the earth have been striving, and which is to establish the commonwealth of Man."

In England there exists a system known as "Rochdale co-operation," the history of which is deeply interesting and instructive, and whose success has been marvellous. That great philanthropist and devoted friend of laboring men, George Jacob Holyoke, who has spent the largest portion of his eventful life in devising and advocating schemes for the elevation and advancement of the toilers of his native

*v*

land, has been largely instrumental in promoting this great industrial scheme.

The character and purposes of this beneficent institution, whose operations, it is said, commenced in a stable, with a wheelbarrow load of goods, will be seen by the following statement of Mr. Holyoke, contained in the March number of the *Journal of Man.* He says, " They now own land; they own streets of dwellings, and almost townships; they own vast and stately warehouses in Manchester, in London, in Newcastle-upon-Tyne, and in Glasgow. They own a bank whose transactions amount to $8,000,000 a year. They possess more than 1400 stores, which do a business of over $160,000,000 a year; they own shares capital of $45,000,000 in amount, and are making now for their 900,000 members more than $15,000,000 profit annually. The mighty power of co-operation has enabled the working class in the last twenty-five years to do a business of $1,800,000,000. Their splendid wholesale society has been buying stations in the chief markets of Europe and America. Their ships are on the sea. The life-boats they have given ride on every coast. They have invested $4,000,000 in the Manchester canal; they issue newspapers; they erect public fountains; they subscribe to hospitals and public charities; they own libraries, reading-rooms, and establish science classes, and subscribe scholarships in the university. Formerly the religion and politics of the working people were dictated to them by their employers, squires, and magistrates. Now, co-operatives have built halls for themselves where they can hear the thing they will on any day they will. No landlord or public authority can lock the door upon them, because they own the place."

Although this statement may seem almost incredible, and more like a romance than a reality, yet there is no reason for doubting its correctness, wonderful as the facts appear. The methods by which such astonishing results have been produced we cannot detail here, but they are all simple, easily understood, and open to the observation of the whole world, none of them being secret or secured by patent. None may undertake to estimate the power and influence of such an association of laboring men, with a membership of nearly or quite a million of men engaged in peaceful business pursuits, working in harmony for their own and others' welfare in an intelligent, systematic way, quietly, without serious friction, and without antagonizing any public or private rights of their fellow-citizens.

Had that great labor association known as the Knights of Labor, organized twenty years ago, and now claimed to number over a million of members, associated themselves together upon the Rochdale co-operative plan, and pursued the methods adopted by their English brothers, we can conceive of no reason why they might not have been equally successful and prosperous; and what a contrast would their condition have presented to what it is now! Instead of many millions of loss of money and time from lockouts and disastrous strikes, they might have accumulated a hundred millions of dollars, and each one himself have become a capitalist as well as a laborer. Instead of the shameful rioting and crime, and destruction of property and unlawful trespassing upon others' rights which have occurred, with all their demoralizing influences upon themselves and the community, they would have been engaged in honorable industrial pursuits that would have led to no conflict with the just rights of any of their fellow-citizens, and which would have brought prosperity, self-respect, and the respect and good will of others. In France the subject of co-operation has occupied the attention and engaged the thoughtful consideration of some of the best minds that country has produced, but as yet the results have generally been more of a speculative than of a practical character. The most successful attempt to establish co-operative institutions in

France that we have information of is that founded by
M. Godin, known as the *Familistere*, near Paris.   In an account of this great family of work-people, published in
the *Chicago Tribune*, it is stated that from his boyhood M.
Godin had been a student and follower of the social ideas
of Fourier and Enfantin, and, having reached a position of
power and influence, he determined to put those theories
into practice.   With this view he erected a large building,
to which additions have since been made from time to time,
until it now has a frontage of six hundred feet.   This he
divided into suites of rooms for his workmen and their
families, and called it the "*Palais Social.*"   At first his workmen did not like the idea.   They thought it would diminish
their independence to live in such an institution.   But M.
Godin persuaded them that the system would make them
really more independent, besides enabling them to live more
cheaply and therefore to save money.

In addition to the main building, various wings and additional buildings have been erected, until more than four
hundred families are lodged in the " Palais Social."   Were
these in ordinary tenements, they would occupy a street
more than a mile long.   The buildings are all of brick and
practically fire-proof, and constructed with every possible
device for the comfort and sanitation of the occupants.
The buildings are four stories high, and each story has a
clear height of ten feet.   There is an abundant supply of
water in every room.   There is also a large court-yard attached to each building, paved with cement and roofed with
glass, serving as a play-room for the children in bad
weather.   The doors of the building are never locked, and
there are no watchmen or special rules, so that all the occupants are as free to come and go and do as they please as
though each family lived in a cottage of its own.   Each
family may rent as many rooms as it pleases, and its apart-
ments are entirely separate from its neighbors, excepting that

they open upon a general hall-way. The cost of the buildings has been about two hundred dollars for each inmate,
and the rent averages about one dollar per month for each
room. M. Godin himself has always occupied rooms there,
differing from those of his workmen in no respect save the
furniture, etc., he put into them.

Connected with the establishment are free schools of
a higher grade than the public schools of France, free
libraries, and reading-rooms; a well-equipped theatre, the
prices of admission to which are from five cents to forty
cents; gardens and parks, co-operative stores at which
everything can be purchased at the lowest possible prices,
and then pay an annual dividend of profit to the purchasers;
a café, a nursery, and numerous minor institutions.

The manufactories cover nearly four acres of ground, and
there are fully twelve hundred persons constantly employed.
The bulk of the business done is the manufacture of stoves,
ranges, furnaces, grates and their settings, coal-scuttles, and
other domestic utensils of cast iron; and it is said that the
finest casting in the world is done there. The magnitude
of the business may be reckoned from the fact that there
are usually on hand, in stock, from thirty to forty thousand stoves and cook-ranges ready for shipment.

The hours of labor are from 6 to 9 A.M., from 10 A.M. to
1.30 P.M., and from 3 to 6.30 P.M., allowing one hour in the
forenoon and one hour and a half in the afternoon for rest
and recuperation, and devoting ten hours to work, which,
by being broken up into three sections, fatigued the men
less than eight hours of continued labor would have done.

The average pay of the workmen has not been much
above five dollars a week, and yet they are better paid than
the hands in most other French factories. But their pay
does not represent all their income, for each workman receives a share of the profits proportionate to his share of
the work of producing those profits. The capital stock of

28

the establishment is nine hundred thousand dollars. The annual dividend of profits to the workmen averages about eight per cent. on this, or seventy-two thousand dollars. This pays about one hundred dollars a year to those who live in the " Palais Social," for of the twelve hundred hands employed, some five hundred are mere outsiders who live in the village of Guise and come to the shops merely for their wages, like workmen in any ordinary factory.

For the aged and crippled there are various pension and insurance funds. There is also a pharmacy fund by which the sick can procure needed medicine without cost.

In the case of M. Godin the attempt has been made by a capitalist and an employer of laborers to put into practice a theory which he and many others believe is capable of solving the great labor question, by raising the laboring man to a condition of assured independence and affording him the means of education and mental and moral advancement, and the motive to strive for the best he is capable of becoming; and this effort appears to have so far resulted in great benefit, both to the employer and employé.

An intelligent and successful manufacturer of machinery, who had himself been a laborer for wages, is reported as saying that "Our present difficulties spring from the fact that our labor reform, though a just and needful one, comes from the wrong side. The reform, to be of any value and to achieve any permanent success, must come from the employer and not from the laborer. But the employing class will not take up that reform until they are pushed to it; therefore I want to see as much agitation of the subject as the country will bear, both by the laborers themselves and all who sympathize with their claims." We can readily perceive how easy it would be to effect all needful reform relating to labor, and to establish the relations of capital and labor upon a just basis, if manufacturers and employers of labor generally would initiate measures adapted to that end; and it seems to us equally clear that such measures, embracing the principle of co-operation, would be equally beneficial to both classes. This subject must and will be agitated throughout the country until the just rights of the laborer and the capitalist will be recognized and respected. Strikes, boycotts, and lawless violence by organized labor associations and their members are not the modes of agitation which right-thinking men want to see or can approve. The evil effects of these we have adverted to in treating of the causes of crime.

Those who claim the sympathy of the wise and good should themselves be just, and opposers of wrong and injustice. Men have struggled *against* each other from the beginning, and the consequences have been injurious to all. If, now, men were wise enough to strive *for* each other, what a contrast would appear! Instead of anxiety, distrust, and hate, and a constant apprehension of evil, we should behold human faces beaming with love and confidence and joy. Order, harmony, peace, and good will would prevail, and we would have a new world wherein contentment would give place to unrest and dissatisfaction. The conflict between capital and labor would no longer exist, and fear of financial ruin and the miseries of hopeless poverty and despairing want would cease to embitter the lives of men. Carlyle truly says, " Men cannot live isolated. We are all bound together for mutual good or else for mutual misery, as living nerves of the same body. No highest man can disunite himself with any lowest. . . . Let a chief of men reflect well on it. Not in having 'no business' with men, but in having no unjust business with them, and in *having* all manner of true and just business, can either his or their blessedness be found possible, and this waste would become, for both parties, a home and peopled garden." In the same book ("Past and Present") Carlyle penned these golden words also, which are worthy to be set in pictures of silver: " The wealth of a man is the number of things which he loves and blesses, which he is loved and blessed by."

In all the great mercantile establishments of the country it is believed that profit-sharing may be adopted to the mutual advantage of employer and employed.  It has been adopted by one of the most astute and successful of men, who is at the head of an immense mercantile establishment in Philadelphia, and we believe with every assurance of success.  We find the following published in the public newspapers in reference to the co-operative principle introduced into this establishment: " The experiment in profit-sharing which Mr. John Wanamaker, of Philadelphia, is making is one which will be watched with much interest.  It marks a new and fraternal era in the labor question when four thousand employés are called together to receive the report of their principal, and to learn the share which they are to enjoy of the profits of the establishment.  As a result of the first year, over fifty-nine thousand dollars have been distributed in monthly dividends, in addition to the weekly salaries.  Ten thousand dollars have been paid over to the trustees as a pension fund for the permanently disabled, whether by reason of old age or accident in the service.  In addition to this, the balance divided in annual dividends amounted to forty thousand dollars."

In an article written by George A. Bacon, of Washington, and published in a Boston periodical in December, 1888, on the subject of profit-sharing, the writer says, " While the economic relations of life are struggling with more or less success to settle themselves upon a basis of equity, it is no less a duty than a pleasure to make public record of each and every instance where the principle of profit-sharing has been practically adopted, knowing that this process of adjustment between labor and capital, between employer and employé,—that this form of mutual partnership, this com-

prehensive scheme of practical co-operation, has every consideration to commend it.

"Briefly outlined, profit-sharing presents itself as follows :
Allow current rates of interest for capital invested. After
paying fair salaries, necessary expenses, etc., divide the
surplus *pro rata* among those who assist in producing it,
adjusting wages to the relative value of each employé.

"Our industrial system is founded upon profits secured
through rivalry. By competition few can succeed, and then
only at the expense of others. In profit-sharing, on the
contrary, all being reciprocally related, each assists the other
and the whole are benefited. A direct pecuniary interest
stimulates industry and increases responsibility. A sense
of personal ownership creates a conserving power in every
community where it exists.

"In a system of profit-sharing, 'strikes,' 'lockouts,' etc.,
become unknown. The relation of boss and laborer, instead
of antagonizing, becomes harmonizing. Instead of war,
peace ensues. Under a well-devised scheme of profit-
sharing the conflicting interests that grow out of competition no longer exist ; they become merged into one
accordant and harmonious whole. The most simple-minded
realizes that his own interests are directly increased in
proportion as he faithfully works for others,—that he becomes a part owner in the labor and materials furnished by
his fellow-associates. The result is that self-reliance and
self-respect and self-improvement naturally follow."

Mr. Bacon refers to the following as instances of profit-
sharing which had come to his knowledge during the preceding year. "About two years ago the firm of Norton
Bros., Chicago, having voluntarily offered to divide a portion
of their profits for the year among their two hundred and
fifty employés who worked continuously for six months,
subsequently divided the sum of thirteen thousand two
hundred and seventy-five dollars among them. Each em-

ployé received over seven and a half per cent. on his year's
earnings, which averaged from five hundred dollars to fifteen
hundred dollars.   This extra amount was from thirty-eight
dollars and fifty cents to seventy-seven dollars and seventy
cents.

"A Cincinnati firm (Messrs. Proctor & Gamble, manufacturers), towards the beginning of last year, proposed to
their help that every six months an investigation should be
made of their business, and that after allowing six per cent.
on their capital, and reasonable salaries to members of the
firm, the remainder should be divided among the employés
in proportion to the capital and wages earned.   This offer
was received with thanks, and a promise was given that no
outside influence should disturb the cordial relations between
them and their employers.

"When the late new proprietor of the *Detroit Evening
Journal*, W. H. Brealey, Esq., took possession of that
paper, a year ago last May, he announced that at the end
of each year his intent was to divide a percentage of the
profits among his employés in addition to their usual
salaries.   And here is a case where the capital is represented by a corporation: President Ashley, of the Toledo,
Ann Arbor, and North Michigan Railroad Company, not
long since submitted the following proposition: That all
officials and employés of the company who shall have been
continuously in its service for five years or more shall, in
addition to the regular wages paid to each, receive an
amount which shall equal the proportion hereinafter named
of such dividend on the capital stock as may be declared by
the board of directors of the company in any one year."

Mr. Bacon also refers to the case of Mr. Wanamaker,
above noticed, and says that "Boston furnishes at least
three notable instances of this beneficent scheme for the
amelioration and encouragement of those in their respective
employ.   Foremost, the *Boston Herald*, to its credit be it

known, has adopted this worthy plan. It can well afford to do it, as it is a very successful concern, but this exceptional action is none the less commendable.

"A popular dealer in fancy goods on Washington Street, gave notice to his help last year that it was his intention to divide the profits of his extensive business with those who had been in his employ one year, each January in future. He will divide one-half the net profits over a certain sum reserved for himself, this to be based on the previous year's business. The employés are to be separated into three classes: those in the first class comprising all who have been in his service five years or upward; the second class those from three to five years; the third class those from one to three years."

Mr. Bacon adds that personally he would go out of his way to trade with such a merchant, and probably there are many others who would do the same.

"The Workingmen's Co-operative Bank, of Boston, is practically on this basis. It has proved to be a successful institution, and justly so.

"In these days of gigantic 'trusts,' 'corners,' 'combines,' etc., heartless monopolies of every kind and character, no one expects that the element of selfishness in men is to be eradicated. Implanted for a wise purpose, it only needs to be wisely directed. But in the economies of life to seek to substitute more righteous and equitable relations for those that generally prevail is always in order. Hence the emphasis given to the foregoing instances of practical co-operation in profit-sharing. Let these examples become multiplied a thousand-fold. The relief that is born of confidence, and which brings to legitimate increase moral and financial success, awaits all such economic action."

Many more instances of the practical adoption of the plan of profit-sharing by employers with their employés might be cited, but those we have referred to are sufficient to indicate the feasibility of adopting it by railroad and other corporations, by manufacturers, and in merchandizing, mining, banking, and various other branches of business. They seem to indicate, also, that when a practical plan of labor reform is introduced by the employers who furnish the capital, it comes from the "right side" and appears to be uniformly successful when fairly and intelligently carried into effect.

The United States Commissioner of Labor, in his report for 1886, treats of profit-sharing as a remedy for industrial depression, and commends it as one of the most hopeful means of harmonizing the interests of capital and labor. He says, "What is known as industrial copartnership, involving profit-sharing, and involving all the vitality there is in the principle of co-operation, offers a practical way of producing goods on a basis at once just to capital and to labor, and one which brings out the best moral element of the capitalist and the workman. This system has been tried in many instances, and nearly always with success. The leading experiments in Europe are well known, among them being the system adopted by Leclaire, a Parisian house-painter ; the methods in vogue with the Paris and Orleans Railway Company; the industrial partnership established by M. Godin at Guise, France; the experiments of Messrs. Briggs Brothers in Yorkshire, England, and other places. In the United States but little has been done in this direction, but wherever the principle has been tried there have been three grand results: labor has received a more liberal reward for its skill, capital has been better remunerated, and the moral tone of the whole community involved raised. Employment has been steadier and more sure. Each man feels himself more a man. The employer looks upon his employés in the true light as associates. Conflict ceases and harmony takes the place of disturbances." This feature, as a suggested remedy for industrial depressions, has in it so much of hope for the future, in the opinion of the commissioner, that he caused specimen articles of agreement which had been adopted by manufacturing companies to be printed in his report for the benefit of all. Report, 281–284. The commissioner says, " The system of profit-sharing means just this: that the proprietor receives for the capital he invests the ruling rate of interest, as part of the legitimate expense of production. He puts in his share, other than capital, his managerial skill, his business accomplishments, and his knowledge of the industry in which he is engaged. The men who work for him receive for their time and for the ordinary display of the skill required the ordinary rate of wages. The workman also contributes, under profit-sharing or industrial copartnership, his liveliest interest, his best skill, and the care of tools and materials. For the skill, knowledge, and management of the proprietor, and for his being liable for the risks of the establishment, he is entitled to the larger share of the profits under this system, while the workman, taking no risks of the enterprise beyond that of employment, is entitled to the smaller share of profits; but the two forces together arrange for a division of profits on some just and equitable basis. This system, simple in itself, humane in all its bearings, just in every respect to all the parties concerned, is the combination of all that is good in the wage system, and all that is good in co-operation as applied to production. . . . It is a pleasure to be able to state that the proprietors of many influential manufacturing establishments in this country are contemplating the organization of their establishments upon this basis. They see the success of the enterprise where this system already has been adopted, and are glad to follow in so just a path."

With so many apparently incontestable facts in favor of the co-operation of capital and labor, under some of the forms of profit-sharing which have been tested and found to be profitable financially, and morally elevating in their effects, it seems reasonable to conclude that as soon as the attention of employers of labor is directed to it, and they come to understand its operation, they will appreciate its advantages, and that they will not long hesitate to adopt it generally. When this shall be accomplished the conflict between capital and labor will cease and their interests become identical.

If this plan had been adopted generally by corporations, manufacturers, merchants, and other industrial institutions half a century ago, the many millions of loss which has occurred from strikes and lockouts would have been saved, and the crime, destitution, and moral degradation which have proceeded from them would have been averted; the material, moral, intellectual, and physical condition of the laborers of the country would have been incomparably better than they now are, and the temptations to crimes against property being removed in a large degree, and general personal good-will among all classes established, comparatively few crimes would be committed. Under the operation of this plan it would soon be found that with the more equal and just distribution of the profits of labor and capital, and the increased prosperity of all classes, the hours of labor might be gradually reduced, so as to afford every one time for intellectual improvement and mental and moral culture. With the multiplied power of machinery in nearly all the industrial arts, increasing the product in many of them from ten to a hundred-fold, it is our opinion that the time is not far distant when from six to eight hours a day will be deemed sufficient, and no more will be exacted. Labor will be then a pleasure instead of a burden, a source of health instead of bodily infirmity or disease, and will be performed cheerfully and well.

Were we proposing some new and untried theory for uniting the interests of capital and labor and avoiding all conflict between them, we should do so with great diffidence, however plausible such theory might appear to us. But in commending a plan which has been tested to such an extent as to demonstrate its practicability and its adaptation as a remedy for the evils complained of both by employers and employés, we feel the most confident assurance that no better, wiser, or more effectual plan has been, or perhaps can be, devised for this purpose than that of profit-sharing, and we believe we can do no better service to the wage-workers of the country than to advise that all labor organizations direct their attention to this subject, and "agitate" for co-operation of capital and labor under a well-devised and well-matured system of profit-sharing. The contrast of such a system with that now prevailing would be as that of light with darkness, of love with hate, of obstruction with helpfulness. The present is one of constant warfare and struggle; that is one of peace and good-will. The present is to the laboring man one of sullen bitterness or despair, and to the capitalist of danger and distrust. The new system is one of cheerfulness and encouragement, of hope and confidence and security to all.

There is perhaps no class of laborers who have suffered more from inadequate remuneration than coal-miners, and none of the efforts which have been made by the various associations and confederations seem to have essentially improved their prospects or condition. Their cries of distress have brought them no permanent relief, and the gleams of hope that have been awakened from time to time by reason of their appeals for justice and appreciation have been disappointing. In 1855 a convention composed of coal operators having mines in Illinois, Indiana, Ohio, and Pennsylvania, and of delegates representing miners employed in the various coal-producing regions of the country, was held in Chicago. At this convention a committee consisting of three mine owners and three delegates representing the miners' organizations was appointed to make a general

public presentation of the objects and purposes of the convention, and to extend an invitation to all those engaged in
the coal-mining of America to lend their active co-operation towards the establishment of harmony and friendship
between capital and labor in this large and important industry.    In the circular letter issued by that committee
they say, " The undersigned committee believe that this
convention will prove to be the inauguration of a new era
for the settlement of the industrial question in our mining
regions, in accordance with intelligent reasoning, and based
upon fair play and mutual justice," and it was the evident
desire of the representatives of the interests both of capital
and labor that this question should be settled upon a broad,
liberal, and just basis.   This address of the joint committee
representing the miners and mine owners is one of the most
remarkable productions which has appeared relating to this
subject, and one of the most temperate and just in its statements and deductions.   It is published at length in " The
Story of Manual Labor," and is worthy of the most careful
consideration, and it is a subject of profound regret that its
recommendations were not more favorably received by some
of those most deeply interested.

Referring to the agencies which had been adopted for the
adjustment of labor disputes, the committee say that " the
history and experience of the past make it apparent to every
intelligent and thoughtful mind that strikes and lockouts are
false agencies and brutal resorts for the adjustment of disputes and controversies arising between employing capital
and employed labor.  They have become evils of the greatest
magnitude, not only to those immediately concerned in them,
but also to general society, being fruitful sources of public
disturbance, riot, and bloodshed.   Sad illustrations of this
truth are now being witnessed in certain of our large cities
and in several of the mining and manufacturing centres of.
the country.    These industrial conflicts generally involve

waste of capital on the one hand and the impoverishment of labor on the other. They engender bitter feelings of prejudice and animosity, and enkindle the destructive passions of hate and revenge, bearing in their train the curse of widespread misery and wretchedness. They are contrary to the true spirit of American institutions, and violate every principle of human justice and Christian charity. Apart and in conflict capital and labor become agents of evil, while united they create blessings of plenty and prosperity, and enable man to utilize and enjoy the bounteous resources of nature intended for his use and happiness by the Almighty."

At a joint meeting afterwards held in Columbus, Ohio, which was largely attended, a proposition was made to raise the wages of miners according to a certain scale, which proposition was adopted by a majority of thirty-one to nine. But some of the mine owners refused to accept it, and thus this most laudable attempt to "adjust market and mining prices in such a way as to avoid strikes and lockouts, and give each party an increased profit from the sale of coal," failed at the moment when it seemed almost sure of accomplishment, and the former evils have continued and increased, to the great loss and injury of both parties and the great detriment of the public morals. Had the noble efforts of those men resulted in the adoption of a system of co-operation by profit-sharing between the mine owners and mine laborers, instead of thousands of the latter now being in such a state of destitution as to be obliged to appeal to public charity to save them from starvation, all might have been living in comfort upon the avails of their honest industry, while the former would have found a source of wealth more valuable than gold in the doing of good to their fellow-men.

# CHAPTER IV.

### CONCLUSION.

THERE are several topics connected with the prevention of crime, some of which have been alluded to in former portions of this work, which we deem it proper to call attention to in this chapter.

*Convict Labor.*                                              .

Much discussion has been had and considerable feeling been exhibited on account of the productive labor of the prisoners in our penitentiaries, and the plan of employing prisoners in some sort of useful labor has been opposed upon the supposition that it created an unjust competition with free labor, and urgent appeals have been made to Legislatures to suppress prison labor for this reason. That this objection is fallacious we think has been abundantly shown. The United States Commissioner of Labor says in his report for 1886, " Convict labor is a disturbing element, affecting the moral apprehension of large bodies of people, and thereby aids in irritating the public mind relative to depressions; but the labor of all the prisons in the country bears so small a proportion to the whole product of the country's industries, that such labor cannot be considered as a prime or influential cause of depressions."

General R. Brinkerhoff, in a paper read before the National Conference of Charities and Corrections in 1877, gives statistics showing the forms of industry pursued in the prisons, the whole number of citizens, and the whole number of convicts employed in these industries, and adds, " From these figures it is apparent, therefore, that the total amount of prison labor actually employed in productive industries in the whole United States amounts, at the farthest, to two and a half per cent. of free labor employed in the same industries. It should be borne in mind, however, that a large proportion of all prisoners are employed in the same industries inside that they previously were engaged in while outside; and as the product of their labor inside cannot be greater than it was outside, how is it possible that their labor should injuriously compete with free labor? It is a fact, however, which should be remembered, that the producing power of convict labor is about one-fourth less than free labor, so that the actual product of convict labor in the United States is less than two per cent. of the total production of free laborers in the same industries." He further says, " The number of emigrants who come to our shores in a single month would be sufficient to supply the industrial position of the suppressed convicts, and by employment outside would soon bring prices and wages to their former level."

It should also be remembered that the convict, by his labor, is earning the expenses of his own support, and perhaps something more, and saving the free industries of the State from so much of taxation. But if it is true that a few industries are injuriously affected by convict labor to an appreciable degree, there are still considerations of overwhelming weight in favor of such employment which it would be a public crime to ignore. To shut men up in prisons for crime without labor, and keep them for long periods in idleness, would be in a high degree cruel and inhuman.

No enlightened prison manager of the present time could be found who would not tell us that prison life without labor would not only defeat all hopes of reformation, but that it would, if long continued, destroy the man, both mentally and physically, and crush out all moral susceptibility They would have to be confined in chains and dungeons, as was the practice a century ago, or surrounded by an army of guards approximating in number that of the prisoners in their charge. Indeed, the idea of such enforced idleness of five or six hundred men in a single prison is too shocking to contemplate. Uncompromisingly opposed as we are to destroying a human life excepting only in self-defence, yet we believe this would be more merciful than imprisonment for several years without some sort of manual labor or other useful occupation.

To be idle in a prison is to experience that "life in death" of Poet Coleridge, to which we have referred in a former chapter. When Carlyle says, "The awakened soul of man, all but the asphyxed soul of man, turns from it as from worse than death," he refers to the condition of those who are without employment, outside of prisons. If to these enforced idleness is so terrible, how much more terrible in chains and dungeons within a prison!

No moral improvement of the man can be hoped for under our penitentiary system, much less his reformation, without labor. "For," says Carlyle, "there is a perennial nobleness, and even sacredness in work. Were he never so benighted, forgetful of his high calling, there is always hope in the man that actually and earnestly works: in Idleness alone is there perpetual despair. . . . The latest Gospel in this world is, Know thy work and do it. The blessed glow of Labor in him, is it not as purifying fire, wherein all poison is burnt up, and all sour smoke itself there is made bright blessed flames? Destiny, on the whole, has no other way of cultivating us. . . . Blessed is he who has found his work; let him ask no other blessedness. He has a work, a life's purpose; he has found it and will follow it.

"Properly speaking, all true work is Religion; and whatsoever in Religion is not work may go and dwell among the Brahmins, Antinomians, Spinning Dervishes, or where it will; with me it shall have no harbor. Admirable was that of the old monks, '*Laborare est Orare*,' work is worship. Older than all preached gospels was this unpreached, inarticulate, but ineradicable enduring gospel; work, and therein have well-being."

Let legislators, and all who possess power and influence in affairs of government and administration, rise to a just appreciation of these inspired utterances of one of the great prophets of modern thought and enlightenment, and the wheels of progress will move onward and upward with constantly accelerated motion, and future generations will bless their memory for the good they have done and the happiness they have secured to them.

*Care for the welfare of those who have been released from prisons and reformatories.*

Under the reformatory system which we advocate, the subject of treatment for crime goes out into the world again carrying with him the assurance that, though he has been capable of committing crime, he has exhibited such evidence of his reformation and disposition to live an honest life, and of his capacity to make himself useful in some industrial pursuit, that he may be safely employed and trusted. Instead of being turned out friendless to take the chances of finding a home and employment, with good moral influences surrounding him, or falling into evil associations and relapsing into crime, those who have had the care and direction of his training and discipline will, in all cases where it is practicable, arrange beforehand for a suitable home and employment for him. Correspondence will be kept up with him, and every encouragement given him until his position is established upon a safe moral basis, and, if necessary for his security at any time, the doors of the institution will be open to him as a temporary refuge. Under our present penitentiary system, when the man has served out the period for which he was sentenced, the institution in which he has served has no further business with him. He takes what is allowed him of clothing, and perhaps the means are furnished him of travelling to his destination, if he has any; and however good his intentions may then be of trying to live an honest life, his chances are small of finding employment and such encouragement as he needs, or providing against want without again resorting to crime, unless some charitable association, organized for such purposes, extends to him a friendly, helping hand. There are a few such associations in the country, and the benefits they have conferred upon this class of persons have been very great, and there are many who bless them for the saving influence they have exercised. If our present system of sentencing criminals to the penitentiary for definite terms is continued, some plan ought to be devised by the Legislature for aiding and encouraging all ex-convicts who are disposed to reform, at the expense of the State; and a temporary asylum should be provided for such as may need it, in order to prevent their lapsing into crime. The man who goes out with a mark set upon him, and finds every man's hand against him, must have become better than the average of mankind if his hand is not turned against every man. Such a one must steal or starve, and it is not surprising that so many who might and should have been saved, return to our penitentiaries for new crimes committed, nor that instances occur in which this is done for the express purpose of being returned to their old quarters. It would surely be for the interest of the State to provide a home and employment for such until something better can be done for them. Through our State boards of charities and corrections, and their agents in each country, a system of communication between the class of persons referred to and a State asylum such as we have suggested may be adopted, by means of which homes and employment might be found for all such as can furnish evidence that they may be safely trusted and employed.

*Exclusion of paupers and criminals of other nationalities from our shores.*

While it is the interest and duty of our government and people to adopt a hospitable and friendly policy, and to encourage good-will and kindly sympathy towards the people of all other nations, it cannot be either wise or humane towards our own people to admit the paupers and criminals of the older nations of the globe to be brought here and dumped upon our shores without limitation or restraint, to be a burden upon our municipalities, or to exert a corrupting influence in our communities. These classes our government has undertaken to exclude, but either because our laws are inadequate or are not enforced with sufficient vigor and faithfulness, multitudes of them are constantly being thrust upon us. It is the duty of every nation to take care of and provide for its own poor, as well as its criminals, and it is unjust that any nation should allow this burden to be cast upon any other people.

Our government has also forbidden the introduction here of foreigners under contracts for labor. The laws enacted for the purpose of preventing the slavery of the immigrant under the former contract system, and the protection of our own laborers against ruinous competition with those whose habits of life enable them to live and labor upon cheaper and coarser food than our own workingmen can subsist upon, and for wages that would not support an American laborer, have been extensively violated or evaded, and seem to require amendment by the adoption of some more stringent regulations. The greed of manufacturers and contractors upon railroads and other great works has tempted them to secure the introduction of great numbers of Bohemians, Hungarians, and Italians, of the class just referred to, in the hope and expectation of making large profits upon their labor. But cheap laborers have not been long in learning that they were not receiving, as they were induced to believe, the current rates of wages of the country, nor slow in adopting the means that the labor organizations here have rendered familiar; and strikes among them, as might have been expected, have been attended with more fierce and reckless brutality and crime than have resulted from any of the thousands of other strikes which have occurred. Their ignorant turbulence and riotous destruction of life and property have made them a terror, not only to their employers, but to the communities in which they have lived. The outrages which they have shown themselves capable of committing may result in discouraging their introduction and employment in competition with our own more intelligent and self-respecting laborers, but this does not compensate for the evil they have done. Another dangerous class of persons to which we have had occasion to refer is composed of those who are known as anarchists. These are the open and declared advocates of treason against all civil government, and it is understood that they are banded together in secret organizations for the purpose of securing their ends by violence or revolution. Associations of this character are dangerous to the peace and good order of society, and their advocacy of such principles borders very strongly upon misprision of treason. It is in the power of Congress to provide for excluding or expelling persons who are known to be advocates of treason, though they may not be guilty of any overt act constituting treason.

*The equal education of the sexes.*

"An eminent French writer has said, ' When you educate a boy, you perhaps educate a man; but when you educate a girl, you are laying the foundation for the education of a family.' He might have added, that to this end the physical training is of equal importance with the mental.

"In these days the subject of the physical training of young men is occupying much attention, and the discussions are broad and full of interest. The fault is that the needs of both sexes in this respect are not equally considered.

"An erect figure, an organization in which the processes of life may go on without the ceaseless disorder of functions at war with each other because of abnormal relations,—in short, the added advantages which a fine physical adjustment gives to its possessor,—are as necessary to the one sex as to the other, and for the same reason. If physical education and consequent improvement are things to be desired, it is not that a number of individuals, as a result of this training, shall be able to perform certain feats of strength or agility, but in its broadest sense it is for the improvement of the race, and the race cannot materially advance physically, intellectually, or morally unless the two factors which constitute the race share equally in whatever tends to its greater perfection. Therefore, if in consequence of proper physical training men can do more work, live longer, and transmit to their offspring a share of this improved condition, women also should be so trained that they can do more work, live longer, and contribute to the higher possibilities of their offspring by supplementing, instead of thwarting, the promise which has been presupposed in the higher development in the male parent." (Dr. Lucy M. Hall, in *Science Monthly.*)

These remarks by a lady physician of some note are very suggestive and worthy of the most profound attention. Since scientific observations and correlation of facts have made us acquainted with the laws of heredity, the physical, mental, and moral education of both sexes assumes an importance and gravity which our more ignorant ancestors did not comprehend, and which is not now generally understood or appreciated. A writer in the London Hospital, treating of the subject of hereditary taints, says, "One result of the labors of physiologists has been the clearing of the mental vision and the gradual comprehension of the great, pervasive, and potential fact of '*heredity.*' 'The sins of the fathers shall be visited upon the children,' said Moses more than three thousand years ago. Probably he comprehended in but a very small measure the significance of his own utterance. Not only do parents transmit to children their mental peculiarities, their moral tendencies, the features of the face, the stoop of the shoulders, and the trick of the gait, but they pass on to them their blood, their brain, their glands, their very soul and life. We do not mean to say that heredity is a tyrant from which there is no escape, and that as is the parent in constitution and conduct so also must be the children to the remotest generation.

"If that were one of the discoveries of physiology, small thanks would be due to the science from overburdened man. But it is not so. The parent himself, as is well known, can modify and make worse or better both his constitution and his character. Similarly, the child's constitution and character may be changed, until, by the operation of the law of heredity itself, a not very remote descendant may be the antipodes of his early progenitors. The discovery of an existing inherited taint of disease or of vice in a child is not a cause for regret, but for thankfulness. The disease taint itself is, of course, to be deplored, and so is the inherited vice; but its early discovery is to be hailed with gratitude as pointing out lines of physical and moral treatment which may lead to the practical enfeeblement of the taint or even to its eradication."

THE END.

PRINTED BY J. B. LIPPINCOTT COMPANY, PHILADELPHIA.

# A LIST OF BOOKS

SELECTED FROM THE

# Catalogue

—OF—

## J. B. LIPPINCOTT COMPANY.

(COMPLETE CATALOGUE SENT ON APPLICATION.)

# LIPPINCOTT'S
# GAZETTEER
## OF THE WORLD.

A COMPLETE PRONOUNCING GAZETTEER OR GEOGRAPHICAL
DICTIONARY OF THE WORLD.

---

**One volume. Imperial Octavo. Embracing 2680 pages.
Price: Library sheep, $12.00; half Turkey, $15.00;
half Russia, $15.00.**

---

New edition. Thoroughly revised, entirely reconstructed, and
greatly enlarged. Containing notices of over 125,000 places, and
giving the most recent and authentic information respecting the
Countries, Islands, Rivers, Mountains, Cities, Towns, etc., in
every portion of the globe, together with a Series of Supplement-
ary Tables of Population, embodying the most recent Census
Returns. It is a large octavo volume of 2680 pages, and contains
the correct spelling and pronunciation of geographical names.

---

---

## J. B. LIPPINCOTT COMPANY,
### 715-717 MARKET STREET,
- - - - - PHILADELPHIA, PA. - - - - -

# LIPPINCOTT'S
# PRONOUNCING
# DICTIONARY
## OF BIOGRAPHY AND MYTHOLOGY,

CONTAINING MEMOIRS OF THE EMINENT PERSONS OF ALL AGES AND COUNTRIES,
AND ACCOUNTS OF THE VARIOUS SUBJECTS OF THE NORSE, HINDOO, AND
CLASSIC MYTHOLOGIES, WITH THE PRONUNCIATION OF THEIR NAMES
IN THE DIFFERENT LANGUAGES IN WHICH THEY OCCUR.

By Joseph Thomas, M.D., LL.D., Author of Thomas's
" Pronouncing Medical Dictionary," etc. New edition,
revised and enlarged. Complete in one volume of
2550 pages. Price: Sheep, $12.00; half Turkey, $15.00;
half Russia, $15.00.

"'Lippincott's Biographical Dictionary' is invaluable as a part of the
smallest permanent working library. It is a treasure-house of information; a
text-book of necessity, embracing many subjects besides biography. Members
of the C. L. S. C. should include it in the formation or building up of a standard library."—J. H. VINCENT, *Chancellor Chautauqua University.*

" There are few noted men and women, past or present, the important facts
of whose lives you cannot learn from this work in a few words. Mechanically
the book is strongly and finely made, and is well adapted to constant and hard
usage, as becomes a book of reference. The directions for pronunciation are
especially valuable. We should add the work without hesitation to the list of
indispensables for every private library; all public libraries will have it, of
course."—*The Literary World* (Boston).

" We must declare it the best as well as the most comprehensive book of its
description, emanating from the pen of one writer,—in any language,—which
has come under our notice. . . . What the comprehensive scholarship, perseverance, energy, and critical accuracy of one man may fairly be expected to do
in this field, our author has amply done."—*The N. Y. Nation.*

*⁎* *For sale by all Booksellers, or will be sent by the Publishers, post-paid,*
*on receipt of the price.*

## J. B. LIPPINCOTT COMPANY,

715-717 MARKET STREET,
· · · · · PHILADELPHIA, PA. · · · · ·

# ALLIBONE'S QUOTATIONS.

By S. Austin Allibone, LL.D. Complete in three volumes.
Price per set: In cloth, $9.00; half Russia, $12.00.
The set contains the following works:

## POETICAL QUOTATIONS.

Covering the entire field of British and American Poetry, from
Chaucer to Tennyson. With Copious Indices. Both Authors
and Subjects alphabetically arranged.

" It will at once rank, as his ' Dictionary of Authors' has long done, as the
first and best book of the kind in the English language."—*Harper's Magazine.*

## PROSE QUOTATIONS.

From Socrates to Macaulay. With Indexes. Authors, 544;
Subjects, 571; Quotations, 8810.

" No well-supplied library can do without this work, and its convenience to
writers and thinkers makes it most welcome to readers."—*New York Evening
Express.*

## GREAT AUTHORS OF ALL AGES.

Being Selections from the Prose Works of Eminent Writers from
the time of Pericles to the Present Day.

" The diversity, style, and classical finish of most of the matter, next to the
food for the mind, moulds almost imperceptibly the channels of thought of the
reader, and creates a love for the higher realms of literature."—*Pittsburgh
Evening Telegraph.*

# A CRITICAL DICTIONARY OF ENGLISH
## LITERATURE AND BRITISH AND AMERICAN AUTHORS,

Living and Deceased, from the Earliest Accounts to the Latter
Half of the Nineteenth Century, containing over Forty-six
Thousand Articles (Authors), with Forty Indexes of Subjects.
By S. AUSTIN ALLIBONE, LL D. Complete in Three Vol-
umes. Imperial 8vo. 3140 pages.

Extra cloth, $22.50; sheep, marbled edges, $25.50; half calf, gilt,
$33.00; half morocco, Roxborough, gilt top, $31.50; half Russia,
$33.00.

*⁎* *For sale by all Booksellers, or will be sent by the Publishers, free of
expense, on receipt of the price.*

## J. B. LIPPINCOTT COMPANY,
### 715-717 MARKET STREET,
- - - - - PHILADELPHIA, PA. - - - - -

# THACKERAY'S COMPLETE WORKS.

These are all Author's Editions, printed in England, from the original plates. The illustrations are all from electros from the original blocks. All the editions contain the author's latest revisions, and the typography, illustrations, paper, and binding are in every way THE BEST. *For sale by all Booksellers. Ask for the Original English Editions.*

## STANDARD EDITION.

Printed from new type, on fine paper, and including some of Mr. Thackeray's writings which have never before been collected. With the exception of the *Édition de Luxe* it is the largest and handsomest edition that has been published. With Illustrations by the author and others. 26 volumes. 8vo. Vanity Fair, 2 volumes; Pendennis, 2 volumes; The Newcomes, 2 volumes; Harry Esmond, 1 volume; The Virginians, 2 volumes; Philip, 2 volumes; Hogarty Diamond, 1 volume; Book of Snobs, 1 volume; Christmas Books, 1 volume; Paris Sketch Book, 1 volume; Yellowplush Papers, 1 volume; Irish Sketch Book, 1 volume; Barry Lyndon, 1 volume; Roundabout Papers, 1 volume; Four Georges, 1 volume; Lovell the Widower, 1 volume; Miscellaneous Essays, 1 volume; Contributions from Punch, 1 volume; Burlesques, 1 volume; Catharine, 1 volume; Ballads, 1 volume.

*Price per volume: English cloth, uncut edges, $3.00; cloth, gilt top, $3.00. In sets: English cloth, $78.00; cloth top, $78.00; three-quarters calf, $150.00; full tree calf, $200.00.*

## LIBRARY EDITION.

With illustrations by the author, Richard Doyle, and Frederick Walker. Complete in 24 volumes 8vo. *Price per volume: English cloth, gilt, $2.00. In sets: Extra cloth, $48.00; half calf, $84.00; three-quarters calf, extra finish, gilt top, other edges uncut, $93.00; tree calf, $120.00.*

## POPULAR EDITION.

Complete in 26 volumes. 12mo. Profusely Illustrated. *Price per volume: Extra cloth, $1.25. In sets: Extra cloth, $32.50; half calf, $65.00; three-quarters calf, extra finish, gilt top, other edges uncut, $78.00.*

## GLOBE EDITION.

Complete in 13 volumes. Crown 8vo. With over 70 illustrations. *Price per volume: Extra cloth, $1.25. In sets: Cloth, $16.25; half calf, $32.50; three-quarters calf, extra finish, gilt top, other edges uncut, $39.00.*

## HANDY EDITION.

Printed in clear type, on fine paper, from a new set of plates (pocket size). Complete in 27 volumes. *Price, per volume: Half cloth, 50 cents; half morocco, $1.00. In sets: Half cloth, uncut edges, $13.50; half morocco, gilt top, $27.00.*

## ÉDITION DE LUXE.

Without exception the largest and handsomest edition that has been published. Containing 248 Steel-Engravings, 1620 Wood-Engravings, and 88 Colored Illustrations. The Steel- and Wood Engravings are all printed on real China paper. The number of copies printed is limited to 1000, each copy being numbered. 26 volumes. With portrait. *$150.00.* *

*\*\* For sale by all Booksellers, or will be sent by the Publishers, free of expense, on receipt of the price.*

## J. B. LIPPINCOTT COMPANY,

### 715-717 MARKET STREET, PHILADELPHIA, PA.

# Charles Dickens's Works

## THE ILLUSTRATED STANDARD EDITION.

### Complete in 30 volumes. Octavo. $2.50 each.

This Edition is printed on a finer paper and in larger type than has been employed in any previous edition. The type has been cast especially for it, and the page is of a size to admit of the introduction of all the original illustrations.

Sketches by " Boz."
Pickwick Papers.
Oliver Twist.
Nicholas Nickleby.
Old Curiosity Shop and Reprinted Pieces.
Barnaby Rudge and Hard Times.
Martin Chuzzlewit.
American Notes and Pictures from Italy.
Dombey and Son.

David Copperfield.
Bleak House.
Little Dorrit.
A Tale of Two Cities.
The Uncommercial Traveller.
Great Expectations.
Our Mutual Friend.
Christmas Books.
History of England.
Christmas Stories.
Edwin Drood and Other Stories.

*Cloth, $60.00\*\*; half calf, gilt, marbled edges, $120.00\*; three-quarters calf, extra finish, gilt top, other edges uncut, $125.00\*; full tree calf, gilt, $175.00.*

## LIBRARY EDITION.

### 12mo. With the Original Illustrations. 30 volumes.

*Each work sold separately in the original red cloth binding. Per volume, $1.50\*. In sets: Cloth, 30 volumes, $45.00\*; three-quarters calf, 30 volumes, $90.00.*

## HANDY EDITION.

### 32 volumes. 16mo. Half cloth, 50 cents per volume. Half morocco, $1.00 per volume.

The clear type, fine thin paper, with uncut edges and neat binding, make these little books as elegant as one need wish, while the low price will enable all lovers of Dickens to possess, at a very small outlay, a good edition of his works.

*\*\*\* For sale by all Booksellers, or will be sent by the Publishers, free of expense, on receipt of the price.*

## J. B. LIPPINCOTT COMPANY,

### 715-717 MARKET STREET,

### - - - - - PHILADELPHIA, PA. - - - - -